## EFFORTS OUSE U.S.

## TO RELEASE S FOR ALLIES

### AY IGNORED EWSPAPERS

OWN CORRESPONDENT

W YORK, Thursday. gh Memorial Day is a oliday in the United ind, as a rule, no newspapers are pub- great is the interest in raordinary fight being y the British and French as they retire from , that all papers brought cial editions this after-

it was noted this was time since 1918 that the of American soldiers in had gone undecorated. rs of public opinion con- their efforts to arouse an people to the dangers front them and make them before it is too late how ely important it is to help ies now at least with sup-

night Dr. James Conant, ent of Harvard University, ast an urgent appeal for id which was made on the ls that it was essential for fence of the United States. itler victory, he said, would t the prelude to the domina- f the world by Hitler. There- he United States should take action possible to ensure r's defeat.

is should include the imme- release to France and and of United States Army Navy 'planes and other imple- ts of war without impairing erican security, repeal of the s preventing United States zens from volunteering for ser- in foreign armies, control of orts with the purpose of stop- g leaks to Germany, and giving ority to the Allies and, finally, operation between the Maritime mmission and the Allies in every y possible under the present vs to expedite the sending of pplies and munitions.

**TURNING THE SCALES**

Such steps, he continued, might p the scales in the Allies' favour, ould be of infinite value in rengthening the Allied morale, and would serve a notice on the orld that our economic resources were now enlisted in the demo- ratic cause."

Dr. Conant urged those who agreed with him to do their part at once to rouse public opinion before it was too late.

A similar appeal was made to-day by Mr. Walter Lippmann, who, writing in the Herald-Tribune, declares: "The task of defending vital interests in the American hemisphere consists in acting now to prevent total catastrophe in Europe and Asia."

Weapons not immediately indispensable to preserve law and order in the United States, he asserts, should be made available to the Allies.

The action taken by the Secretary of State, Mr. Cordell Hull, in eliminating the red tape involved in wheeling United States 'planes across the Canadian border, has met with emphatic approval, and it is believed that this will do a great deal to speed up deliveries.

It is suggested that under favourable weather conditions big bombers can now be flown from ... to Britain

# 37 'PLANES SH BY ONE SQU

## NEW DEFIANTS DEFEAT MESSERSCHMITTS

R.A.F. fighters over the French and Belgian coasts shot down 61 enemy aircraft, including 25 bombers, and probably brought down 23 others on Wednesday, it was officially stated in London last night.

**No fewer than 37 of the Nazi 'planes were shot down by a single squadron of 12 Defiant fighters. During the past three days this squadron has destroyed 50 enemy aircraft.**

Ten of our fighters, stated an Air Ministry bulletin, are missing, but one of the pilots, although wounded, has since returned safely. All 12 of the Defiants are safe.

In the Defiant gun-turret two-seater fighter it is clear that the R.A.F. has a design triumph comparable to the Spitfire and Hurricane fighters, which with their eight-gun converging fire are the most formidable single-seat fighters in the world.

The Defiant is a departure from previous fighter designs, for instead of its armament being confined to six guns firing forward it has a rotating gun turret which enables it to fire in any direction. The guns are synchronised so that the stream of bullets is interrupted to avoid hitting either the propeller or the tail of the machine.

The thrilling exploits of the Defiant Squadron were described in a later Air Ministry bulletin.

**TOO MANY TO COUNT**

On their after-lunch patrol over Dunkirk they met more German fighters and dive-bombers than they could count. They first sighted seven Messerschmitt 109's, they immediately attacked, and one of the Messerschmitts was shot down.

Hardly had this fight finished when the Defiants were surprised by four more Nazi fighters diving on them out of the sun, and firing a stream of cannon shells.

One of the Defiants was hit but was able to reach home safely. The gunner, apparently believing that his machine had been vitally hit baled out over Belgium. Except for him every Defiant pilot and gunner in the squadron returned safely.

After a dog-fight between the remaining Defiants and the other Messerschmitts, the Nazi fighters disappeared.

Then the British squadron saw two formations of nine Heinkel bombers that were attempting to bomb Dunkirk, but all their bombs fell into the sea. They were attacked by Hurricanes, so the Defiants looked for other quarry.

**PARTING SHOT**

Circling above them, ready to dive and attack, were a number of Messerschmitt 110 twin-engined fighters. There was another dog-fight, in which 16 of the Nazi ... destroyed.

## WORRIED OVER CASUALTIES

### GERMAN SCHOOLS AS HOSPITALS

FROM OUR OWN CORRESPONDENT

ZURICH, Thursday.

The German Press is featuring a long list of atrocity stories about alleged treatment of German war prisoners. Despite British and French official denials, allegations of maltreatment and murder of prisoners continue.

There are two explanations. First, Hitler wants a free hand in practices of which he accuses others. Secondly, the German public has become appalled by the tremendous casualties and is now realising that man-power is sheer cannon fodder. It is therefore desirable to work up hatred for the Allies to sustain German morale.

The Germans admit that their casualties in Flanders continue at an increasing rate owing to the stubborn British and French fighting, but no figures are given. The defeat of this Allied army was declared to be an easy matter after the Belgians desertion. The heavy losses are therefore awkward to account for.

Hospitals in the interior of Germany are filled to overflowing. Despite carefully planned organition, hundreds of hospitals have had to be improvised in school buildings. These are being so hurriedly installed that it is obvious that the number of beds necessary was hopelessly underestimated by the military authorities.

## COUSIN OF THE KING KILLED

### LORD F. CAMBRIDGE

Lord Frederick Cambridge, cousin of the King and heir to his brother, the Marquess of Cambridge, has been killed in action while serving with the B.E.F. in France, it was learned in London yesterday. He was reported missing a few days ago. The Marquess of Cambridge is also serving with the B.E.F.

Lord Frederick, who was 32 and unmarried, was a nephew of Queen Mary, his father being her elder ... He was a captain in the

4

S

IT

ONE

## "FORMIDABLE"

## ELEVEN VICTIMS IN FIRST FIGHT

### SIX NEW D.S.O.s

A young squadron leader, whose daring made his squadron "a formidable fighting unit"; another who is officially described as "an incomparable fighter commander"; and a third whose unit has brought down more than 60 enemy 'planes figure in an R.A.F. honours lis issued last night.

Two of these squadron leaders and an acting squadron leade and a flight lieutenant receiv both the Distinguished Servic Order and the Distinguishe Flying Cross.

The list includes six awards the Distinguished Service Orde 27 Distinguished Flying Cross two bars to the D.F.C., Distinguished Flying Med and two bars to the D.F.M.

The new D.S.O.s are: Sq Ldr. E. M. DONALDSON, Sqdn.-L J. S. DEWAR, D.F.C., Sqdn.-L J. O. W. OLIVER, D.F.C., A Sqdn.-Ldr. J. R. KAYLL, D.F Flt.-Lt. W. M. CHURCHILL, D.F Flt.-Lt. R. H. A. LEE.

The officers who also receive D.F.C. have the initials their names.

**FIRST FIGHT "BAG"**

Sqdn.-Ldr. Donaldson, wh born in the Federated States, is 28 years of age. official announcement state he "Inspired in his squadro a fine fighting spirit that, first encounter with enemy nine aircraft of his squadro troyed six enemy aircraft, further five were believed t been destroyed.

"This officer's high coura his inspiring qualities of ship have made his squadro midable fighting unit. himself, shot down four aircraft."

Before the intensive op started Sqdn.-Ldr. Dewar his right shoulder in a seve accident. Despite this he h regularly and has led his s in destroying more than aircraft.

Sqdn.-Ldr. Oliver, now home, commanded a squ France which has acco more than 50 Nazis.

"He was an inc fighter commander," official announcement, personal example in the on the ground was a inspiration to his pilots. fact, necessary to res from flying again after had been shot down; a landed by parachute."

**SQUADRON'S 62**

Flt.-Lt. Churchill's sq brought down 62 ene

Flt.-Lt. Lee, in his ment, was seen at 200 tail of a Junkers 89 bei to intense fire from over enemy occupied t escaped from behind lines after being arr upheld the highest tra Service." He is 2 the D.F.C.

# DEFIANT

# DEFIANT

*The Untold Story of the Battle of Britain*

Robert Verkaik

ROBINSON

ROBINSON

First published in Great Britain in 2020 by Robinson

3 5 7 9 10 8 6 4



A CIP catalogue record for this book is available from the British Library.

ISBN: 978-1-47214-355-6

Typeset in Adobe Garamond Pro by Hewer Text UK Ltd, Edinburgh
Printed and bound in Great Britain by Clays Ltd, Elcograf S.p.A.

Papers used by Robinson are from well-managed forests and other responsible sources.

Robinson
An imprint of
Little, Brown Book Group
Carmelite House
50 Victoria Embankment
London EC4Y 0DZ

An Hachette UK Company
www.hachette.co.uk

www.littlebrown.co.uk

*To all the pilots and gunners who flew and fought in two-seater fighters during both world wars.*

BBC: 'If circumstances so forced you to live through that period again, being in the same position and the same command, would you have done anything differently?'

Hugh Dowding: 'Well, all I can say is, she would have been my uncle.'

BBC interview with Hugh Dowding, Commander-in-Chief of Fighter Command during the Battle of Britain, 12 July 1968 (*And if my auntie had balls she would be my uncle.* It is fruitless to speculate about counterfactual situations).

# CONTENTS

# INTRODUCTION

I GREW UP NEAR Hawkinge airfield on the Kent Downs overlooking the harbour town of Folkestone. Today it is the site of a Battle of Britain air museum. Across the road is a cemetery where the gravestones of both RAF and Luftwaffe aircrews are neatly laid out side by side. This is the final resting place of twenty-eight-year-old Arthur 'Arch' Hamilton, who was killed just after 12 p.m. on 19 July 1940. On that day he was an air gunner with No. 141 Squadron, which suffered the greatest loss of life and aircraft in a single combat during the Battle of Britain.

I have long been fascinated by the story of No. 141 Squadron and the massacre of the Hawkinge 'Defiants'. I was led to believe that the pilots and gunners died in vain because they were flying a flawed aircraft. But when I began uncovering the truth about what really happened on that day I discovered that there was much more to this story and to the part played in the Battle of Britain by Fighter Command's newest fighter, the Boulton Paul Defiant.

In the spring of 1940 all that stood against a Nazi invasion were three front-line fighters. Much has been written of the heroic feats and sacrifices of the RAF pilots who took off in their Spitfires and Hurricanes against the larger Luftwaffe air forces. But what of the third British fighter, the Defiant?

The genesis of Britain's first monoplane fighters reflected RAF thinking that Germany would send waves of heavy, undefended bombers to attack British cities. It was a strategy rooted in the experience of the First World War when Britain had been left almost defenceless against the Zeppelins and long-range biplane bombers of the German air force which had set ablaze British towns and cities.

But British military aviation thinking was bitterly divided. On one side of the argument was the Air Ministry, supported by former First World War fighter pilots, who wanted to confront the bombers using the newly developed state-of-the-art machine gun turrets; on the other was the dour, but meticulous, head of Fighter Command, Hugh Dowding, who favoured single-engine fighter planes with guns in the wings.

The aircraft which partly accommodated both views was the Boulton Paul Defiant – a single-engine, two-seater monoplane with a revolving machine gun turret housed behind the pilot and operated by a gunner.

As late as 1938 Sholto Douglas, the Assistant Chief of the Air Staff, ordered Dowding to equip fifteen of his squadrons with Defiants.

After the Defiants' spectacular successes over Dunkirk, Fighter Command came under even greater pressure to throw more Defiant aircraft into the battle. By the preliminary stages of the Battle of Britain, the Air Ministry still hoped to build enough Defiants to turn the fortunes of the war in favour of Britain and blast the Nazi bombers out of the skies.

The Defiants' kill-rate had also partly helped convince Hitler and his generals that before the Germans could launch an invasion against Britain the Luftwaffe must have total air superiority. But opposition from Fighter Command as well as crippling production hold-ups meant the Boulton Paul Defiant was unable to fulfill its promise. After sustaining heavy losses, the turret fighter was later unceremoniously withdrawn from the front line of the Battle of Britain. Discarded as an RAF embarrassment, the Defiants' story was not allowed to mar the glorious victory won by the Spitfire and the Hurricane.

RAF high command, whose negligence contributed to the losses of the Defiant crews, shamelessly distanced itself from its third Battle of Britain fighter. The public was encouraged to believe that the Defiants' success over Dunkirk only came about because the Luftwaffe fighter pilots mistook them for Hurricanes and, attacking them from behind, the Germans had fallen prey to the rear-firing turret machine guns.

But this, and many other stories which have grown up around the Defiant, masks some very inconvenient truths.

# PROLOGUE

TODAY IT IS impossible to imagine the excitement and exhilaration of those heady years of the first man-made flight.

American brothers Orville and Wilbur Wright harnessed the soaring spirit of humankind by turning the dreams of the pioneer aviators into a wonderful reality. That first historic flight of 1903 covered just 852 feet and lasted 59 seconds. Yet only six years later the French flier Louis Blériot had piloted an aircraft which carried him across the English Channel.

During these early days of experimental flight, the British and German contribution to aviation achievement was almost conspicuous by its absence. That emphatically changed with the conflagration of the Great War, sucking in all human endeavour to the ultimate contest of nations.

Great Britain had started slowly and initially relied on the French aircraft industry, especially for engines. When the country went to war in July 1914, the British 'air force' numbered no more than thirty serviceable machines. So it is hardly surprising that Germany raced to a commanding air superiority, denying the Allies access to vital aerial reconnaissance over the static battlefield. These early skirmishes saw the emergence of the first German aces who shot down the more cumbersome British and French twin-seater aircraft.

Soon the pattern of aerial combat was established where single-seat fighters, such as the Albatross flown by Manfred von Richthofen, sought out and destroyed the enemy's spotter planes, whose defensive armament often amounted to no more than an observer sitting behind the pilot brandishing his pistol. When fighters were later deployed to defend these reconnaissance patrols, the observers were armed with machine guns. These were the first dogfights where young 'knights of the sky' fought to the death in gladiatorial combat.

My Uncle George was one of them. And his journey from his birthplace of Hull to the skies over the Western Front was a circuitous one.

George Heseltine was born in 1895 and after leaving school at the age of fourteen took jobs as a clerk in Hull and then London. But his intended vocation had always been the priesthood, and in the year war broke out he had been accepted as a Jesuit novice. So, setting his ecclesiastical pursuits to one side, George signed up to the East Yorkshire Regiment. He was commissioned and transferred to the Kings Own Scottish Border Regiment and sent to Gallipoli where he was badly wounded in the bitter fighting to oust the Turks from the Dardanelles. The invalided George was repatriated to England but, refusing to sit out the war, he volunteered for the Royal Flying Corps (RFC) and after completing pilot training was posted to the Western Front.

George was soon back in the thick of the action, flying a Fe2d (Farman Experimental) with No. 20 Squadron. The Fe2d was known as a 'pusher' aircraft because the propeller faced backwards and was positioned behind the pilot and observer, giving the impression it was 'pushing' the aircraft through the sky. Pushers were the first stars of the First World War, their flying exploits regularly featuring in the early 'Biggles' books. Like George, Biggles' creator Captain W. E. Johns was wounded in the trenches at Gallipoli before enjoying a new lease of life as a pilot with the RFC on the Western Front.

George later wrote in his diary that he loved his 'pusher' because the unusual placing of the engine meant his Lewis gunner had a 'magnificent arc of fire, 180 degrees in all directions'. Sitting behind the gunner in an open cockpit, George must have felt very exposed, but he swore that of all the fighters serving on the Western Front, the Fe2d was the one the Germans feared the most.

Writing in his diary at the time he observed: 'Their planes were twenty to thirty miles an hour faster than our old buses, which were the heaviest and most cumbersome, but still the stoutest machines in the front. The Hun "scouts" could outclimb and outpace us with ease, but they only had one fixed gun firing forward. So we had to stick together and cover one another and at all costs keep nose-on to the enemy if we could.'

After signing up with the RFC in 1917 George didn't have long to wait for his first tangle with the German flying circus led by the legendary 'Red Baron', Manfred von Richthofen. At 16.35 on 5 May 1917, at just twenty-one years old, wrapped in woollen jumpers and a leather coat strapped down to his ankles, my uncle was on 'offensive patrol' at 10,000 feet over Ypres with his gunner Lieutenant Frederick Kydd, a trainee dentist in civvy life, sitting in front of him. They were among a flight of five aircraft (the sixth British machine had turned back with engine trouble) following their leader Captain Jimmy Thayre, one of the RFC's highest scoring aces with seventeen victories to his name, over the German lines.

I'll let George take up the story: 'We were rumbling along in that bright May sky when a couple of specks approached from starboard. Might be ours, I thought. Whilst Kydd and I were making up our minds I saw Thayre in the leading Fe waving to me then shaking his fist, and making what Sir Winston Churchill has since patented as the Victory Sign, in the direction of the two. We turned with him to attack.'

But almost as soon as George had made the turn Lieutenant Kydd was excitedly pointing to the sky above them where he had spotted eight more Germans lying in wait.

'It dawned on me then, and no doubt on our leader Thayre,' wrote George, 'that the two might be a decoy, a trick that the famous circuses of von Richthofen and von Burlow were known to use. The next thing I realised was that everywhere I looked I could see fighters and so far as I could tell they were all Huns [flying Albatrosses, the biplane fighter favoured by von Richthofen]. I was trying to stick as close as possible to Thayre and I saw that the others were all following the two of us closely round.'

This follow-my-leader tactic, known as the Lufbery Circle, had been developed by the Fe2s to protect themselves against the superior German fighters.

'Suddenly,' George wrote in his diary, 'I saw a Hun go down to [Captain Francis] Cubbon's guns – black smoke trailing behind him. I was watching that, feeling a bit queasy because it always "might have been me", when to my surprise a Hun flashed almost straight across our nose – but Kydd had evidently seen him coming and fired when he was 50 feet away. He caught the Hun full broadside on and the machine went into a steep dive, turned over and belched smoke.'

George was so excited with their first kill that he stood up in the open cockpit and patted Kydd on the shoulder. But the five British fighters were now strung out, no longer in protective contact with one another.

'We were desperately trying to keep together,' wrote George. 'The air seemed full of Huns, and above the spatter of our guns, and the Huns, I could hear the "woof" or doggie bark of anti-Archie aircraft shells bursting below us.'

George's Rolls-Royce Eagle engine was on full throttle as he tried to turn away from the nippier German fighters. He turned one way and then the other while Kydd kept up the rat-a-tat-tat on his Lewis gun. Then suddenly the British machine gun jammed. Kydd frantically tried to clear the chamber and reload the belt of bullets but it was no use. So he stood up and lifted George's own gun into his front seat just as a Hun began a diving attack from behind.

Recalled George: 'He [Kydd] at once trained the gun on him and fired over my head – a rotten experience for me I can assure you. I watched his eyes, for they showed me the direction of the Hun and I tried to turn away to shake the Hun off – when Kydd suddenly let the gun go and leaned over to me shouting – I could not hear above the roar of the engine – but it gradually dawned on me he was shouting "fire". I gave the thumbs up sign and patted him on the shoulder, thinking he had downed another Hun but he looked wildly alarmed, pointed above my head and seized my head to twist it around and make me look up and behind. In doing so he dragged my flying helmet over one eye but with the other I saw enough. My own centre section was on fire.'

Kydd stood up, his legs straddling George's cockpit, and tried to batter the fire out with his hands – but at 75 mph it was no use.

Recalled George: 'He struggled back into his own cockpit and crouched in the bottom – front gun useless, he could only reduce the wind resistance as much as possible and "wait for it", poor devil, whilst I dived for the ground, defenceless.'

The Fe2d had a warning bolted onto the front of the pilot's instruments saying 'do not dive above 110 mph'. George could only helplessly stare at the needle as it crept round to 130 mph, which was as steep as he could dive while forcing the joystick forward with his knee.

'She would either burn out up there or break up on the way down and so I put my faith in the makers – Boulton and Paul – and my trust in God.'

But now one of the German machines had noticed the burning British fighter and decided to follow it down to make sure of the kill. It looked as if George and Lieutenant Kydd had flown their last sortie. Then suddenly Captain Thayre and his fearless gunner, Captain Francis Cubbon, appeared in the sky and were diving to the rescue. They caught the German and Cubbon dispatched him with a short burst of machine gun fire. The Fe2d held firm, and with the fire now out George somehow managed to land in a field just on the right side of the front line.

Twenty-three years later, aerial combat had barely changed. The pilots, now sealed into their bullet-proof cockpits, may have been flying faster monoplane fighters wielding more fearful armament but the tactics employed to defeat the Hun were just the same. By 1917, George and his pioneer fighter pilots had perfected the Lufbery Circle, a defensive turning circle that became equally useful to another British fighter during the Battle of Britain. The Boulton Paul Defiant, a direct descendent of the Farman Experimental, was an equally sturdy two-seater fighter and built and designed by the same famous aircraft manufacturer. It too would outfight the faster German fighters as the British pilots put their trust in God and their faith in Boulton Paul.

George was badly burned in the crash landing but he noted in his diary that he hardly cared as he and Kydd had claimed their first two kills in their first combat.

Lord Hugh Trenchard, the head of the RFC and later the 'father of the RAF', sent a personal telegram to George and the rest of the crews, wishing them 'many congratulations' for taking part in a 'great fight carried out with such determination and inflicting such heavy casualties on German formations superior in numbers'.

*The Times*, which wrote up the combat in blazing glory, said George's Fe2d and the other four machines had taken on twenty-seven German fighters, sending eight to earth, 'crashing, crippled or in flames'. But the newspaper had stern words for the German fighter who had mercilessly chased George's burning machine to the ground, only to be cut to pieces by Captains Thayre and Cubbon diving on behind.

'It was just retribution,' the newspaper proclaimed. 'The unwritten laws of this marvellous game prescribe that no honourable fighter attack an enemy in flames. Such an enemy is out of the fight, and has trouble enough for a brave man. The German who dived for our burning machine knew that he was doing an unchivalrous thing, and it may be that that knowledge unnerved him so that he paid the penalty.'

Not long after the fire had been extinguished on George's aircraft, *The Times* reporter was on the scene to describe the miraculous escape: 'Strangely enough our burning aeroplane got home. I have seen the wreckage, with the reserve petrol tank on the roof bearing two bullet holes on one side and great ragged tears on the other where the bullets passed out. The whole tank is scorched and crumbled. The flames had burned away the whole central span of the upper plane. The thick rear main spar was charred and burned through, and two ribs were completely severed and hung with loose blackened ends. Yet like a great blazing meteor it crossed our lines and came to earth . . . and as another airman said to me in admiration "he made a perfectly topping landing".'

When Uncle George came to stay with us for Christmas in the late 1970s he was well into his eighties. He was quite a short man, and in old age had shrunken into his baggy grey suit trousers held up by a pair of wide braces. I remember once being told by my mother that Uncle George was waiting to talk to me in the sitting room. I cannot tell you what he said, but I doubt very much it concerned the time he took on the Red Baron in his fighter plane over France. By now he was a gruffly pious old boy who had a reputation for boring the pants off anyone who'd listen. No one bothered to tell me that he had once been a real-life Biggles, whose exploits I had been so excitedly gripped by in my early teens. Instead I remember him sitting opposite me at Christmas lunch, his festive hat sliding down his forehead, as my brother and I surreptitiously flicked peas in his general direction in the hope they would be caught in the crown of his paper hat.

No. 20 Squadron became the highest-scoring and most decorated British squadron on the Western Front. Two months later, one of its crews claimed the greatest scalp of them all when a Fe2d shot down Manfred von Richthofen in another bitter fight with a 'circus' of Albatrosses. Richthofen was wounded in the head and forced to land near Wervicq. But he lived to fight and die another day.

George's injuries sustained in Gallipoli and in the air over Ypres finally ended his active participation in the First World War. But he was not the only soldier to join the RFC after being badly wounded in the trenches.

Sydney Carlin, like my Uncle George, also hailed from Hull where his father was a tallow chandler (candle maker). From an early age Carlin had dreamt of becoming a soldier and in 1907 on his eighteenth birthday he joined the Royal Hussars. But he soon found that parading around Hull lacked the military adventure he had been seeking, and so left the army for a life of farming.

In 1914 he answered the nation's call to arms and marched off to his old regiment's recruiting office where he was signed up and dispatched to Belgium as part of the advanced cavalry screen with the British Expeditionary Force. By the spring of 1916 the hopelessly exposed cavalrymen had been relegated to fighting in the trenches with the rest of the British Tommies. Carlin's unit suffered heavy casualties in the Battle of the Somme, and on 17/18 July 1916 he was seriously injured by shrapnel in his left leg which was later amputated. Unwilling to be invalided out of the war, Carlin decided to apply to join the RFC and paid for his own flying lessons to help support his case.

His persistence paid off and he won a Flying Officer commission on 12 March 1918, joining 74 'Tiger' Squadron in northern France. The RFC had replaced their slow and cumbersome Fe2ds with the latest SE5A fighter plane. Carlin's commanding officer, Mick Mannock, Britain's highest-scoring ace, christened his new one-legged pilot 'Timbertoes' which stuck for the rest of his life. Despite initial problems with landings, which resulted in some aircraft being written off, Carlin escaped injury and went on to destroy five enemy planes and six air balloons, for which he was awarded the Distinguished Flying Cross (DFC). But on 21 September 1918 Carlin was shot down and taken prisoner.

At the end of the war Sydney Carlin and Uncle George were honourably discharged from the RFC because of their disabilities. They both returned to Hull and sought solace from their war service in their love of farming. George went on to forge a career as a journalist and became a close acquaintance of G. K. Chesterton, Wyndham Lewis and Hilaire Belloc. He later helped found the Distributists, a Catholic socialist movement. Carlin left Britain for a colonial life as a farmer/soldier in Kenya.

When Britain went to war with Germany twenty years later George Heseltine and Sydney Carlin were among the first to volunteer. George became a squadron leader with RAF intelligence. But Carlin, who was now fifty years old, served as a gunner in the turret of Britain's newest fighter, the Boulton Paul Defiant, from where he shot down more Germans and could claim to be the oldest British gunner in the Second World War.

# Chapter 1

# FIRST OF THE FEW

THE FORMATION OF the Brieftauben Abteilung Ostende ('Ostend Carrier Pigeon Detachment') cynically disguised its true purpose. Germany's new generation of long-range bombers could fly from bases in Belgium where they were capable of launching terror raids on London.[1]

These first bombers were commanded by the German Naval Staff and the rationale for introducing them into the conflict was clearly set out by the Grand Admiral Alfred von Tirpitz, who declared: 'The measure of the success will lie not only in the injury which will be caused to the enemy, but also in the significant effect it will have in diminishing the enemy's determination to prosecute the war.'

A bombing campaign directed against London was finally approved on 7 January 1915, after initial resistance from the Kaiser who feared killing his own relatives in the Royal Family. But he needn't have worried – such pinpoint bombing was well beyond the prowess of the Kaiser's air force.

In the first raid of 19–20 January 1915 two Zeppelins targeted Humberside but were diverted by strong winds, and dropped their bombs on Great Yarmouth, Sheringham, King's

Lynn and the surrounding villages. Four people were killed and sixteen injured. The operations that followed were more destructive, although no more accurate.

British defences against the Zeppelin threat were uncoordinated and divided between the Royal Navy Air Service (RNAS) and the Royal Flying Corps (RFC), with the Navy engaging enemy airships approaching the coast and the RFC taking responsibility once the enemy had crossed the coastline. This mirrored the division of command of the German airfleet which was similarly split between the Army and the Navy, although both launched Zeppelins against Britain.

The first British squadron assigned to the home defence of London was No. 19 RNAS based at Sutton's Farm which later became RAF Hornchurch, Essex, a fighter station at the heart of the defence of the capital against the Luftwaffe in the summer of 1940. No. 19 Squadron is today No. 39 Squadron, based at RAF Waddington, which flies Reaper drones out of the Middle East.

Britain's military commitment to the Western Front and the sporadic nature of the German air attacks meant that by February 1916 there were just eight squadrons defending the whole of the British Isles.

One of the RFC commanders tasked with protecting the homeland from the German bombs was a young officer called Hugh Dowding who, twenty-four years later, would come to the aid of the British nation as it faced the Nazi onslaught. By the start of the second year of the war Dowding, stationed in France, had acquired a mixed flying record. He had shot down five enemy aircraft but had also crashed a single-seater Bleriot (after becoming dizzy from inhaling exhaust fumes) and been embarrassingly lost on patrol on several occasions.

In those days the standard RFC fighter was a Be2c, a twin-seater crewed by a pilot and a gunner. The two-seater pilot/gunner fighter was favoured more by the British who strictly adhered to the conventional wisdom that the division of duties allowed the pilot to concentrate on the business of flying while the observer navigated and fired the guns. It was an aerial combat concept that would continue to dominate fighter tactics well beyond the end of the war.

Dowding recalled his own experience during a mission in one of these first fighters: 'My observer was in the front seat, and we were armed only with a Lewis gun which he could fire backwards or sideways. We were well across the enemy lines when we were attacked by a large German formation. My observer was kneeling on his seat facing backwards and I was flying straight and level to give him an easy shot at a German flying behind and to the left of us.' He continued: 'We were getting shot at all the time but my observer did not fire. A bullet came in under my arm and went between my hand and just nicked my knuckles . . . then I saw that my observer's face was full of blood.'

Dowding immediately tugged on the joystick and pulled the aircraft out of the fighting before safely landing back at the airfield. He and his observer had only suffered superficial wounds and were very fortunate to survive. But the experience badly damaged Dowding's confidence in the twin-seater fighter aircraft. Throughout the conflict the Be2cs were easy prey for the German fighters, especially the Fokkers.

British fighter strategy was largely determined by General Trenchard, who sought to gain air superiority over the battlefield by flying continuous offensive patrols behind enemy lines. He did achieve his objective but for a very high casualty rate.

During the Somme campaign the British lost 500 pilots and 800 aircraft while the German total aircraft losses were just 400. To Dowding's mind this was an unnecessary cost in human life. So he resolved that as soon as the Somme offensive had calmed down he would put his concerns directly to Trenchard. Dowding, still a relatively junior officer, sent a communiqué to headquarters saying that the strain of continuously flying offensive patrols was taking a heavy toll on the pilots. He later told Robert Wright, the author of his authorised biography: 'I thought it very reasonable that the squadrons engaged in intensive operations should be periodically relieved, as was done in other branches of the Service, and asked Trenchard if this could be done.'

But Trenchard reacted badly to Dowding's intervention, raising questions about his subordinate officer's ability to press home orders while he held an 'obsession with the fear of casualties.'[2] Trenchard started referring to him as a 'dismal Jimmy' and arranged for Dowding to be posted off the front line in January 1916.[3]

Dowding was recalled to England and given command of 7 Wing at Fort Grange Gosport, in Hampshire, where he had a role in the home defence of the south of England. The demotion, however, did nothing to dampen Dowding's tendency to question superiors over military policy and tactics. In almost his first contact with the Air Staff in London he complained that none of his under-powered aircraft, 70 hp Renault-engined Be2cs, were suitable for the job of repelling the German raiders. When his complaint fell on deaf ears he decided to switch his attentions from aircraft to aircrew, later saying: 'I remember writing round to all the better-known public schools and asking the headmasters to help us secure suitable applicants for commissions in the RFC, not necessarily the boys at the top of the school, but members of the football team and athletes and tough characters in general.' Dowding's plea was met with a collective ambivalence: '. . . some schools responded wholeheartedly, while others (including my own old school) were less than helpful. The fact was of course that the RFC (in modern argot) was distinctly Non-U [non-upper class].'[4]

Throughout 1916 German bombers continued to menace the British homeland. One of the biggest raids came on the night of 2 September when the Kaiser sent twelve German Navy and four Army airships to attack London. The Navy Zeppelins were much more susceptible to stormy weather and all twelve had to withdraw after being blown off course. That left just two of the Army's airships heading for the British capital, the LZ98 and the newly commissioned Schütte-Lanz SL11.

Fighters from Sutton's Farm, the RFC air station tasked with the defence of London, were ordered up into the night sky to seek out and destroy the attacking enemy raiders. At around 02.15 a Be2c piloted by Lt William Leefe Robinson made contact with the lumbering SL11. Robinson made three attacks against the enemy airship, on each occasion emptying a drum of ammunition from his Lewis gun. On the third pass the airship burst into flames and plummeted to the ground near Cuffley, Hertfordshire, killing all the crew. It was the first rigid airship shot down on British soil, for which Leefe Robinson received the Victoria Cross.

Airships, mostly Zeppelins and the more advanced Schütte-Lanz, carried out a further fifty raids on Britain during the war, dropping five thousand bombs, killing 557 people and injuring another 1358.

Of the eighty-four airships that took part, thirty were either shot down or lost in accidents, a rate of attrition that soon became unacceptable to the German high command. After the loss of SL11, the German Army withdrew from combat operations, leaving the German Navy to carry on a scaled-down airship bombing campaign.

The next year the German Army air force, the Luftstreitkräfte, returned to the fray with a specially developed aircraft – a long-range bomber capable of flying so high the British fighters could not reach it. This twin-engine Gotha had a wingspan of almost 80 feet, the length of two buses and as long as a Lancaster bomber. Equipped with huge fuel tanks, these new jumbo bombers had a flying range of 500 miles which meant no target on the British mainland was safe. Eighteen of them could carry the same payload as three Zeppelins – and three airships had never succeeded at reaching London in the same raid.[5]

On 25 May 1917, twenty-three Gothas took off from two aerodromes near Ghent in Belgium to bomb London. But as they crossed the British coast, cloud cover over the capital forced the commanders to select a secondary target upon which to drop their bombs. Their new destination was the port of Folkestone in Kent and the nearby Shorncliffe army camp. At around 5 p.m. bombs began falling on the town, killing ninety-three civilians and soldiers and injuring many more. One bomb exploded in the road where my grandparents lived, killing a young woman married to an army surgeon. The material destruction and loss of so much life, including many children who had been playing in the high street, was a deep shock to the nation. But for the people of Folkestone it left a particularly bitter taste. In 1875 the town's fishermen had sailed to the rescue of the stricken SMS *Grosser*

*Kurfürst* after it had collided with another German warship in the channel. Dozens of German lives were saved by the fishermen. Understandably the good folk of Folkestone believed themselves safe from indiscriminate bombing raids.[6]

Such sentimental history mattered little to the German high command who, after Folkestone, stepped up their air attacks, leading to many more daylight raids and an ever-increasing death toll. They also introduced a new, mightier bomber to the campaign. The Giant, or Riesenflugzeug, was the largest aircraft built during the First World War. Powered by four engines it carried an even bigger payload than the Gotha.

The Gothas and Giants dropped more than 220,460 lb of bombs, causing the deaths of two thousand civilians. Compared with the carnage and destruction on the Western Front the German air raids made no material difference to the war – except in one respect. The British public was terrified of them. During the first few raids, Londoners had lined the streets and parks gazing up in wonder as the procession of giant German biplanes crossed the capital's skyline. But the stark horror of the randomness of the falling bombs soon caused three hundred thousand Londoners to seek refuge in the underground stations. Others left the capital for the safety of the countryside, some even choosing to sleep in open fields rather than face the German bombers in their homes.

Public outrage forced Prime Minister David Lloyd George to recall his air chiefs from France and make them account for the shameful abandonment of Londoners to the terror of the daylight raids.

This prompted a collective redoubling of military effort. Scores of anti-aircraft batteries, mostly modified ship guns, were sited around London while the RFC and RNAS sent up hundreds of patrols to meet the invaders. But even these numbers made little impression on the high-flying Germans. In one attack the British had ninety-two fighters in the air but failed to hit a single enemy bomber. The anti-aircraft guns fired more than fourteen thousand rounds without scoring a hit, apart from against the civilian population who were now being injured by both the German bombs and the shrapnel raining down on them, fired by their own guns.

It was only when Trenchard allowed state-of-the-art fighters to be co-opted from the Western Front that the home defenders started to make an impact. On 22 August 1917, fifteen Gothas arrived over the Kent coast in a planned attack on Margate and Dover. Three were shot down and the other twelve were forced to turn back because of a combination of high winds and concentrated anti-aircraft fire. Like the Zeppelins, the German long-range bombers were susceptible to determined fighter aircraft, directed by ground control, during daylight raids. Mounting German losses forced the enemy to switch to night raids, which caused even more terror and were even more difficult to stop.[7]

During the war years, Germany's bombing offensives had repeatedly exposed the inadequacy of Britain's home defences. Parliament was entitled to know why the Army and Navy were unable to protect British citizens in their own homes and so ordered an urgent inquiry into the scandal.

It fell to the South African 'Boer' Jan Smuts, now employed in the British Army as a Lieutenant General, to begin the task of putting the home defences in order. In August 1917 Smuts completed a detailed report setting out the failures of the Army and Navy air forces. His key recommendation was the creation of a separate air service, subordinate to neither the Navy nor the Army and answerable to a newly constituted Air Ministry. He quite rightly calculated: 'The day may not be far off when aerial operations with their devastation of enemy lands and destruction of industrial and populous centres on a vast scale may become the principal operations of war, to which the older forms of military and naval operations may become secondary and subordinate.'[8]

But the establishment of the world's first independent standing air force was opposed by the military. Neither the Navy nor the Army were prepared to give up their claim to run an auxiliary and bespoke air force. And if Smuts had hoped for support from the flying officers in the field he was in for an unpleasant surprise.

Trenchard, who had fought the Boers in South Africa before the First World War, had been in charge of the Royal Flying Corps in France since 1915. He may have held a grudging respect for an old adversary like Smuts whom he had once chased across the African plains. But he violently disagreed with some of the conclusions in the Smuts report, of which he had received an early copy. Trenchard could sense victory on the Western Front and what Smuts was proposing threatened his and the RFC's part in that triumph. Moreover, the disruption caused by the creation of a new air force mid-war might even lose Britain its hard-won air supremacy.

Trenchard had intended to make his opposition forcefully known the next time he had a chance to speak directly to the Cabinet. That moment came more quickly than he was expecting and under less propitious circumstances. The success of the German bombers had led to increasingly louder calls for Britain to retaliate in kind, leaving Lloyd George little choice but to summon the field commander of the RFC from his duties in France.

Trenchard set off for London by air on 2 October 1917 but was forced to make an emergency landing at Lympne in Kent after his flight of aircraft had been mistaken for a German air raid and come under heavy friendly fire. When he finally arrived in Whitehall and came before the Cabinet he quickly discovered there was only one subject on the ministers' minds – military retribution against the Germans in their own homes. Fortunately he was able to tell them the first RFC bomber airfield at Ochey near Nancy was now operational. Lloyd George urged him to begin bombing as soon as possible.

In December 1917 Britain's most famous fighter station was also cleared for operations. Biggin Hill in Kent was about to play the first of many vital roles in the air defence of the nation. It had been equipped with the new Bristol two-seater fighter flown by No. 141 Squadron, a squadron which would go on to feature in the Battle of Britain – but, as we shall later see, with disastrous results.

The Bristol, which replaced the slower Fe2ds, was powered by a 250 hp Rolls-Royce Falcon engine, giving the fighter a top speed of 125 mph and a ceiling of 20,000 feet. The crews who flew with 141 hailed from all corners of the Empire – Australia, Canada, New Zealand, Rhodesia and, in Lieutenant Hardit Singh Malik, a Sikh from Rawalpindi. They were adventurous young men who soon became known in the locality as much for their exuberant high jinks on the ground as their achievements in the air.

In fact, the landlord of the Railway Hotel in Staplehurst, 10 miles from Biggin Hill, had grown accustomed to serving the young pilots who regularly made 'emergency' landings near the town. One wing commander, who had genuine engine trouble and was forced to use a nearby landing strip, arrived at the hotel to seek assistance only to be greeted by a row of a dozen Bristol fighters neatly lined up in the car park.[9]

Biggin Hill was a key station in the London air defence, responsible for the North Kent sector. As the Germans had now restricted their raids to the hours of darkness, 141 became a squadron of night fighters patrolling a beat between the airfield and the River Thames at Joyce Green.

Biggin Hill 'boffins' had been secretly developing a new ground-to-air and air-to-air radio transmitter system and the pilots of 141 Squadron were to be the night-flying guinea pigs. Information on the enemy's movements taken by coastguard stations, ground observers, searchlight crew and patrolling aircraft was now fed into Biggin Hill's operations room. This data was used to plot the course, altitude and number of approaching enemy aircraft and then to direct the Bristols to their targets using a ground-to-air wireless.

To ensure close cooperation between the squadron and the ground defences, the headquarters of the anti-aircraft company was moved to the airfield's North Camp. This permitted better coordination between the fighters and the area's sixteen searchlights which illuminated the enemy bombers so 141 could attack them.[10] The searchlight crews relied on stethoscopes clamped to their ears to locate their targets. By balancing the sound of the drone above they flashed open the searchlight shutters as soon as the noise bored a vibration into the centre of the operator's forehead. Occasionally it worked and a Gotha would suddenly be caught in the beam of light, exposed in the sky above London. The precise location of the Gotha could then be transmitted to the RFC intelligence officer who ordered the Bristols into the air.

All these developments became the unsung forerunners of the sector control system that was to play such a vital role in the Battle of Britain twenty-two years later.

However, this rapid improvement in ground-to-air enemy aircraft detection coincided with a drop-off in the number of German raids, leaving 141 with little opportunity to put the technology to the test. Instead the pilots had to make do with practising close formation flying and offering their aircraft as targets for the anti-aircraft batteries to try out their guns. Captain Norman Dimmock told his son after the war: 'We used to get very bored flying around all morning in formation, so to pass the time we would pretend to be a band. I would brace up in the front seat and tap the wing prior to conducting, and everyone would go through the motions of playing one instrument or another.'[11]

On 17 October 1917 Trenchard honoured his promise to Lloyd George. Before lunchtime six de Havilland bombers took off on the first British long-range bomber raid against Germany. Later in the day Handley Page bombers of the RNAS joined the de Havillands in the attack. Their target was the Burbach iron foundry near Saarbrücken. It was the turn of the German population to experience the horror of being bombed from the sky.

Two months after these first British raids Trenchard was recalled to England for a meeting with Lord Rothermere, the media mogul whose family owned *The Times* and *Daily Mail* newspapers and who Lloyd George had appointed as his Air Minister. Lloyd George had given Rothermere the job of implementing Smuts' recommendation for the establishment of a new independent air force. And Rothermere had made no secret that he wanted Trenchard to be its first Chief of the Air Staff.

But the scheming Rothermere intended to use the new air force and its Chief of the Air Staff to effectively wage a political war against Field Marshal Haig, the commander of the British Army in France. To oust Haig, Rothermere asked Trenchard if he would be willing to hold back the air force from supporting Haig's land forces. Trenchard refused but still accepted the job offer, reasoning that he could best serve the interests of the air force inside the tent.

He later recalled: 'I warned them that I would not fight against the Army and the Navy during the war, but the arguments got hotter and more unpleasant.' And he was in no doubt that: 'I should have to fight Rothermere and Northcliffe [Rothermere's press baron brother] from the day I took the job'.[12]

Relations between the Air Ministry (led by Rothermere) and the new head of the air force went from bad to worse as the Whitehall civil servants bombarded Trenchard with orders and counter orders as well as meddling in the long-range bombing campaign against Germany. The Air Ministry had begun life as an insurgency department in government, a reputation it lived up to long after the war.

At the end of January 1918, Trenchard asked for a private meeting with Haig in France. Haig wrote in his diary for 26 January: 'General Trenchard came to dinner, he could think and talk about nothing else but the rascally ways of politicians and newspaper men.' In his own diary on 11 February, Trenchard added: 'The great curse of this place is too many officers doing different jobs . . . in fact of the 207 officers in Bolo House [Air Ministry HQ in London] only twenty-nine were pilots.'[13]

By the close of March, Trenchard had had enough and wrote to Rothermere offering his resignation, but Rothermere talked him out of it.

The war in Whitehall was soon to be eclipsed by critical developments on the Western Front. During the weekend of 22–24 March the German Army had taken the British by surprise and launched a major offensive, forcing Haig to retire his forces behind the River Somme.

Rothermere quickly looked to turn national disaster into a personal triumph and he wrote to Trenchard: 'No more reinforcements for Haig. Get back as much Air as you can from France for the defence of England, whatever the Army do.' Rothermere appeared to want to abandon the Army and Haig to their fate and in so doing turn the British retreat into a rout, setting up the conditions for a premature Battle of Britain.

Trenchard refused and suggested Rothermere take some time off from his 'onerous' responsibilities. Rothermere had lost two of his sons fighting in France and Trenchard suspected this had taken a far heavier toll on his mental health than the Air Minister was prepared to admit. Instead Trenchard ordered all available aircrews to France to bolster Haig's position. Disaster was averted and the British halted the German advance.

A week later, on 1 April 1918, the Royal Air Force came into existence, exactly six months after the Air Force Bill had received Royal assent and less than one year since Lt General Smuts had set out the urgent need for an independent air service.

It could not have happened at a less auspicious moment. Its minister was conspiring to use the new service to bring down the head of the Army, even at the risk of losing the war, while its Chief of the Air Staff had already tendered his resignation. On 13 April Rothermere changed his mind and accepted the loss of Trenchard, remarking: 'In getting rid of Trenchard I flatter myself that I did a great thing for the Air Force. With his dull and unimaginative mind and his attitude of *je sais tout* he would within twelve months have brought death and damnation to the Air Force.'[14]

Trenchard was succeeded by Major General Frederick Sykes. A fortnight later Rothermere also resigned and was replaced by Sir William Weir.

At Biggin Hill, blissfully unaware of the Air Staff political scheming, the dawn of a new air service was not exactly greeted with universal enthusiasm.

The antagonism of the RFC pilots and gunners of 141 Squadron reflected the contempt in which the RNAS was held by the Army. Fiercely proud of their young heritage and hard-won military achievements, the RFC crews strongly resented a merger with the Navy fliers, whom they regarded as an inferior branch of the flying service, waging war in obsolescent aircraft against submarines. 'Just don't let them send any of those bell-bottomed buggers to our squadron,' said one 141 pilot, 'they had better be a very Silent Service if they come near us.'[15]

When the RFC pilots discovered that their new uniforms were to be blue (the Navy's colour), they felt utterly betrayed by the new Air Ministry.

There was more than pride at stake. Under its new commanding officer Major Brian Baker, 141 Squadron had become a well-drilled and highly effective fighter unit.

On 19 May 1918 Baker and the crews of 141 Squadron, now a newly formed RAF squadron, faced their sternest test. The Germans had assembled the largest number of aircraft ever to take part in a long-range bombing raid. Thirty-eight Gothas, three Giants and two smaller bombers set off from their Belgium airbases on a moonlit night and headed for the north Kent coast. At 22.30 holidaymakers enjoying a moonlit swim at Margate heard the plane engines overhead and saw a flare float down over the sea, signalling the commencement of the German bombing run up the Thames estuary. In response maroons were fired off in London to warn the population of the impending danger. But it had been so long since the last big raid that few Londoners took any notice.[16]

The searchlights and anti-aircraft guns of London's newly strengthened home defences turned the night sky into a reassuring fireworks display.

Within minutes of the first bomber crossing the coast, Biggin Hill ordered its nine Bristol Fighters into the air. The pilots now looked to the new enemy location system to direct them to the Gothas and Giants which were approaching the city in eight waves at five-minute intervals.

German bombs were scattered across the outskirts of the capital as the bombers weaved their way through the defensive barrage of anti-aircraft fire. Pilot Edward Eric Turner and his observer Henry Balfour Barwise were flying at 12,000 feet above Charles Darwin's home in Downe in Kent when they saw a Gotha silhouetted against the moon trying to slip home after dropping bombs on Rotherhithe, Peckham and the Old Kent Road. Turner used the glare of the Gotha's exhaust to position his Bristol above the enemy aircraft. After gaining sufficient height he pushed on the joystick, sending the plane roaring down towards the target. In the first sweep Turner fired incendiary tracer and armour-piercing bullets into the Gotha's belly, while Barwise used his rear-mounted Lewis gun to rake it from nose to tail as soon as the Bristol had completed the pass. But the Gotha appeared to have absorbed the initial punishment and continued on its homeward course. The British fighter had not given up and Turner attempted to repeat the attacking manoeuvre. This time the German pilot was wise to the attack and side-slipped steeply to upset the tailing Bristol with his slipstream. But it was already too late. Barwise's bullets had scored a hit on the petrol tank as well as causing considerable damage to one of the Gotha's engines. As the Gotha struggled to maintain height it was spotted by another British fighter, a Sopwith Camel flown by Major Frederick Sowrey from 143 Squadron. Sowrey, an ace fighter pilot who had recently transferred from France, fired two drums of bullets at the Gotha, wounding the pilot, before the German bomber helplessly drifted down on to the lee side of the Kent Downs, crash-landing near Harrietsham. The pilot and observer were dead, but the rear gunner miraculously escaped with just a broken arm.

When Turner and Barwise returned to Biggin Hill to celebrate their victory they were met by a muted reception. Sowrey had also claimed the kill. The decision as to which pilot would be credited with the German bomber was to be decided by an inquiry headed by a Wing HQ investigation. The rules of attribution were quite clear – the aircraft which had fired the first shots would be able to bag the prized Gotha. Fortunately staff officers were able to interview the surviving German gunner who emphatically told them that it was the Bristol machine guns which had scored the first hits against his aircraft. Biggin Hill had won its first kill and the news set off considerable celebrations at the airfield. It was followed swiftly by a message from the Lord Mayor of London, which the squadron commander, Major Baker proudly read to all the crew: 'The citizens of London are filled with admiration and gratitude for the splendid defensive measures taken by the Air Services against the enemy's attack and will be glad if their appreciation and thanks will be conveyed to those who gallantly and successfully protected the capital on that occasion.'

Turner and Barwise were both awarded the DFC and later took possession of the Gotha's Spandau gun, which remained an honoured squadron trophy long after the two World Wars.

Of the forty-three German aircraft that took off from Belgian airfields that night, only nineteen managed to penetrate the London defences. Three, including 141's Gotha, were shot down by British fighters, three more were lost to heavy anti-aircraft fire and another two crashed due to engine trouble.

The British estimated that 2700 lb of bombs were dropped, although the German figure was 3200 lb. The total civilian casualties were forty-nine people killed and 177 injured.

The 19 May bomber raid was to be the last launched against the British mainland until the start of air hostilities which culminated in the Battle of Britain in 1940. The Bristol, a two-seater fighter crewed by a pilot and rear gunner, had proved to be a very effective bomber destroyer. When the Germans returned twenty-two years later it would be the next generation of airmen attached to 141 Squadron who would be tasked with the defence of the realm in another two-seater fighter aircraft – the Boulton Paul Defiant.

# Chapter 2

# REARMAMENT

THE MONTHS LEADING up to the armistice of November 1918 were empty ones for No. 141 Squadron. The diminishing threat of the German bomber menace meant the aircrews spent the summer endlessly practising formation flying drills. Newspaper reports of how their RAF colleagues in France were shooting down the Hun in daily aerial combats only added to their frustrations. The bored crews devoted more of their time to drinking in the mess playing rowdy games, and then at weekends organising charabanc trips to London or the seaside.

In an effort to distract his pilots, the squadron's commanding officer Major Baker, a battle-hardened fighter pilot with twelve enemy kills to his name, restricted the crews to base and introduced rugby and cross-country paperchases to help the men run off their nervous energy. But the young pilots were not so easily engaged and the fighter crews started competing in reckless flying dares resulting in aircraft prangs, some involving serious injury and even loss of life.

Finally London's home defence headquarters was forced to intervene. It was decided the best way of maintaining morale and discipline among the idle home crews was to hold an inter-squadron flying competition. The squadron which proved to be the most proficient in formation flying, aerobatics, wireless telephony and gunnery would be awarded a silver cup and honoured with the title 'Cock' squadron, which gave the pilots the right to sport the figure of a fighting cock on their aircraft. No. 141, which considered itself the premier squadron, sailed through to the finals held on 22 September at Sutton's Farm, home to 78 Squadron which had already been eliminated from the competition.

On the day more than a hundred aircraft were lined up across the airfield and the great and the good of metropolis London and the home counties were in attendance to witness the spectacle. Among them was Lord Weir, Minister of Air. After a slow start in formation flying 141 had it all to do. In the gunnery trial each squadron's top marksman had to fly his aircraft from a height of 3300 feet and dive onto a ground target. No. 141 was quietly confident in its choice of pilot, Lieutenant Thomas Langford-Sainsbury, a very experienced flyer who went on to command the fighter station at RAF Thorney Island during the Battle of Britain. But after the other squadrons had made reasonable scores Langford-Sainsbury's guns jammed. On the third dive he rescued the situation, opening up with his Vickers machine gun and obliterating the target. However, it was in the final event that 141 showed its true colours. Baker's insistence on months of painstaking practice in relaying countless messages by wireless telephony paid off. The accuracy of the final transcribed messages was so close a match that the other squadrons accused 141 of cheating. No. 141 Squadron happily accepted the challenge of a second test in which they repeated the result.

Lord Weir commended 141 as the star fighter squadron of the home defence and awarded Major Baker a live fighting cock. Clutching their trophy and cockerel the jubilant crews mounted their Bristols and flew back to Biggin Hill.

A few weeks later and the war was over. In celebration, the Biggin Hill pilots took the WRAFs and any other girls who would go with them on victory joyrides around the airfield. Then they headed off to London to join the wild celebrations. Officers from 141 dragged the guns in Hyde Park down the Mall and left them under Admiralty Arch. As the drink continued to flow they commandeered a taxi, drove it to Piccadilly and jammed it into the entrance of the Criterion restaurant where it immediately burst into flames. They capped their exuberance by setting light to a coffee bar under Nelson's Column before heading off to the Savoy to drink themselves into oblivion.

Great Britain had begun the war with just thirty front-line flying machines. At the end of hostilities in 1918 the RAF was the most powerful air force in the world, in possession of over twenty thousand aircraft, 103 airships and a third of a million personnel.

But the war had drained the national coffers, leaving peace-time Britain unable to afford such a large standing Army, Navy and now an air service. So the government embarked on a demobilisation programme across all the services. For the RAF, the most junior of the services, abolition was in the air.

Prime Minister Lloyd George, never a fan of the air service, made Winston Churchill the new Minister for War and, signalling his contempt for the newly established RAF, told him: 'You can take the air with you in either case. I'm not going to keep it as a separate department.'[1]

Churchill was ambivalent about the independence of the RAF. He could see that it had played a role in the winning of the war but he was less sure about its long-term survival without the support of the Army or the Navy. His first ministerial action was to summon Trenchard to the War and Air Office to discuss the future of the RAF. Trenchard, fed up with scheming politicians, had already resigned his commission, and after putting down a soldiers' mutiny in Southampton had gone on holiday. But Churchill was in great need of his counsel. After all, Trenchard was the airman who had led the air service to air superiority and ultimate victory in France.

Trenchard, with absolutely nothing to lose, arrived in London for his meeting with Churchill and passionately argued the case for retaining the RAF as a separate fighting arm of the military. Churchill was so moved by Trenchard's plea that he offered him his old job, Chief of the Air Staff. He also asked Trenchard to write down a blueprint for the new service.

Trenchard went back to his London flat and scribbled eight hundred words on foolscap paper which he duly posted to Churchill. Those eight hundred words would turn out to be the most important written in RAF history and would preserve the RAF as a separate fighting force fit for the home defence of Great Britain in its greatest hour of need.

Group Captain Peter Townsend, who fought in the Battle of Britain, summed up Trenchard's document in his quintessential account of the battle, *Duel of Eagles*: 'The memorandum was the work of a prophet and a professional. Independence was to be the basic principle of the new RAF. Trenchard envisaged in one stroke its fundamental needs: technical experts for development and research of the aeronautical science; training colleges for officers and technical apprenticeships. The officer cadet colleges would provide permanently commissioned officers to form roughly one third of the strength while the remaining two thirds would be "short service" officers with a five-year commission. This would build up a reserve at minimum cost. An Auxiliary Airforce of "weekend flyers" would provide a permanently active backing to the regular squadrons . . . officers must learn to be more than "air chauffeurs"; mechanics must become masters in their trade.'

Townsend concluded: 'The memorandum laid out so exactly the needs and functions of the new service that fifteen years later (practically unchanged in form) it would provide the basis of the RAF's immense expansion schemes . . .'[2]

But that was for later.

Young men serving and surviving in the RFC and the RNAS had achieved high ranks in a relatively short period. Flying aeroplanes for a living was more than a career, it was a calling. While the mobilised soldiers and sailors might have been anxious to return to the lives they had before the war, the men of the RAF were not.

Lloyd George's government approached the task of culling numbers with dispassionate efficiency, capping the RAF officer corps at fifteen hundred. It meant that six-and-a-half thousand officers, all holding temporary commissions or seconded from the Army and Navy, had to apply for permanent commissions, knowing that only one in four would be successful. The Air Ministry actually only kept open one thousand and sixty-five officer posts, publishing the first list of the successful applicants on 1 August 1919, 75 per cent of them on short-term (two to five years) commissions. The service as a whole had been reduced in strength to thirty-five thousand personnel.[3]

None of this pleased Trenchard, who had just begun his second term of office as Chief of the Air Staff, and he complained: 'I have been left with two heaps of rubble. One of bricks and mortar, the other of men.'[4]

Trenchard was also facing renewed territorial claims over his planes from the Navy and the Army, whose high command sensed the vulnerability of the weakened RAF. Churchill, who had become obsessively preoccupied with defeating the threat of the Bolsheviks in Russia, left Trenchard to fend off the predatory advances on his own, which he did with commendable single-mindedness.

One of the officers waiting to hear whether he was to be kept on was Hugh Dowding, now in charge of No. 1 Training Group at RAF Kenley, near Croydon. He suspected his application had not been supported by Trenchard, with whom he had fallen out during a number of 'unpleasant' incidents when his tendency to speak out earned him a reputation for being awkward and militant. It looked as if he might have to resign himself to returning to the Artillery.

The German air force, as the vanquished foe, was to absorb far worse cuts. For its officers this was very hard to accept. Consensus of feeling among the young pilots was that they didn't believe they had lost the war – defeat had been imposed upon them by the gutless generals. This was a sentiment especially felt by Hermann Göring. Göring had won a reputation as an ace fighter pilot who had finished the war commanding Richthofen's famous Circus after the death of its eponymous leader. Some thought Göring to be a courageous commanding officer, others regarded him as reckless flyer whose refusal to turn away from the enemy had needlessly cost the lives of many brave pilots and reduced the Circus to a shadow of the force it was under Richthofen.

On the day the Armistice was signed, Göring received an order to surrender his aircraft to an American unit. He ignored it and instead flew the Circus back to Darmstadt in Germany. It was the French who eventually caught up with him, but in one last act of defiance he destroyed all his machines by ordering his pilots to take part in a mass crash-landing.

Göring and Dowding were to later meet as adversaries in the greatest air battle ever fought. But in 1919 both men had every reason to believe their flying careers were over. At least Göring could rationalise his fall from grace. For Dowding, who had been on the winning side, it was difficult to reconcile his unblemished war record with an uncertain military future.

Having won the war, the Allies threw themselves into administering the peace. For the French this meant squeezing the pips of the German economy and its military until they squeaked. Under the terms of the Treaty of Versailles the German Imperial Army was liquidated and replaced with the Reichswehr force limited to a hundred thousand service personnel. And there was a strict prohibition on a German air force.

However, the newly appointed head of the Reichswehr, General Hans von Seeckt, had no intention of honouring the Allies' terms of surrender. There would be an air force but it would be one that wasn't visible to the Allies. Von Seeckt made sure that one hundred and eighty committed air force officers were secreted within the new German defence ministry in the surviving army units. Among them were Albert Kesselring, Hans-Jüergen Stumpff and Hugo Sperrle, who in 1940 would command the three Luftflotten which formed the German air assault on Britain. Göring had already left the country and taken up a desk job in charge of a Swedish airline.[5]

Meanwhile, in London, Trenchard was embroiled in his own battle with the government and the heads of the Army and the Navy over the viable future of the RAF. The dispute was finally resolved by the mediation of Arthur Balfour [6], whom the Cabinet had asked to settle the question of RAF independence once and for all. He concluded that for as long as it was possible to envisage military operations in which only aircraft were deployed there was a strong case for a separate air force. Balfour's pronouncement was now welcomed by Churchill who presciently declared: 'If war on a great scale broke out, the Power which had made the most intensive study of aerial warfare would start with an enormous advantage . . . To keep this new arm, with its measureless possibilities in perpetual thralldom to the Army or Navy will rob it of its most important developments.'[7]

RAF independence may have been secured, but it was unrecognisable to the fighting force it had been at the climax of the war. The one hundred and eighty-five squadrons of 1918 had been reduced to a paltry twenty-eight. Only seven of these were based in the UK of which just three were reserved for home defence. The rest were mostly serving in the Middle East and Africa helping to hold together the Empire. Should a hostile power have chosen 1922 to launch an assault against the British homeland, just thirty-six aircraft stood in its way. By stark contrast France retained 126 squadrons.[8]

These woeful aircraft figures were soon leaked to and seized upon by the press. *The Times* called it a 'betrayal' and the *Observer* decried it as the 'supreme blunder since the Armistice'.

While the British had failed to take advantage of their dominant military position after the war, the Germans were determined that the Treaty of Versailles would not hold them back. On 16 April 1922 Germany signed the Treaty of Rapallo with the newly established Bolshevik Russian state. In a secret section of the treaty it was agreed that three Russian air bases, well away from the prying eyes of the British and French, were to be handed over to the Germans to develop their aircraft and train their pilots. It was at an airfield near Lipetsk that the Germans began the clandestine evolution of their new air force.

At the same time, unaware of the hidden implications of the Russian pact, the Allies lifted the restrictions on the German civil aircraft industry, putting Junkers, Dornier and Heinkel back in business. Crucially it meant the First World War fighter aces of the old German air force had plenty of modern aircraft to fly. These were the men who would later comprise the pilot officer corps of the Luftwaffe. The civil gliding schools, that were unaffected by the treaty nor merited much Allied concern, provided the essential training for the select ranks of the next generation of German aircrew.

The German public remained proud of the part played by their gallant air force during the war. Tales of heroism in the skies over the Western Front were immortalised in the literature of the day. They even had their own version of Biggles. But special reverence was reserved for their greatest fighting ace – Baron von Richthofen. On 20 November 1925, bells tolled across the country when the body of the Red Baron was repatriated from a French cemetery to his final resting place in Potsdam where thousands came to pay their respects at his state funeral. Conspicuous by his absence was the last leader of the Circus, Hermann Göring, who after being wounded in Hitler's 1923 failed coup of the Beer Hall Putsch was now being treated for a morphine addiction in a clinic back in Sweden.

The exploits of Britain's own brave fighter pilots, like my Uncle George, commanded far less celebratory attention. Instead Trenchard intended to rebuild the RAF around the bomber squadron, not the fighter. In a speech he gave in Cambridge, in the same year the Germans were paying homage to their fallen eagle, Trenchard reasserted his belief that the bomber was the key aircraft of any modern air force. Defence, he argued, was largely pointless: 'The airplane is the most offensive weapon that has ever been invented. It is a shockingly bad weapon of defence . . . although it is necessary to have some defence to keep up the morale of your own people, it is infinitely more necessary to lower the morale of the people against you by attacking them.'

For Trenchard the sole purpose of having an air force was to bomb the enemy into submission. However, he did accept one vital concession to defence by allowing the cities of London, Edinburgh and Glasgow to organise their own volunteer citizen pilots who under their own resources would be able to spend the weekends training to fly.

In 1927 Göring, taking advantage of a government amnesty, returned from Sweden, cured of his drug addiction, and started work as a Lufthansa agent in Berlin. When Hitler visited the city Göring met the leader of Germany's new national socialist movement, impressing upon him that his contacts and money could be very useful to the Nazi Party. Hitler did not demur and agreed to support Göring's party candidature for the Reichstag.

But Germany was now in the deepest grip of an inflationary recession. German housewives filled wheelbarrows with marks just to buy a loaf of bread. Six million people were out of work.

Hannes Trautloft, a young German from Saxony, was one of them. He had grown up among the forested hills where his father worked as a ranger. Here he had watched the gliders soaring over the Wasserkuppe, its high plateaus so perfectly suited to the training of young pilots. At his school in Schloss Bieberstein he helped build a glider from scratch. And after leaving school the young Trautloft dreamt of only one thing – to become a pilot with the Reichswehr.[9]

The fact that so did every other German teenager seemed to make no difference to him. So he wrote directly to the colonel of his regional regiment and was invited, along with three hundred young men, to a physical training day. Trautloft later recorded in his diary that he grabbed the attention of one of the selection officers by throwing a 'grenade' so far that it landed in a puddle of water, splashing the senior commander. He was told that he had passed the physical test and also showed the necessary aptitude to be a pilot. The odds on Hannes Trautloft being one of the lucky few to be offered a place on the pilot training course had considerably shortened. A year later he was invited to report to the Schleissheim pilot school where he was joined by twenty-nine other idealistic hopefuls. When Trautloft found out he was one of the ten Germans chosen to make the secret trip to Lipetsk in Russia he could barely contain his excitement.

The Lipetsk German flying school was staffed by former First World War fighter aces flying fifty specially ordered Dutch-built Fokker D XIIIs, unbraced biplanes powered by British 450 hp water-cooled Napier Lion engines. They could reach a top speed of nearly 150 mph and they were armed with two machine guns. In addition, the school had a few light Albatros trainers from First World War days. Trautloft and the other trainee pilots spent four weeks of intensive flying in groups of seven cadets.[10]

As part of von Seeckt's plan for rebuilding the German air force, Trautloft and the other pilots were then quietly placed among Germany's army units. Trautloft was sent to a Jäger Battalion at Magdeburg. Others joined cavalry battalions. These clandestine pilots were told to never disclose the fact they had been trained at Lipetsk. For Trautloft this was more difficult as his commanding officer was obsessed with air warfare. Occasionally, Trautloft was granted special leave, ostensibly to return to his family. In reality he was sent on a refresher course at the flying school at Brunswick. When Hitler became Chancellor of the Third Reich in 1933 the only change the pilots noticed was a subtle addition to their uniform – a pair of eagle wings sewn into the lapel of the tunic. These were the German elite fighter pilots, members of the German Air Sports Association, who seventeen years later would lead the attack on Britain.

Hannes Trautloft was no different from the thousands of British young men who left school consumed by the same excitement and wonder at the prospect of flying an aeroplane. One of them was William Arthur Richardson, born on 19 July 1903. These two young pilots were destined to meet over the English Channel in one of the most decisive encounters of the early stages of the Battle of Britain.

William Richardson was born in Hong Kong where his father was working as a marine engineer on the China railways. When he was five years old he was sent back to boarding school in England in the care of his uncle. He never saw his parents again. They contracted diseases and died in China when William was in his early teens.

After school, he joined the family typewriter ribbon-making business but he hated it and begged his uncle to pay for a one-way ticket to Australia where he hoped to find adventure. In Australia, he spent three years working as a 'jackaroo', rounding up sheep and honing his skills as a horseman and an expert shot with a rifle. He even won a few horse races.

Returning on a steamer to England he fell into conversation with a British pilot who told him that if he was still seeking real adventure he should join the RAF because they 'will pay for your flying lessons'.[11]

Richardson joined the RAF on a short service commission in March 1930, a year before Trautloft had answered the call of the Reichswehr. He arrived at No. 5 Flying Training School, RAF Sealand, north Wales, fresh from his month of 'square bashing' at RAF Uxbridge in Middlesex. Many of the young pilot cadets had already flown solo in gliders at an Elementary Flying Training School where they were inducted into the RAF. Pilots thus arrived at Sealand as Acting Pilot Officers (APO) and upon satisfactory completion of intermediate training became qualified Pilot Officers (PO) and were posted to a squadron or Operational Training Unit. Richardson's instructor was Kenneth 'Bing' Cross, who would go on to lead the RAF's forlorn efforts to support the Army in its disastrous Norway campaign. Among the other APOs was Harvey Heyworth, a Battle of Britain Spitfire pilot who later became one of the RAF's most experienced jet-engine test pilots.[12]

At Sealand the young pilots' flying skills were exhaustively tested. They had to show they could take off into wind, carry out low flying, make steep turns and forced landings as well as fly at night. Richardson took to flying like a duck to water. The aircraft chosen by the RAF for their new recruits were twin-seater biplanes, the Avro Tutor and Armstrong Whitworth Siskin. So in the early 1930s British and German pilots (in their Fokkers) were being trained on remarkably similar aircraft, a model hardly changed since the end of the First World War.

But this parity in air weaponry was about to change. In 1933 Hitler made Göring head of his Air Ministry. Under Göring was Erhard Milch, a low-ranking observer gunner in the great war with an extensive combat record.

It was Milch who is credited with founding the Luftwaffe, the air force of Nazi Germany. Göring could be an inspirational leader and hard task master but he was not interested in detail. Milch had a natural capacity for organisation and took a close interest in the production and supply of aircraft as well as the selection of the new pilots.

Under the rearmament programme Germany developed new aircraft which would lead the world in military aviation. The Heinkel 70 (He 70) was about to break the international speed record. Willy Messerschmitt was close to perfecting his 108, the forerunner of the superb Me 109, a state-of-the-art fighter that would dominate aerial combat in the early years of the coming war. Hitler's rise to power meant the Nazis could now abandon the pretence of clandestine rearmament, which included leaving the Soviet airbase of Lipetsk. The moment had come for men like Trautloft to leave their army units and join secret fighter squadrons.

All this time Britain remained negligently oblivious to the growing threat to its air power superiority. The Germans found it very easy to pull the wool over the eyes of some very senior Air Staff who should have been less gullible. British aviator and former First World War soldier, Lord Willoughby de Broke, jointly led a group of aircraft owners and parliamentarians invited by Göring to review the state of the German aircraft industry. They happily accepted German assurances that rearmament, especially in the air, was out of the question. Lord Willoughby would more than make up for his oversight in the summer of 1940 when he was duty controller in the No. 11 Group Operations Room at RAF Uxbridge, the epicentre of the Battle of Britain.

Under the careful direction of Milch, leading German aeronautical companies, including Heinkel, Dornier, Junkers and Messerschmitt were encouraged to adapt their civil models into military bombers and fighters which would become the backbone of the Luftwaffe. By the end of 1935 Germany had almost four thousand aircraft at its disposal.[13]

The only element the Germans lacked was aircraft engine technology to power their new machines. It was the unwitting British who provided the solution. Britain's Napier had already equipped the Fokker D XIII trainers with a suitable engine which the Germans had put to such good use in Lipetsk. Next it was the turn of Rolls-Royce. Early models of the Junkers 87 Stuka (Ju 87) and the Messerschmitt BF109 (Me 109) were powered by the famous Rolls-Royce Kestrel engine. In hindsight it is of course easy to criticise British companies for being so compliant in the rearmament of the German air force. But in the mid-1930s the world was still in the grip of a recession and all business was welcome. However, the British had been canny enough not to give up all their engine secrets. The Rolls-Royce Merlin, which would later be used to power the Hurricanes and Spitfires in the defeat of the Luftwaffe, was twice as powerful as the Kestrel, a prize that was jealously and secretly guarded by the Whitehall air chiefs.

The British also held another critical advantage over the Germans – a human rather than a mechanical one. In 1930 the Cabinet appointed Hugh Dowding to be in charge of RAF supply and research.

# Chapter 3

# BOMBERS IN COMMAND

TODAY WE ARE used to our skies being criss-crossed by a multitude of civil and military aircraft. But in the early days of aviation, the wonder of flight captured the fears as much as the excitement of the public. Films like Howard Hughes' *Hell's Angels* and *Flash Gordon,* as well as H. G. Wells' book *War in the Air*, portrayed the inability of cities to defend themselves against the unstoppable destructive power of the aeroplane.

Looking back to the years before the Second World War, Harold Macmillan, then a senior member of Churchill's government, said: 'We thought of air warfare rather as people think of nuclear warfare today.'[1]

It was Hugh Trenchard who had passionately advocated for the bomber, believing that the next war would be won by the nation which was capable of dropping the most bombs on the enemy civilian population. In 1932 Prime Minister Stanley Baldwin gave Trenchard's military doctrine a popular voice when he addressed the House of Commons on 10 November, declaring: 'I think it is well also for the man in the street to realise that there is no power on earth that can protect him from being bombed. Whatever people may tell him, the bomber will always get through. The only defence is in offence, which means that you have to kill more women and children more quickly than the enemy if you want to save yourselves.' And he warned that in the next war the aeroplane would 'wipe out European civilisation'.

In the run-up to the Second World War the men in the Air Ministry were paralysed by a post-victory complacency after the last conflict. Instead of looking to redesign a new fighter aircraft the British focused on an offensive strategy for winning the next war. They blindly placed their faith in Trenchard's doctrine of a war fought between fleets of bombers, each passing each other in the sky on the way to bomb their enemy's home. Victory would not be achieved by the physical damage done to the enemy's industries but the terror caused by the hundreds of thousands of civilian deaths. Trenchardists did not believe that a formation of fortified bombers could be disrupted, never mind destroyed, by squadrons of machine gun popping fighters.[2]

In 1928, under the aegis of the newly created Air Defence of Great Britain, there were to be thirty-five bomber squadrons and as few as seventeen fighter squadrons. The only form of defence was to be attack.

World leaders and their air marshals of the interwar years were in the thrall of the all-conquering biplane. The biplane had transformed the way wars were fought and at the end of hostilities in 1918 helped to usher in a golden age of civil aviation. Its combination of modernity and affordable adventure opened up the skies to men and women aviators all over the world. The biplane looked set to dominate the business of flight for many years to come.

But rapid advances in aircraft and engine development meant governments who relied on a fixed policy of aerial warfare were being quickly left behind. The Germans had already equipped themselves with twin-engine monoplane bombers, faster and more heavily armed than the RAF's biplane fighters. Britain was perilously undergunned and unprepared for the next air war.

In 1923 Stanley Baldwin's government created a bureaucratic post on the Air Council for the 'supply and research' of the RAF. This was not a highly prized role but a bureaucratic backwater where the Air Ministry could shunt senior air officers who had served their time and usefulness.

In 1930 the job was given to Hugh Dowding. After the sudden death of his first wife in 1920, Dowding devoted himself to his professional work. Despite his public school background he was not a particularly 'club-able' fellow and had a reputation for being stuffy and aloof. But this didn't seem to bother him and he set about his new job with customary efficiency and fastidiousness, always directly speaking out about ideas or practices which did not stand up to scientific scrutiny.

That was especially true when it came to the doctrine of aerial warfare.

In the summer of 1930 Dowding was asked to take part in an air exercise in which bombers were to attack Britain. Dowding commanded the fighter defence. By deploying his fighters in standing patrols, and with the assistance of a rudimentary early-warning system, he succeeded in intercepting every raid launched against him during the simulated combat exercise. He had proved, to himself at least, that the bomber did not always get through. However, the air games umpires overcompensated for the firepower of the bombers and downgraded Dowding's fighters' 'hits' on the attacking force so that he was ruled to have suffered unsustainable losses and victory was awarded to the bombers.[3]

It was a telling lesson, much better understood by Dowding than the Air Ministry. Dowding dedicated the next few years to creating a home defence that could defend itself against any bomber threat. During his nine years' tenure at the Air Ministry, Dowding laid the groundwork for the RAF's victory in the Battle of Britain. He acquainted himself with all aspects of fighter defence, training, research and development. Moreover, he understood the importance of radar and the urgent need for a new kind of fighter.

In 1936 the government decided to divide the RAF into Bomber and Fighter commands, the former being the much more prestigious of the two services. Dowding was given the job of leading Fighter Command. The Air Ministry's military air strategy had hardly changed since the end of the First World War and remained fixated on the power of the bomber. In the 1930s this fixation was justified by the threat. Intelligence reports reaching Whitehall spoke of Hitler's plans for a fleet of state-of-the-art giant bombers the like of which the world had never seen.

The man in charge of the German super-bomber programme was Generalleutnant Walther Wever, the Luftwaffe's first Chief of Staff. He had persistently advocated for a long-range bomber fleet and in 1936 approved secret plans, codenamed Ural, for two new aircraft. One was the four-engined metal-constructed Dornier (Do) 19, an 84-foot long behemoth of a bomber with a 114-foot wingspan and carrying a ten-man crew, including five gunners. The second was the Ju 89, of similar dimensions but with just five crew.

The Do 19 and Ju 89 were both designed to be heavily fortified and capable of reaching targets as far as Scotland from bases in Germany. Had they been available to the Luftwaffe in 1940 they would have been able to fly from airfields in France into the heart of England, presenting the RAF with a very different kind of adversary. These long-range four-engine bombers mirrored Britain's own designs for bomber aircraft like the Halifax, Stirling and later the more famous Lancaster bomber.

The Air Ministry top brass, responsible for meeting the challenge of the new breed of bomber destroyer, had done their flying in the First World War. The two-seater biplane, which continued to be the staple of the RAF fighter squadrons throughout most of the 1930s, was comfortably familiar to them.

This was particularly true of Wing Commander Arthur 'Cissie' Maund, the man in charge of flying operations. He took the view that single-seat fighters would not be able to tackle large formations of super-bombers. In October 1931 he set out his theory in a paper called 'Bright Ideas Fighters' which he presented to the Deputy Chief of the Air Staff, Charles Burnett. In it he proposed a new kind of fighter capable of breaking up the bombers before they reached their target. This, he argued, required a large number of fighters capable of directing unified and coordinated fire into the belly of enemy bombers. And to achieve this, argued Maund, the pilot had to be free to manoeuvre his aircraft without concerning himself with the operation of the machine guns.

Maund's ideas took hold and quickly became accepted orthodoxy among the Air Staff. Its greatest champion was

Geoffrey Salmond who in 1933 became commander-in-chief of Britain's air defence. In response to the 'Bright Ideas' paper he wrote: 'It will be recognised that in practically all the proposals put forward by the various officers under my command there is a note of pessimism as to the ability of present-day fighters to compete successfully with hostile bombing formations. This is a clear warning that there is something wrong in our policy. I would suggest that the fixed-gun single-seater fighter which is the cause of this pessimism was designed in the first instance rather for the needs of air fighting in France in 1916 to 1918 than for the purpose of home defence fighting.'

In a strong call for an aircraft equipped with the similar free-guns deployed by biplanes in the First World War, Salmond added: 'A pilot cannot aim his gun and at the same time maintain his position in formation.'[4]

A few months after writing these words Salmond was dead, succumbing to a short battle with cancer. He was replaced by his brother, John, another air force veteran from the First World War. John Salmond[5] firmly endorsed his brother's views on the future of the RAF fighter.

In a seamless procession of Air Defence chief appointments, the Salmond doctrine was followed by the higher echelons of the Air Council. Indeed Salmond's successor, Air Marshal Sir Edward Ellington, thought it would be impossible to avoid collisions between friendly fighters while undertaking formation bomber attacks if the pilot also had to fire the guns. Even Dowding, who was consulted about the new ideas for attacking bombers, could see merit in the general thesis but remained cautious about the aircraft industry's ability to deliver such an aircraft.[6]

In 1932 an Air Ministry memorandum was issued which set out the criteria for the new bomber destroyer. Britain's advanced fighter was to be all things to all air forces – able to both engage fighters and bring down bombers with coordinated fire.

After considering a number of proposals, the Air Ministry settled on an adaption of the successful Hawker Hart bomber as the fighter that could best match its requirements. Its firepower consisted of a single rear .303 (7.7 mm) Lewis Gun with two fixed .303 (7.7 mm) Vickers machine guns fitted in the nose. The aircraft was powered by a supercharged Kestrel IS engine. The new fighter not only proved to be faster than the RAF's reliable Siskins and Bulldogs but it also packed a bigger punch. After its first flight on 10 February 1933 the Air Ministry ordered 232 of these new Hawker Demons.

But the Air Ministry was not completely satisfied with its new fighter. One further technical advancement was required, which the Air Staff believed would allow their fighter to effectively counter an attack by a mass formation of giant enemy bombers. An enhanced turret was to be fitted to the rear seat to protect the gunner from enemy return fire as well as provide a stable platform from which to operate the guns.

Squadrons of turret-armed fighters would be able to approach a fleet of enemy bombers from below or from the side and coordinate their fire – much like a fleet of naval frigates in Nelson's day. The strict division of roles between the flying of the aircraft and firing the guns allowed the pilot to concentrate on manoeuvring the fighter into the best position for the gunner to engage the enemy. Although this idea was presented as a modern concept in aerial combat it relied on the same tried-and-tested separation of duties employed by the twin-seater fighters of the First World War, like the Fe2d and Bristol.

Such easily understood air tactics were as reassuring to the air marshals as they were to the veteran First World War pilots like my Uncle George.

However, early trials found the manually operated turret to be too heavy and cumbersome for the gunner to move during flight. So the Air Ministry sought out a design that would enable the gunner to deliver accurate fire while facing turbulence at high speeds and in battle conditions. The answer would turn out to be a newly developed hydraulically powered turret.

The company chosen to build the powered-turret Demons was Boulton Paul, then based in Norwich. Boulton Paul had enjoyed a good First World War. Its aircraft had a reputation for being sturdily built (as my Uncle George had so vividly testified in the battle with the Red Baron's Circus flying his Fe2d in 1917). The company was well known to the Air Ministry because it had built more Sopwith Camels (550), the first truly British designed and manufactured fighter of the First World War, than any other company.[7] And crucially, Boulton Paul already had experience in the use of turrets.

After the war the company had developed a twin-engine bomber biplane, the Overstrand, which was the first RAF plane to have an enclosed and powered turret fitted with a machine gun. Movement of the nose turret was driven by pneumatic motors, elevation and depression of the gun by hydraulic rams. It was crewed by a pilot and three gunners, one perched in the enclosed nose turret and one each in the open dorsal and ventral gun positions. The Overstrand enjoyed the same smooth handling of the earlier Boulton Paul P.7 Bourges, but despite proving to be an excellent aircraft for bombing and gunnery, only one squadron ever flew them.

Nevertheless, the Air Ministry now firmly recognised the turreted machine gun station to be a state-of-the-art weapons system. And here Boulton Paul was well in front of the competition. These early designs were the brainchild of Boulton's chief engineer, John Dudley North, who during the First World War had been superintendent of the aviation department of the Austin Motor Company which was churning out the RE.7 and RE.7 biplane light bombers. He had joined Boulton Paul in 1917 as a young, dynamic aircraft designer, and had set up the company's experimental division.[8] On 23 November 1935 the company directors, headed by North, purchased a revolutionary electric hydraulic turret designed by the French company Société d'Application des Machines Matrix (SAMM). Housing four Darne machine guns,[9] it was far in advance of any powered turret being developed in the UK. So it came as a pleasant surprise to North when the French defence ministry rejected it for its own air force.

North later recalled: 'As the result of continental publicity afforded to the Overstrand as the first aeroplane in military service with a powered gun turret, we received a communication from a small French company (SAMM) giving particulars of a powered gun turret developed by the engineer and suggesting to us that we might like to purchase the British Empire rights.' North immediately left for Paris accompanied by his chief test pilot Cecil Feather who had been instrumental in the early development of the Overstrand. 'It appeared to me,' North later wrote, 'that the SAMM development was so much in advance of anything we or Nash [the other British company working on turrets] had done.' A ground trial of the SAMM turret confirmed North's enthusiasm and so the company acquired the rights.

The British Government immediately expressed their own interest. 'On the strength of this,' reported North, 'I was able to place an order for two experimental turrets especially designed for English guns and incorporating certain inventions of my own; the contract gave us an extended option to acquire the British Empire rights on the terms already put forward.'

North was not just an engineer; he was also a good businessman, and through his contacts at the Air Ministry he knew that the government was looking to develop a totally new fighter that would challenge the world view of aerial combat. 'On the basis of this advance information,' wrote North, 'I prepared the general design of the Defiant. This design received an official approval and the directorate decided to proceed with its development as a private venture with some assistance from Rolls-Royce with the reasonable expectation of receiving an experimental contract when the ministry specification was ready. The company then acquired the services of Mr H. V. Clarke, the chief designer, in July 1935 to carry out the design.'[10]

With the completion of the purchase of the French turret the Air Ministry was confident they now possessed the technical means to equip a fighter capable of delivering the overwhelming firepower necessary to defeat the threat posed by Germany's long-range bomber programme. But in 1936, Walther Wever, the mastermind of the Nazis' strategic super-bomber, was killed in a flying accident and Germany's plans for a long-range heavy bomber died with him. The Do 19 and the Ju 89 remained prototypes and Wever's successor, Kesselring who favoured medium bombers, quietly dropped the super-bomber project.

So the Germans, almost by accident, switched their attention and resources to two new kinds of military aircraft – the dive-bombing Ju 87 Stuka and a faster, agile fighter, the Me

109. And instead of the cumbersome super-bomber, the Luftwaffe bomber force would be equipped with tactical medium bombers which required less manpower and materials and were capable of working more closely with the Army.

But for the British, completely unaware of Germany's change in tact, the need to find a modern fighter capable of taking on the anticipated fleets of German super-bombers seemed more urgent than ever.

The Air Ministry had commissioned detailed research on the effects of long-range bombing operations against British cities. Estimates of the number of civilian deaths from a week of German bombing raids ran into hundreds of thousands. Those responsible for the defence of the realm read the reports with grim alarm. They could well imagine the public outcry if the bombers got through and the RAF had been impotent to stop them.

In the rush to commission a new bomber destroyer, senior members of the Air Staff convinced themselves that their new fighter would not need any forward-firing machine guns.

The enemy they faced would have to fly from Germany and would be bereft of fighter escort, leaving the new British fighter with the sole objective of shooting down heavily gunned super-bombers. One of the chief architects of this aerial combat doctrine was Air Vice Marshal Christopher Courtney, who in 1935 was promoted to Deputy Chief of the Air Staff. He began his military career in the Royal Navy where he had learnt about naval gunnery from which he based his fighter thinking. Courtney saw no reason for fitting the aircraft with downward-firing and forward-firing guns. After all, he argued, a fighter attacking the vulnerable underbelly of an enemy bomber needed upward fire, not downward fire.[11]

In March 1935 Courtney wrote to his boss Ellington informing him that the Air Ministry's Air Flying Committee now officially recommended it was 'undesirable to split the armament between the pilot and the air gunner, since the opportunities of fire by the former to be very few and far between under the conditions of tactical employment visualisation for this aeroplane'.[12]

Ellington agreed. Instead of forward guns he suggested beefing up its turret armament by developing a second prototype fitted with the more destructive cannon rather than machine guns. However, not everyone was happy with the idea of a fighter that couldn't fire directly forwards. Even the most feeble of the First World War fighters had a front machine gun.

In April 1935 Ellington approved Air Staff requirement F.9/35, a full specification setting out the precise requirement for the new free-gun fighter. The two vital stipulations for the fighter were that it must have a 'battery of guns amidships' and be able to fly 20 mph faster than the fastest bomber of the day.

Invitations were sent to every aeronautical company in the country,[13] including Supermarine, who were busy developing the Spitfire, and Hawker who were almost ready with their Hurricane.

North knew the contract for his untested Defiant was far from a done deal and Boulton Paul would have to compete with companies who already specialised in front-firing machine guns.

When North used his unofficial channels to approach the Air Ministry about his design he was told by Wing Commander E. D. Davis, the assistant director of armament, that to be sure of securing a commission he might wish to offer a forward firing capability.[14] North duly ordered his designers to incorporate a fixed forward firing position for the turret where the guns could be operated by the pilot pressing a button in the cockpit. However, Boulton Paul didn't get around to synchronising the forward fire with the engine so that if the pilot ever had cause to fire the turret guns in this way he would shoot off his own propellers. No one at the Air Ministry appears to have challenged this idiocy.[15]

The competing company tenders for the F.9/35 contract were whittled down to five and then reduced to two – Boulton Paul's Defiant and Hawker's own design, the Hotspur, which would feature a turret designed by Nash & Thompson.[16]

This pitched Boulton Paul and Hawker against each other to see who would produce the best prototype and win the biggest order. The Royal Navy simultaneously placed an order with Blackburn Aircraft for its own version of the turret fighter, the Roc.

Like the Spitfire, the turret fighter was an all-metal aircraft with a compressed elliptical wing, but in profile it bore a close resemblance to the Hurricane. The fuselage was designed to have easily subcontracted sections that could be bolted together, making it simpler to reproduce and repair than a Spitfire.

To meet the government's anticipated demand for its new fighter, Boulton Paul moved its production from Norwich to Wolverhampton where there was a large pool of motor car engineers working on some of the country's glamorous models such as the Sunbeam and the Star. The nearby Goodyear plant offered a ready supply of tyre fitters. All could be tempted away from the auto-manufacturing factories by increased wages and bonuses as well as the chance to contribute to Britain's new and exciting aeronautical industry.

Having gathered his workforce, North looked for test pilots to fly his revolutionary plane. In 1936 he engaged the services of George Skelton, an experienced Australian pilot. The young pilot had learned to fly in South Africa before signing up for the RAF in 1930. He first trained on Bristol Bulldogs with 32 Squadron at RAF Kenley, Surrey, and later Westland Wapitis with 30 Squadron in Iraq. In 1936 he was promoted to Flight Lieutenant (Flt Lt) and placed on the Reserve Class C which allowed him to work with Boulton Paul while still being employed by the RAF. When war was declared Skelton joined 264 Squadron, later flying Defiants in their very first combats.

The Defiant prototype was tested by Boulton Paul in August 1937 and was delivered to Martlesham Heath, Suffolk, home to the RAF's Aeroplane and Armament Experimental Establishment, in December.[17] Here the Defiant, still minus its turret, underwent rigorous testing as RAF pilots put it through its paces. Back at Wolverhampton, North and his design team waited anxiously for the results. They needn't have worried. The Defiant's sleek look, from nosetip to tailplane, was beautifully smooth, with the cockpit and gun turret space streamlined with the fuselage. More importantly its performance exceeded both Boulton Paul and Air Ministry expectations. The Defiant was credited with a top speed of 323 mph[18], as fast as a Hurricane, and could climb to around 30,000 feet in just seven-and-a-half minutes. The performance report written by Robert Saundy, the Deputy Director of Operational Requirements, concluded: 'The Defiant is a peculiarly viceless and straightforward aeroplane to fly.'[19]

The commanding officer at Martlesham Heath went even further, declaring the turret fighter to be 'the finest built aircraft that has come to Martlesham Heath.'[20]

It meant that North's design was up and flying and well ahead of the rival tender, the Hawker Hotspur, which wouldn't undergo its first test for another ten months. When the Hotspur finally arrived at Martlesham Heath early trials showed 'there really is nothing to choose between the Defiant and the Hotspur in performance.'

However, Air Ministry minutes reveal that Hawker had by now all but abandoned its commitment to the Hotspur so it could focus on the Hurricane, gambling that the government would give the fixed gun fighter priority over the turret fighter. In January 1938 Robert Saundby wrote to the new Chief of the Air Staff, Cyril Newall, giving the nod to the Defiant.

He told Newall: 'Whereas Boulton Paul have been most enthusiastic about their design, Hawkers have shown less interest in the flying trials of their first prototype . . . and appear to show more interest in fixed-front gun fighters. I therefore think the risk in accepting the Defiant is small and we should accept the risk.'[21]

It was a decision which would have important implications for the coming Battle of Britain. Had Hawker given the turret fighter its full attention it might well have beaten Boulton Paul to the contract. Encumbered by the additional production demands placed upon it, Hawker would have been unable to equip Fighter Command with the number of Hurricanes that proved so decisive in the battle.

Meanwhile, the Defiant was fitted with its turret and underwent further testing at Martlesham Heath. Results from the second trials were proving to be just as positive as the first. Despite the turret's considerable drag and additional weight the Defiant's top speed was only reduced by 17 mph, slower than the Hurricane Mk 1 but faster than North had anticipated. This was almost entirely due to its superb Rolls-Royce Merlin engine, which also powered the Spitfire and the Hurricane. The Air Staff declared themselves more than satisfied with their new bomber destroyer.

But while the Air Ministry forged ahead in its quest to re-equip the RAF with twin-seater gunships, developments in civil aviation were taking a very different course.

The contraction of Britain's aircraft industry after the war forced companies to compete for overseas business and contracts tended to be won by companies whose aircraft performed best at international air shows. The most prestigious of them all was the Schneider Trophy, devised by a French industrialist who offered a prize of £1000 to the company who could build the fastest plane. Victory at the Schneider guaranteed sales. On the final three occasions the race was staged the trophy was won by a small Southampton-based aircraft design company called Supermarine.

In 1931 the Supermarine seaplane set a new world speed record of 380 mph. Then a few days later the Supermarine S.6B smashed through the 400 mph speed record. This rapid development in civil aircraft performance was outstripping all military advances. None of this had gone unnoticed by Hugh Dowding, head of the Air Ministry's Supply and Research.

The challenge for Dowding and those in the Air Ministry who recognised the need for the fastest plane available was how to turn a super-fast lightweight civil aircraft into a high-performance British fighter. Supermarine's Reginald J. Mitchell, who had designed the Schneider winner, began work on meeting the Air Ministry's requirements, but it turned out to be a far from straightforward task. His first effort, Type 224, flew on 19 February 1934 reaching a disappointing maximum speed of only 228 mph and taking a lumbering nine-and-a-half minutes to climb to 15,000 feet. Such poor performance figures dampened enthusiasm in Whitehall where many of the air chiefs had always remained unconvinced about the viability of a single-seat monoplane fighter. Mitchell's first design only confirmed their own prejudices, prompting the government to commission another biplane fighter, the radial-engined Gloster Gladiator.

Similarly, Hawker, which had gambled everything on a fixed gun fighter, had also failed to impress the Air Ministry with its early designs of the Hurricane. This lukewarm support left the company no option but to continue its development at its own expense. The Hawker Hurricane made its maiden flight four months before the Spitfire, posting a speed of 320 mph.

The obsessive Mitchell refused to give up on his own aircraft and continued tirelessly refining his design. On 5 March 1936 the prototype (K5054) took off from Eastleigh Aerodrome. This time performance lived up to the early expectation of the Schneider Trophy with the aircraft attaining a top speed of 347 mph. What was remarkable was that the new plane had achieved such a high performance while fitted with four .303 Browning machine guns in each wing. These results helped convince Dowding that the new generation of modern RAF fighters must be based on a monoplane design.

Yet as late as the summer of 1937 all the RAF squadrons were flying biplanes. And during the national exhibition at RAF Hendon in the same year every aircraft featured in the military displays was a biplane. Dowding later recalled in an interview with the BBC in 1968 that the Air Ministry remained fixated with biplanes, remarking: 'If it hadn't been for the Schneider Trophy there wouldn't have been any machines flying in Fighter Command other than the Gloster Gladiator biplane. That would mean we couldn't have fought the war because the bombers could just fly away from them.'

By contrast, the German squadrons were already mostly equipped with monoplane fighters. In 1937 the Me 109 was not only capable of outperforming the prototype Hurricane and Spitfire, it was about to be tested in combat conditions in the Spanish Civil War.

However, it was the Luftwaffe's second fighter, the Messerschmitt BF110, flaunted and promoted by Hitler's head of propaganda Josef Goebbels, which was stirring up interest at the Air Ministry. The air marshals were concerned that a twin-engined fighter like the 110, carrying such potent firepower, would be able to blast the RAF bombers out of the skies. The fact that it had been developed behind the 109 only added to the Air Ministry's suspicions that it would prove to be a superior fighter. When British intelligence got hold of the 110's performance data in 1938 their fears were realised. With the Daimler Benz 601 engine, the 110's maximum speed increased to 336 mph and had a range of approximately 680 miles. Bristling with machine guns and cannon, including a rear-firing gun, the plane was everything the British top brass wanted for themselves.

# Chapter 4

# MARCH OF THE MESSERSCHMITT

On 1 March 1935 the Nazi Party enacted a decree which for the first time permitted the airmen of the Luftwaffe to openly salute their Führer. Adolph Hitler's secret new air force was finally free from the shackles of the Treaty of Versailles.

Six days later nineteen infantry battalions supported by Göring's bombers entered the Rhineland, marking the first time since the end of the war German forces had set foot in the region. In a ham-fisted attempt to play down the Nazi aggression, Göring told the British press that Germany's only intention was to build an air force to defend the Fatherland: 'The objective is not the creation of an offensive weapon threatening other nations, but rather a military aviation strong enough to repulse attacks on Germany,' he told the *Daily Mail*'s man in Berlin.[1]

But Göring's assurances did little to calm nerves in Westminster. Although the Royal Navy remained master of the sea the threat of an attack by air still played on the fears of the nation.

On Sunday 24 March Sir John Simon, the British Foreign Minister, arrived in Berlin for talks with Hitler. In almost the first exchange between the two men, Simon asked Hitler directly: 'What is the strength of the German air force?' The Nazi leader tellingly replied: 'We have reached parity with Britain.'

Although the casual menace of Hitler's boast was intended to shock, the German desire to rearm was already well known in Whitehall. The year before, Winston Churchill, MP for Epping, warned the Commons that his 'private sources' had informed him Germany had already begun building an air force two thirds the size of the RAF's Home Defence Force. He warned his fellow MPs: '. . . with our enormous Metropolis here, the greatest target in the world, a kind of tremendous fat cow . . . tied up to attract the beasts of prey.'[2]

Churchill had conveniently forgotten that when he was head of the Treasury in the 1920s he had been responsible for cutting in half the Home Defence's fifty-two squadrons. Now his warnings drew jeers from the opposition who accused him of warmongering.

On 17 July 1936 the Spanish Civil War broke the fragile peace of Europe. Göring immediately counselled Hitler to support the leader of the Fascist cause, General Francisco Franco, to 'defeat communism' but also to 'test my young Luftwaffe'.[3]

Hitler needed little encouragement and ordered the dispatch of a Condor Legion comprising units of the Army and the Air Force. The Luftwaffe's contribution was initially restricted to transporting Franco and his troops from North Africa across the Iberian Peninsula. But soon the Germans had established a formidable expeditionary force.

Göring now turned to Hannes Trautloft to head up the Jagdgruppe 88 (J/88), the German Condor Legion fighter group. Trautloft, the young idealist who had dreamt of flying since his childhood days watching the gliders soaring over Wasserkuppe, was now an experienced pilot stationed in Spain in command of a small fighter force. The Germans had brought mostly transport and medium bomber aircraft. But Trautloft led a flight of six He 51 fighters, a biplane whose First World War design would have been easily recognisable to the Red Baron himself.

It was in an He 51 that Trautloft scored his first victory: 'Three Breguets [obsolete Spanish biplanes] attacked our lines by throwing bombs at us from the aircraft. I shot one down in a copybook manoeuvre,' bragged Trautloft in his memoirs of his exploits in the Spanish conflict.[4]

A few days later Teutonic triumphalism turned to professional embarrassment when he became the first German pilot to be shot down in a military action since the end of the First World War. His victorious adversary was a French-built Dewoitine 500 fighter, a single-seat, open-cockpit monoplane, a handful of which had been sold to the Republican forces.

Trautloft recalled in his diary: 'As I was descending in my parachute I felt a bit of an idiot. I was wearing an open shirt, shorts and tennis shoes. I finally came down on a farmhouse, crashing backwards against a wall and immediately came under fire from both sides.'[5]

He waited until dark before crawling to a nearby olive grove where he was surrounded by a battalion of Nationalist soldiers: 'A sergeant stuck a pistol in my stomach and punched me in the mouth. I reached for my passport to try to show him I was on his side but I was punched again before I could present it. So I decided that my only hope was to try to remember the only Spanish I knew and I shouted "viva Franco" to which the sergeant threw his arms around me.'[6] This encounter between

Trautloft's biplane and the modern French fighter emphasised the urgent need to blood the Luftwaffe's own monoplane.

In December 1936, four prototype 109s were delivered to the Condor Legion to counter the Russian SB twin-engine bombers and the I-15 and I-16 fighters flying with the Spanish Republican forces. However, the rushed introduction of the new German fighter got off to a poor start.

The first 109 crashed on take-off. The second was damaged on landing. It soon became clear that the Nazi fighter suffered from extreme torque forces,[7] making it swerve to the left on contact with the ground. It was fortunate for the Luftwaffe commanders that the Spanish conflict presented them with an opportunity to tweak some of the 109's teething problems in combat conditions against inferior aircraft.

Trautloft went on to record three more confirmed victories flying in his 109, giving him a total of five kills. For his service in the Spanish campaign Trautloft was awarded the Spanienkreuz in Gold mit Schwertern.[8] Moreover, he was responsible for developing tactics for the deployment of the 109 in future combats.

Trautloft and the other young German pilots stationed in Spain were the first aces of the age of the monoplane.

They had gained invaluable experience flying the 109 in battle, a critical advantage they would have over their Czech, Polish, French and, eventually, British adversaries in the air fights to come.

In England the life of the pilot serving with the RAF was more akin to membership of a country flying club. The young airmen, many on short commissions, treated their slim silver Hawker Fury biplanes like their sportscars, racing each other across the skies of southern Britain.

One of them was James Bailey. Like many of the amateur flyers of the interwar period he came from privileged stock. Bailey was privately educated at Winchester College, the same school as Hugh Dowding. His father, Sir Abe Bailey, a Johannesburg gold millionaire, was closely acquainted with both Winston Churchill and the Liberal statesman and foreign secretary, Sir John Simon, who (as we discovered earlier) had challenged Hitler on the size of his air force.

Bailey junior had learned to fly in the Oxford University Air Squadron at the same time as Richard Hillary, a Spitfire pilot who wrote a seminal autobiography of a Second World War fighter pilot, *Last Enemy*, before he was tragically killed in action in 1943. Bailey's humorous claim was that he was the only pilot in the RAF whose mother had clocked up more flying hours. Lady Bailey was a pioneer of women's aviation who had flown across South Africa in a De Havilland Moth. Her stories including crash-landing in Spain and Russia and being lost in the Sahara for four days.[9] Bailey spent his privileged youth playing polo and shooting partridge. Later, at Oxford, he broadened his pastimes to drinking and philosophizing.

While Hannes Trautloft was shooting down Republican bombers and learning to accept the arbitrary cruelties of war, Bailey was discussing the rights and duties that a democracy bestowed on a citizen: 'There were a group of us,' he later wrote, 'who met to discuss the most junior questions in philosophy such as "When is it right to revolt?" and "What is meant by a state?" "If a man is outside the contract and has no vote does he have to obey the law?"'[10]

These were indeed innocent times for the amateur English flyer. Recalled Bailey: 'It was a perfect year, that year before the storm broke. I was possessed with an hydroptic, immoderate thirst for human learning, and by the great feast that was the university, delighted. I enjoyed an equal passion for country sports – polo in the summer, pike fishing and game shooting in the winter. So it occurred to me that I was close to that bliss for which the faithful must wait all their lifetime . . . It was thus a year of magic.'[11]

Like many British aristocratic youth Bailey had visited Germany and joined a group of Luftwaffe cadets on a walking holiday. He could not have known that just a few months later he would be trying to kill them and they trying just as hard to do the same to him.[12]

There were three ways a young British flyer could join the RAF as a pilot. The first was through Cranwell College in Lincolnshire, a standardised training programme established by the Chief of the Air Staff, Sir Hugh Trenchard, at the end of the First World War. Cranwell was the RAF's answer to Sandhurst which educated the Army officer corps. The Lincolnshire location was chosen because Trenchard argued: 'Marooned in the wilderness, cut off from pastimes they could not organise for themselves, the cadets would find life cheaper, healthier and more wholesome.'[13]

That didn't stop the trainee pilots from finding ways to circumvent Trenchard's strictures. Some even used their time away from home to visit the less-than-wholesome local brothels. T. E. Lawrence, better known as Lawrence of Arabia, was stationed at RAF Cranwell just after the war in 1926, where he wrote a revised version of his autobiography *Seven Pillars of Wisdom*. He mentioned the nearby village of Navenby in a letter to a friend at the time, saying: 'I'm too shy to go looking for dirt. That's why I can't go off stewing into the Lincoln or Navenby brothels with the fellows. They think it's because I'm superior: proud, or peculiar or "posh", as they say: and it's because I wouldn't know what to do, how to carry myself, where to stop. Fear again: fear everywhere.'[14]

Another young flyer was John Banham, born in Royston, Hertfordshire, in 1913 and educated at The Perse School, Cambridge. After working in an electrical company he joined the RAF in 1935 on a short service commission and trained in Hawker Harts and Furies. Later that year, after three weeks of square bashing at Uxbridge, Banham was sent to 19 Squadron where he flew Gloster Gauntlet biplanes. He noted that the pilots were still wearing 1918 RAF uniforms: 'Ten of us (officers) lived in one hut like a dormitory. But later married officers lived off of the aerodrome. Officers were not allowed to get married unless you were a squadron leader or you were over the age of thirty. And we all had to dine in full mess kit four days a week. On Wednesday you could dine in a suit. But we all had first-class batmen who made life very easy for us.'[15]

Many cadets began their careers in the RAF on short commissions of six years. John Banham and William Richardson, who had signed up in 1931, were typical of those who joined the air service in the inter-war period on a short-term commission and, provided their backgrounds and countenance were deemed suitable, went on to be granted a permanent appointment. This informal vetting process ensured that those who filled the RAF's top ranks continued to be plucked from the same public schools and the higher strata of society as those who took part in the First World War. There was no riff-raff in the RAF.

In the years leading up to the outbreak of war the entry requirements were slightly relaxed, although the class barrier was still in evidence. Instead of a professional commission, young pilots could sign up for the Auxiliary Air Force which had been established by Trenchard in 1925. The Auxiliary airmen trained at the weekend and treated membership as an extension of their gentleman's clubs. The financing and servicing of a modern biplane was not cheap. As a result the Auxiliaries tended to come from even wealthier backgrounds which afforded them the means to support their hobby. The RAF regulars referred to them as 'pampered pimpernels', but by the time of the Battle of Britain they proved their flying skills were a match for any of the men of the professional air corps.

But there were few pilots, amateur or professional, who could match the instinctive flying skills of pilots like Douglas Bader or his friend William 'Dickie' Richardson. Bader and Richardson had been pulled out of their squadrons and chosen to form part of an air aerobatic display team based at RAF Hendon.[16]

Flying silver-painted Gamecock and Bulldog biplanes, they were the Red Arrows of their day performing shows all over the country. The young pilots thrilled the crowds with their acrobatics and even off duty couldn't resist performing dare-devil stunts. Richardson had his aircraft number taken by a police officer who caught him flying his plane just a few feet above Reading High Street. But in 1931 tragedy struck. On 14 December, at Woodley Airfield in Berkshire, Bader, Richardson and a third flier, egged on my fellow pilots, agreed to demonstrate their low flying routines. Coming in on a fast and low approach to the airfield, Bader, performing a slow roll, misjudged his height and allowed his Bulldog wing tip to touch the ground. The plane immediately turned over and crashed onto its back. Bader was rushed to the Royal Berkshire Hospital, where both his legs were amputated. Richardson and Bader would have been court-martialled had Bader not been due to play rugby for England and so the RAF hushed it up. Less than ten years later, both pilots were Squadron Leaders flying very different fighters in the Battle of Britain.

A third entry route to the RAF, opened up in 1936, attracted flyers from less privileged backgrounds. The RAF Volunteer Reserve (RAFVR) took in civilians recruited from the neighbourhoods of Reserve Flying Schools. Recruits were restricted to men of between eighteen and twenty-five years of age who had been accepted for part-time training as pilots, observers and wireless operators. Its principal and timely object was to provide a reserve of aircrew for use in the event of war. By September 1939, the RAFVR comprised 6646 pilots, 1623 observers and 1948 air gunners/wireless operators.[17] Since these men were not strictly 'gentlemen' in officer recruitment terms most of them joined the squadrons as sergeant pilots. At the height of the Battle of Britain a third of fighter pilots had been trained by the RAFVR. Competition for places was tough, with as many as fifty applicants for each commission.[18]

Although Jim Bailey was a South African toff he preferred the idea of a more socially mixed pilot training cadre. So the summer before the war he enrolled at the Volunteer Reserve Centre at Oxford. As he stood in line waiting to see a recruitment officer he remembered one of the other men turning to him and saying: 'It is better than clerking anyway.'

Summing up the motivation of the ordinary men who joined up to fly fighters, Bailey recalled: 'I was to discover in the following years that men without my opportunities fought chiefly for enjoyment. Life in the industrial cities of Europe in those days was church-going, petty and poor which was in itself so intellectually, legally and sexually restricted, the cannonade provided many a young man with a welcome change.'

Bailey was eventually dispatched to Cranwell on 30 December 1939 where he trained on Hawker Harts and Hinds, by now vintage biplanes but excellent for teaching the basics to novice flyers. Bailey's instructor was an 'ill-tempered' Rhodesian who proved to be a 'first-class' teacher, demanding, though not receiving, absolute precision in the handling of his aircraft. Bailey later wrote: 'I believe that I owe my life to this exactness.'[19]

Another late arrival was Eric Gordon Barwell, who after leaving Wellingborough School fell into a job with the family rubber manufacturing and engineering business. But with war clouds gathering, Barwell decided to enlist with RAFVR in Cambridge in July 1938. The following year he gained his wings. Bailey, Richardson, Barnham and Barwell all went on to serve their country flying Defiants in the Battle of Britain.

The RAF also attracted scores of young men from the Commonwealth looking for excitement and a vocation in the mother country. By the start of hostilities as many as one in ten pilots hailed from Commonwealth nations. The greatest number came from New Zealand which contributed 129 (4.4 per cent) pilots to the Battle of Britain.[20] The most famous was Keith Park, who led No. 11 Group which felt the full force of the Luftwaffe attacks and who Dowding later credited with winning the Battle of Britain.

Another was John Rushton Gard'ner, born in Dunedin on New Zealand's South Island in 1918. He boarded at the historic Nelson College in Nelson City on Tasman Bay. While still at school, he paid 10 shillings of his savings to take a joyride in a biplane over Nelson. After that he was hooked and learned to fly while still in his teens. He was one of the first Kiwis to sail to England in December 1938 to join the RAF. Among those sailing with him was Colin Gray (later group captain), who became New Zealand's 'Top Gun' of the Second World War, racking up twenty-seven 'kills' at the controls of his Spitfire.

Gard'ner joined 141 Squadron in Scotland where he trained on Gloster Gladiators and Bristol Blenheims before transferring to Defiants and taking part in one of the first engagements of the Battle of Britain.

The Defiant squadrons had a disproportionately high number of Kiwi pilots and gunners. They may have assimilated better than the Poles and the Czechs but even among the Commonwealth and British pilots there were cultural and language differences to overcome. One English pilot, having heard Gard'ner talking about the 'Beast Leagues' assumed he was referring to some Kiwi sport involving animals. In fact, Gard'ner was talking about the legs of a woman who had ventured into the airmen's canteen.[21]

Gard'ner and the rest of the small, gallant band of Kiwi aircrew would make a contribution to the Allied war effort far out of proportion to their number.

In the same week that tensions between Republican and National factions in Spain boiled over into civil war, Hugh

Dowding arrived at Bentley Priory in Stanmore on the outskirts of north London to take up his position as head of Fighter Command. He had not been everyone's first choice, overcoming powerful critics, including Trenchard who profoundly disagreed with his approach to fighter strategy.

Trenchard saw the RAF (bombers and fighters) as an offensive arm of the military which had to be maintained on a permanent offensive footing. Dowding offered a very different perspective, arguing that the primary and most important role of Fighter Command was to defend the nation from any air or naval threat. In this belief he was uncompromising.

Underlying Dowding's philosophical differences with Air Staff members like Trenchard were personal animosities left over from Dowding's war service in France and at home. Some of these were a result of professional rivalry and jealousy. But Dowding's fastidious and stubborn temperament made these disagreements worse than they needed to be, and in some cases provoked Air Staff officials into conflict with their Air Officer Commander-in-Chief of Fighter Command.

This would not have mattered so much in any other branch of the military. But the Air Ministry had grown into a toxic government department where senior airmen ruthlessly sought to carve out careers for themselves, often where there were none. Dowding, who had long ago acquired the nickname 'stuffy', was hopeless at playing politics, a business for which he held nothing but disdain. It meant he was often cut out of decisions or had his recommendations countermanded merely because it was Dowding who had given them.[22] Such was the hostility shown towards Dowding that a memo privately circulated among senior officers of the Air Staff described Fighter Command as 'a one man show led by a man with inadequate mental ability and a very slow brain who treated his staff badly.'[23]

But those who succeeded at the politicking were invariably the most out of touch with technological advances in aerial combat. What Dowding lacked in political nous he made up for by being commendably well informed about all developments in aircraft and aeronautical science.

By the time he was given his chance in 1936 he had been Air Member for Supply and Research for five years, serving longer than any other officer who has ever held the post. Those invaluable years of service gave Dowding a root-and-branch understanding of the workings of the air force and its attendant services and an unrivalled estimation of the challenges he faced during a time of rapid technological change.

By 1936 Dowding had used his time on the Air Council to put in place the key elements of a separate system of fighter defence for Great Britain. In doing so he was fortunate to be able to build on a template of fighter and anti-aircraft gun defence established during the First World War by Major General Edward Ashmore, another RFC veteran.

Ashmore arranged defensive weapons into three rings around the capital – searchlights and anti-aircraft artillery in the outer ring, fighter aircraft in the middle ring, and more anti-aircraft guns in the innermost ring in the city. He also set up a large plotting table at Horse Guards in the heart of Whitehall. Information from spotters was relayed to this central room where wooden blocks were placed on a large map to indicate the location and altitude of aircraft. The controllers relayed this data to one of twenty-five regional plotting centres, who re-created the portions of the map relevant to them and passed the information to the fighter squadrons and anti-aircraft batteries.

After the war Ashmore improved the system further, founding the Royal Observer Corps, a civil defence organisation intended for the visual detection, identification, tracking and reporting of aircraft over Great Britain.

This would all prove vital to the future of fighter defence. But it was Dowding, the first technocrat to lead a branch of the military, who had the foresight to mix technical knowledge with detailed organisation and combat experience. Hindsight would show that his most critical contribution was to recognise very early on the importance of radar, or radio direction finding (RDF) as it was known then. In the first years after the war Britain had been locked in a technological arms race with Germany, France, Russia and America to find a practical use for radio waves to detect objects beyond the range of sight and sound.

But Britain held the advantage after scientist Robert Watson-Watt found a way to use radio technology to provide advance warning to airmen. Through his investigations into lightning, Watson-Watt became an expert on the use of RDF before turning his inquiry to shortwave transmission. But a radio wave system for tracking aircraft remained elusive.

Then in 1935 Britain's lead was cut when German scientists came close to making their own breakthrough. The first British intelligence knew about German advances were sketchy reports of experiments for a radio-based death ray. Although UK scientists found the death ray to be a Nazi fantasy they discovered through their own investigations that the radio interference caused by an aircraft could be used for the basis of a radio location system. As soon as Dowding was made aware of the discovery he set up the Daventry Experiment of 26 February 1935, which, using a powerful BBC shortwave transmitter, for the first time gave a modern air force the ability to detect a bomber flying overhead. Dowding immediately authorised more funding and by the summer of 1935 RDF was able to warn of bomber-sized targets at ranges of 60 miles.

Dowding ensured that the British discovery was given the highest top-secret classification. But in October 1937 the RAF received a rather nasty surprise.

A Nazi delegation led by Göring's number two, Erhard Milch, had been invited to lunch with Dowding and some of his staff officers at Bentley Priory. It followed a reciprocal invitation to visit the Luftwaffe HQ which had been taken up by Fighter Command in January of the same year. The German guests were greeted warmly and the RAF band played Nazi marches in their honour. Halfway through the lunch Dowding and his staff were stunned into silence when Milch asked them: 'How are you getting on with your experiments in the radio detection of aircraft approaching your shores?' With no apparent need to be coy, he added: 'We have known for some time that you are developing a radar system. So are we and we think we are a jump ahead of you.'[24]

Milch's Teutonic indiscretion convinced Dowding of the urgency in prioritising radar and placing it at the heart of his home defence programme. He set about establishing a chain of radar stations that stretched from Orkney in the north to Weymouth in the south. This provided radar coverage for the entire Europe-facing coast of the British Isles, able to detect high-flying aircraft over northern France. But once aircraft had crossed the Channel, the sea-facing radar stations were blind. Although Dowding had foreseen this, his recommendation for a set of inland radar stations was blocked by the Air Ministry.[25]

By early 1939 the key elements of Dowding's defence system were already in place. On 11 August Bomber Command was asked to launch a series of mock attacks using aircraft returning from exercises over France. The initial reports of Dowding's effective defences gave Fighter Command confidence for the battle to come. Dowding noted: 'Daylight raids were normally tracked and intercepted with ease and regularity.'

The German high command, however, had grossly underestimated the importance of radar. So although the Germans had a radar capability, its own programme had been allowed to stagnate. German policy assumed all ground and air hostilities would be short, and that the overwhelming strength of the Luftwaffe would ensure that incoming enemy aircraft would not present a tangible threat to Germany.[26]

But radar fundamentally changed the concept of aerial warfare by giving unprecedented early warning of enemy intruders, enabling fighters to be directed to the location of the bomber formations without the need for standing patrols that had dominated air warfare in the First World War. What German intelligence had so comprehensively failed to grasp was that with the help of radar, Britain had created the most destructive fighter defence system in the world.

Yet without a modern fighter aircraft to capitalise on these innovative developments Britain's home defence remained vulnerable. And in 1936 Air Ministry thinking was still very much focused on the bomber rather than the fighter. Chief of the Air Staff Edward Ellington told his deputy in November of that year: 'Every fighter is a loss to the striking force – the true defence against air attack.'[27] In the same month George Pirie, Deputy Director of Operations, announced that the Air Ministry had planned to commission sixty-eight bomber squadrons but only foresaw a need for twenty-one fighter squadrons. This ratio was partly based on the misapprehension that bombers flown against the enemy would not need to be escorted by fighters.[28]

In 1936 both Britain's bomber and fighter squadrons were still reliant on biplanes. Many senior members of the Air Ministry wanted to keep it that way. But, as we discovered in Chapter 3, Dowding and more enlightened RAF officers among the Air Staff had set in train the conversion of biplane squadrons to ones equipped with the faster monoplane.

After a series of tendering rounds and air trials the Air Ministry had settled on Hurricanes, Spitfires and Defiants as the three single-engine strike aircraft in their front-line home defence. The only question was how many of each aircraft type should equip Fighter Command's thirty-eight fighter squadrons.

In June 1936 the Air Ministry placed an order for six hundred Hurricanes. But production deliveries had been delayed by roughly six months due to a decision to refit the Hurricane with the high-performance Merlin II engine, leaving the Merlin I for the Fairey Battle and the Hawker Henley. It wasn't until December that the first four Hurricanes entered service with No. 111 Squadron at RAF Northolt.

On 3 June 1936, the Air Ministry also placed an order for 310 Spitfires. Full-scale production of the Spitfire began at Supermarine's facility in Woolston, but it quickly became apparent that this order would also suffer from delays. Supermarine was a small company, already busy building Walrus and Stranraer flying boats, while Vickers-Armstrong,

Supermarine's parent company, was preoccupied developing the Wellington bomber.

The obvious solution was to subcontract the work to other aviation manufacturers. But Vickers-Armstrong was reluctant to hand over its flagship Spitfire to outside concerns, and so was slow to release the necessary blueprints and subcomponents. When the Air Ministry threatened to drop the contract and make the firm build Bristol Beaufighters instead, the company saw sense. Reassured by the new promise of cooperation the government placed a further order for two hundred Spitfires on 24 March 1938.[29] The Hurricane production programme was now well under way. And in mid-1938 the first production Spitfire rolled off the assembly line, flown by Jeffrey Quill on 15 May 1938, almost twenty-four months after the initial order.

Having won the battle to equip his squadrons with monoplanes, the Commander-in-Chief of Fighter Command now considered the choice of armaments for his new fighters.

The Hurricanes and Spitfire prototypes were all specified to be fitted with four machine guns, two in each wing.[30] But it was clear, as long ago as 1936 when Dowding became head of Fighter Command, that firing rifle bullets into the massive hulks of enemy bombers was not going to bring enough of them down. This was especially so when the Germans started strengthening their aircraft with metal, defensive armour plates.

Squadron Leader Ralph Sorley, who had been posted to the Operational Requirements Branch at the Air Ministry, found that Spitfires and Hurricanes would only be able to get in a two-second burst during an attack where two aircraft were closing in on each other at a combined speed of more than 600 mph. So the Air Ministry once again turned its attention to its third fighter, the turret-armed Defiant.

A turret fighter capable of firing four coordinated machine guns accurately at a vulnerable part of an enemy aircraft might achieve better results. Even more promising was the prospect of a Defiant armed with a cannon. The larger cannon shells, which were later used to great effect by the Luftwaffe fighters, would have a much better chance of downing a bomber. But the design of the Hurricanes and Spitfires meant wing-mounted cannons caused a dangerous recoil to the aircraft.

A gun-firing turret offered a much more stable firing platform and was now an integral part of the Air Ministry's counter-bomber strategy.

As the Government began prioritising its home defence fighter force the Defiant enjoyed influential support among the senior Air Staff. The two most enthusiastic proponents for the free-gun fighter were Sholto Douglas, Deputy Chief of the Air Staff, and Donald Stevenson, Deputy Director of Home Operations. Douglas and Stevenson, in common with most of the air marshals, had both served as fighter pilots in the First World War. Donaldson finished the war on the Western Front, the commanding officer of No. 5 Squadron, flying Bristols, the most advanced two-seater machine-gun fighter of its day.

The two Air Chiefs were so convinced of the virtues of the turret fighter that they insisted a third of Home Defence fighter squadrons be equipped with Defiants. Donaldson was even prepared to argue for Defiants over Spitfires and Hurricanes. A paper circulated among the senior Air Staff in the spring of 1938 considering the comparative merits of single and two-seat fighters in Home Defence set out a persuasive case for new fighter tactics to be built around the attributes of the Defiant.

Indeed the RAF's own *Manual of Air Tactics* also published in 1938 stated clearly that the advanced speed of the new breed of fighters made dogfights impossible because of the 'effect of gravity on the human body'. Instead fighters must concentrate on shooting down bombers.[31]

A second Air Staff paper[32] went even further, asserting that the 'fixed-gun fighter' was limited to mounting attacks against the heavily protected stern, making it more difficult to secure surprise and restricting the number of fighters combining in multiple attacks. By contrast, the movable turret gunfighter, flying on a parallel course to the bomber, could attack the enemy bomber from any direction.

Stevenson, who authored the paper, wanted the Defiant to be the RAF's primary strike aircraft at home and overseas, insisting: 'It must carry offensive and defensive armament to enable it to penetrate into enemy territory.' He also set out the conditions for increasing the proportion of Defiant squadrons from a quarter to a third of RAF fighter units, which he said must be undertaken if 'Germany is considerably increasing the armament of her projected bombers and including adequate armour protection'. He argued: 'Since the two-seater fighter has the great advantage over the single-seater fighter, being able to bring a high concentration of fire to bear thereby destroying aircraft and breaking up the formation to enable single seaters to take on targets singly and under the best tactical conditions provided turrets and 20 mm gun equipment are satisfactory, there is a strong case for a higher percentage of two seaters.'[33]

Stevenson and Douglas were so impressed with the Defiant that they had already set their sights on the next generation of free-gun fighter, a twin-engined fighter and ground-attack aircraft fitted with four cannons housed in the Boulton Paul turret. The new fighter, under specification F.11/37, would have a speed of 370 mph and a service ceiling of 35,000 feet. Stevenson told Douglas: 'As you are aware the restrictions imposed by production in any event prevent a revision of this ratio at present. When nine squadrons have been equipped with the Defiant under scheme L and when the F.11/37 comes along this situation will ease. If you would kindly approve the above, we would review the ratio when either of the conditions of the preceding paragraph are fulfilled.'[34]

The procurement of the Defiant had been largely carried out behind Dowding's back, adding to his suspicion that he was being frozen out of key decisions being made by the Air Ministry.

He was right. The reason Douglas was so unwilling to engage with Dowding on the Defiant was because the Air Ministry had already committed Fighter Command to the new fighter and he knew or sensed Fighter Command's opposition. Having already set in train an order of 450 Defiants from Boulton Paul he was not going to 'change horses' mid-production.

If Dowding was difficult, Douglas had a reputation for being headstrong and unwilling to compromise once he had made up his mind up. He could also be insubordinate. In the First World War, serving as a Second Lieutenant in the Royal Field Artillery, he had a serious falling out with his commanding officer and transferred to the Royal Flying Corps, joining No. 2 Squadron as an observer. During his three years' service he had not particularly distinguished himself in the air. He couldn't call himself a fighter ace, because he had shot down fewer than the requisite five enemy aircraft during the war and in peacetime had done his reputation serious harm by crashing a DH9a biplane into an airfield hangar in front of Trenchard[35].

Dowding and Douglas had known each other since 1920 when their roles were reversed and Dowding was the superior officer. Indeed, Douglas recalled how 'stuffy' Dowding had reproached him for his slapdash approach to his paperwork.[36] Where Dowding was stand-offish and remote Douglas was gregarious and sociable, qualities that he was prepared to exploit to outflank his more experienced RAF colleague.

When it came to Air Staff doctrine, Douglas was a self-declared 'heretic',[37] which he claimed was borne out by his opposition to Trenchard's view that air warfare was all about the bomber. In this at least he sided with Dowding's priority for the RAF to be supplied with sufficient fighter squadrons to defend the nation from bombers. Douglas stated in his autobiography: 'I felt we needed a much broader approach in our thinking to the use that was to be made of all types of aircraft.'

But according to historian Vincent Orange, the deputy air chief lacked the fighter experience to be able to properly evaluate the effectiveness of the Defiant, Hurricane and Spitfire: 'Douglas who had a very high opinion of his own merits later claimed to have been a "well-known fighter pilot and an expert on air fighting when in its infancy". Neither claim will stand close scrutiny. He did indeed serve throughout the war – as did many of his contemporaries – in combat, training or command duties, but he met with virtually no success in aerial combat.'[38]

Even so, Douglas's view of modern combat fighters remained rooted in his own limited experience on the Western Front. He later wrote: 'after some hair-raising experiences we found that it was necessary for us, if we were to engage the enemy on anything approaching equal terms, to fly underneath his formations so as to lure him into attacking us; and then we would trust to the good shooting of our observers to pick off the Huns as they came diving down to the attack.'[39]

On 26 April 1937 the Condor Legion, headed by Oberstleutnant Wolfram Freiherr von Richthofen, a cousin of the Red Baron, led the fateful air bombardment of the Spanish town of Guernica. In a series of terror raids, bombs dropped from Ju 52s, Do 17s and He 111s caused devastation and 1654 civilian deaths. The Nazi bombers, unopposed, had indeed got through. In London news of the attack confirmed the military's worst fears – a series of prolonged bombing raids by modern aircraft would result in unsustainable casualties.

Two days later a panicked Air Ministry placed an official order for the first eighty-seven Boulton Paul Defiants. As this was prior to the first flight of the Defiant prototype, the aircraft had effectively been ordered off the drawing board.

Not everyone had been bowled over by the Defiant. There were plenty of senior RAF pilots who still harboured concerns about its lack of forward-firing weapons and its comparatively inadequate top speed. Dowding was one of them. On 25 June 1938 he wrote to Douglas setting out his serious reservations about the Defiant and the Air Staff's plan for equipping his squadrons with the slower two-seater fighter.[40] He complained that by the time the Defiant came into service they would be 'semi-obsolete' because, he argued, their provenance had more to do with the air battles over the Somme in the last war than a modern home fighter defence.

Not mincing his words, he griped: 'I am not suggesting that the Commander-in-Chief of Fighter Command should be given dictatorial powers over such matters, nor do I suggest that the advice of a succession of commanders-in-chief always be consistent, but I do think that the user, or potential user, should have an opportunity of making his voice heard at appropriate stages when fighter aircraft are being produced and allotted.'

He continued: 'You say that we cannot have less than nine squadrons of Defiants because we are committed to an order of 450 machines. I'm very sorry to hear it but I most earnestly request then no more be ordered until you have a chance of seeing what they will do. The first essential of a fighter is performance and the second is hitting power. In both these respects the Defiant is inferior to contemporary fighters, and in speed it is estimated to have only 5 mph advantage over the Dornier 17 with the Benz engine . . . when we get the Defiant in a year's time, or whenever it may be, it will already be semi-obsolete . . .'

Dowding was also dismissive of the conditions Stevenson set for the performance role of an offensive fighter: 'I see no reason why a fighter should carry defensive armament to enable it to penetrate into enemy territory. Provided that it has adequate speed, that is the best form of defence.' And he 'energetically refuted' Stevenson's idea of using fighter squadrons, one to break up the bombers and the other to engage the fighters (although this is exactly what Dowding and Park ordered their squadrons to do during the Battle of Britain). Nor did he think the Defiant suitable for the Field Force because of 'its very poor zone of fire in the lower hemisphere', although he did concede its use in support of the Army was not actually any of his business.

Finally he reproached the Air Staff for commissioning the

cannon turret fighter, saying: 'We ought to have carried out the most careful experiments to prove the value of the gun before we adopted it in anything but experimental types and we have acted in woolly imitation of woolly continental air forces.'

To settle all these issues he asked the Air Staff to call an urgent conference, otherwise 'I shall wake up in a year's time to be told that I am "committed" to having fifteen squadrons of something with a 20 mm gun, whereas I can tell you now that I do not want any and so perhaps save a large sum of money.'

Understandably, Dowding's letter was badly received by Stevenson and Douglas. Douglas wrote privately to Stevenson saying he utterly disagreed with Dowding's assessment of the requirements for an offensive fighter: 'Experience in the last war,' he wrote, 'shows that even fighters of high-performance are liable to interception if they penetrate far into enemy territory . . . I am still of the opinion therefore that for work over enemy territory a two-seater fighter is best.' Nevertheless, Douglas did accept the need to consult Dowding on their future policy since the 'user's views' should be taken into account.

Stevenson replied to Douglas on 26 July 1938 reiterating his belief that the Defiant had the best chance of breaking up German bomber formations of five-hundred-plus aircraft formations over London: 'It is obvious that the ability to attack large formations from practically any angle, particularly those in the rearward and downward arcs which is confirmed by the movable gunfighter is a great advantage. We cannot yet say in these circumstances what proportion of two seaters to single seaters should be in the fighter force, but our conclusions are that it would have been most unwise to have accepted a reduction of the present ratio.'

Stevenson also dismissed Dowding's comparisons with the

Somme which he said 'doubtless refer to the Fe2b', the fighter flown by my Uncle George. He confided in Douglas: 'At this time not only was this aircraft [Fe2b] obsolete in regard to performance, but defensive fire could only be brought to bear by the air gunner standing up in his cockpit and firing over the top of the main plane since the aircraft was a pusher. Its replacement, the Bristol Fighter [which Stevenson had flown] had an unimpeachable record of air fighting from that time right up to the end of the war.'

Stevenson also disputed Dowding's claim that the Defiant had an inferior performance to the single-seater fighter, adding: 'As you know the Defiant is slightly faster than the Hurricane with the same engine.' Stevenson's last assertion was not borne out by trials of the two aircraft which found the Hurricane to be faster.

Dowding's persistent resistance to Air Ministry fighter policy meant the Air Marshal's were in no rush to keep him informed of their plans. In fact throughout the summer months Dowding heard nothing more from Stevenson and Douglas on how many of his squadrons would be equipped with each fighter type. At the end of the summer Dowding wrote to Sholto Douglas once again requesting a reply to his June letter in which he had asked for the numbers of each fighter type to be prioritised for home defence.

Douglas' office told him he could expect his answer in two months. But none was forthcoming so he wrote once again: 'I know the Air Ministry is preoccupied,' he told Douglas, 'it always is about something, but surely it is wrong that in four months it should have been possible to deal with the very important matters raised in my letter of June 25th.' This time Dowding did get a response from Douglas, but only a holding letter saying that Douglas' deputy would be in touch in due course.[41]

Douglas and Stevenson knew they could not indefinitely keep the head of Fighter Command in the dark about his own squadron deployments.

And so on 16 November 1938 the Air Ministry gave Dowding the chance to air his views at a conference hosted by Richard Peirse, Deputy Chief of the Air Staff and Director of Operations and Intelligence. At the top of Dowding's agenda was the question of how many of his front-line squadrons would be equipped with the 'semi-obsolete' Defiants. But if he hoped Peirse would be an objective arbiter on the Defiant issue he was to be disappointed. Instead Peirse endorsed the Air Staff view that they should remain committed to nine squadrons which might be increased if 'operational requirements' demanded it.

But Dowding hadn't quite given up on trying to kill off his third fighter before it had a chance to enter service. He told the gathered Air Chiefs that given the advent of radar surely the two-seater fighter would be best suited to a night-fighting role. However, this endorsement only bolstered the Defiant's credentials as a dual-purpose fighter. The head of Fighter Command had more joy with the cannon gun, telling the conference that the results had been disappointing, describing how the 20 mm shell 'exploded on impact with the outer parts of an aircraft and had no penetrative power, although in certain circumstances such as impact against a wing close to a tank, battle damage might be done'. Douglas conceded that the 'air fighting committee' would have to make final recommendations on the suitability of the RAF's new weapon. In the meantime no orders of the F.11/37 were to be signed off until the destructive qualities of the cannon gun had been properly established.

The conference also recommended that for practical reasons all auxiliary squadrons would be equipped with single-seat fighters. This was welcomed by Dowding, partly because it would delay the rapid deployment of the Defiant squadrons by ensuring civilian gunners and pilots would be unable to train together. But Dowding left the conference knowing he had only succeeded in slowing the march of the Defiant.

At the heart of this clash of fighter policy between Dowding and the Air Ministry was Douglas' and Stevenson's unshakeable belief that single-seat fighters would be restricted to attacking the enemy from astern. It was a view supported by the head of Bomber Command, Sir Edgar Ludlow-Hewitt, who stuck his oar in to pronounce that the Defiant would emulate 'the tremendous success of the Bristols of the last war'.[42] Any reference to the last war was guaranteed to antagonise Dowding who knew that rapid technological advances meant the next aerial conflict would have no bearing on the last.

Yet in many ways the Defiant was as much a product of state-of-the-art aeronautical design as the Spitfire and the Hurricane. No other air force in the world had developed such a capability. And advocates of the Defiant believed the turret fighter gave the RAF a critical advantage over the Luftwaffe in the lead up to the next war. Soon they would have the chance to find out if they were right.

# Chapter 5

# THREE FIGHTERS

Hours before news of the peace terms agreed under the 1938 Munich Agreement between Britain and Germany had filtered through to RAF fighter stations, PO John Banham was sitting in his newly equipped Spitfire ready to respond to an imminent German air attack. 'It was a fearful flap,' he later recalled. 'We had the only three Spitfires available in the country at that time. We had no gunsights, but they were loaded up with guns and we were ready to go if needs be.' Banham, who had only had a handful of hours in his Spitfire, knew that although the new Browning guns were still proving troublesome the three Spitfires were fully expected to meet the Nazi menace.[1]

This anxious wait on the RAF runways for the German bombers had forced the Air Staff to grasp the nettle.

Just days before, on 12 September 1938, Adolf Hitler had flown to Nuremberg to address mass crowds of Nazi supporters. His intention was to lay the groundwork for an invasion of

Czechoslovakia on the pretext of liberating the eight hundred thousand German-speaking population living in the neighbouring Sudetenland which had been annexed to Czechoslovakia under the terms of the Versailles settlement.

Hitler whipped up the rally by falsely claiming the Czechs had executed Sudeten Germans and were planning to force hundreds of thousands of 'Germans' from their homes. Days before Nuremberg, the Nazi leader had secretly ordered his generals to prepare for Operation Green, the conquest of Czechoslovakia. A total of 750,000 German soldiers were amassed on the border. His military invasion was a calculated risk and Hitler half expected the French and the British to try to stop him. Hitler's generals were nervous, believing Germany was not yet ready to wage another European war.

However, the weakness of the Anglo-French alliance, whose military forces had been under-invested for years, meant Germany had little to fear. Autumn 1938 would turn out to be the season of appeasement. In a series of emergency meetings with the British Prime Minister, Neville Chamberlain, Hitler goaded and bullied the British leader, threatening conflict unless the British succumbed to his territorial claims. Chamberlain now faced the hard choice of either directly confronting the Nazi leader and risking all-out war or giving in to his demands.

The threat posed by Germany's newly armed air force weighed heavily on his mind. It was a fear grounded in reality. Göring had stationed two thousand aircraft on the German-Czechoslovak border, the greatest build-up of air strength since the end of the First World War. Among the young officers with the fighter squadrons waiting to support the planned invasion of Czechoslovakia was Oberleutnant Hannes Trautloft. Even now, on the brink of war, it never occurred to Trautloft that he would be required to fight. Indeed part of the potent strength of Hitler's appeal among his airmen was that the Führer kept achieving his aims without spilling German blood.[2] But Trautloft, in common with his fellow pilots, harboured deep misgivings about an attack on Czechoslovakia. He felt sure that if Hitler continued to push the French and British, war would come and he was nervous about where that war might lead Germany.[3]

One of Chamberlain's closest political allies and friends was Sir Howard Kingsley Wood, the Secretary of State for Air. Drawing on the latest Air Ministry intelligence reports, Kingsley Wood warned Chamberlain that Hitler could call upon a force of fifteen hundred bombers to mount an air assault on Britain and in the first three weeks of this campaign the public should expect half a million casualties. Cowed by the fearful strength of the Luftwaffe bomber fleets and likelihood of mass casualties, Chamberlain, backed by his Cabinet, made peace with Hitler under the terms of the Munich Agreement on 29 September 1938. News of the peace terms was greeted with equal relief in Germany and Britain.

In the closing months of 1938 John Banham and the rest of the RAF guinea-pig pilots desperately put the Spitfire through its paces. 'I had just been down to Martlesham Heath where they were being tested,' Banham recalled of his first encounter with the Spitfire. 'I was shown the taps and then told to fly it. I think I had half an hour. It was a tremendous thrill. So different from a Gauntlet, although visibility was restricted in a Spitfire because of the forward engine. We took delivery of the first Spitfire at Duxford in the next few weeks. It was still being developed so we were told to fly it, from first light to dusk, so we went in relays just to get the hours in.'[4]

It took until the end of November 1938 for Banham's squadron to be fully operational with Spitfire Mark 1s. The other RAF units were in an even more parlous state. A few fortunate squadrons were already equipped with Hurricanes but the majority were still making do with biplanes, like the Hawker Fury. The Defiant and its revolutionary turret still hadn't made its maiden flight. If Britain had gone to war with Germany in the autumn of 1938, Fighter Command would have to rely on just 565 fighters, most of them obsolete biplanes. Of the ninety-odd Hurricanes available, all of them were useless above 15,000 feet because their guns froze.[5]

Munich had seriously concentrated minds at the Air Ministry about how they might defeat an armada of Luftwaffe bombers. Approval was given for an immediate and dramatic step-up in the production of fighter aircraft to meet the coming threat. Ever since the creation of Fighter Command in 1934 the Air Ministry had announced a succession of aircraft production schemes. Previous plans had prioritised British bombers over fighters. The most recent, scheme J (to be completed by the end of 1939) allowed for 1442 bombers against 532 fighters.[6]

Dowding, with the support of Sir Maurice Hankey, who sat on the Committee of Imperial Defence, and Thomas Inskip, Minister for the Coordination of Defence, now helped to guide the government towards a greater commitment to Fighter Command. On 7 November the senior Air Staff met with ministers to approve scheme M, an even greater programme of aircraft manufacture which was to lead to 2550 front-line aircraft by 31 March 1942.

While this proposal meant more Hurricanes and Spitfires, it also meant more Defiants. Dowding had demonstratively failed to dissuade the government from lending its support to the free-gun turret fighter. This was partly because as a novel aerial concept it had captured the imagination of both air marshals and politicians.

None more so than Winston Churchill who, just a few months before Munich, wrote to Neville Chamberlain, sharply criticising the preference for the Hurricane and Spitfire over the Defiant. He told the Prime Minister of the day: 'We have concentrated upon the forward-firing fixed-gun fighter. The latest developments increasingly suggest that hostile aircraft can only be engaged with certainty on parallel or nearly parallel courses, hence that the turret type of equipment will be paramount.'[7]

Dowding had been pestering the Air Ministry for nearly five months to make clear to him exactly how many Spitfires, Hurricanes and Defiants he was to be given.

Douglas now responded in terms, telling Dowding[8] Fighter Command's total strength was to comprise thirty-eight squadrons, of which at least nine squadrons must be equipped with Defiants. This should not have come as much of a surprise to the head of Fighter Command who had been repeatedly told by the Air Ministry that nine was a bare minimum. He may not have liked it, but there was little he could do apart from huff and puff.

In February 1938 the Air Ministry ordered 202 Defiant Mk Is, followed by another 161 aircraft three months later. And in December 1938 the Air Ministry placed an order for a further 150, raising the overall total number of Defiants to six hundred. Before the start of the Battle of France, 563 Boulton Paul

Defiants were being earmarked for RAF fighter squadrons.[9] When the Germans broke through Allied lines and reached the French coast in June 1940, this figure had risen to 650.[10]

Munich had not only focused British minds. In the weeks after the two nations had stood on the precipice of war, Germany's military leaders were also busily preoccupied with the rearmament of their own air force.

By the summer of 1939, the Luftwaffe had equipped nine Jagdgeschwader (fighter wings) of Messerschmitt Bf 109E and four Zerstörergeschwader (destroyer wings) of the Messerschmitt BF 110 heavy fighter. The Luftwaffe's offensive capability was just as formidable, comprising eleven Kampfgeschwader (bomber wings) equipped mainly with the He 111 and the Do 17Z, supported by four Sturzkampfgeschwader (dive-bomber wings) primarily armed with the much-feared Ju 87B Stuka.

Although the Me 109, Do 17, He 111 and Stuka were by now well known to British military intelligence, less was understood about the 110.[11] Designed by Willy Messerschmitt, the 'Zerstörer' could reach speeds of 336 mph. In the nose, it carried four .311 caliber machine guns and two 20 mm cannon, with an additional machine gun in the rear of the cockpit to defend against stern attacks.

Among Whitehall Air Staff, the Me 110 had taken on an almost mystical aura. This was partly because the fighter bomber was last off the Luftwaffe production line and had yet to be tested in combat. The 110 was of particular interest to Douglas and Stevenson who wrongly reasoned that squadrons of heavy bomber destroyers would determine the outcome of future air campaigns. And of course the 110 drew immediate comparisons with the RAF's own bomber destroyer. Like the turret fighter, the rear gunner was free from flying responsibilities, allowing formations to attack in strength from all directions and strike a knockout blow against a British bomber force. What the two air chiefs had conveniently forgotten was that most of the 110's armament, four cannons and four machine guns, was packed in the front and was delivered by the pilot. The rear gunner, whose primary role was navigator, had control of a single twin-barrel MG 81Z machine gun. But Douglas and Stevenson were convinced that if the RAF was going to compete on terms with the Luftwaffe, it would need a comparable aircraft to the 110.

At the same time questions were being raised in Parliament about whether the Spitfire and Hurricane would be obsolete just as they entered service.

During a debate on British air power on 9 March 1939[12] Sir Hugh Seely, who the following year was made a minister in the Air Ministry, told the Commons: 'These Spitfires and Hurricanes are not, as it is thought, new machines. They were considered as far back as 1933 and 1934, and a good many things have happened since then . . . I would ask the Minister to consider the policy that is being developed of the single-seater fighter with eight small Browning guns and to consider whether the two-seater fighter which has a far heavier cannon will not have to be the policy for the future.' He argued that in a modern fighter: 'It is necessary to have a heavier gun in a machine which can be manoeuvred to make an attack on the bomber not merely from one position, namely, exactly behind, where the armour is, but from the sides as well. There has been a description in the papers of the Defiant machine which is built by Boulton and Paul and has a gun, but that is only one machine. We are building Hurricanes and Spitfires, and I hope that the Minister will not think that it will be wasting money if he has to scrap what has been done in order that he may be able to move with the times.'

At the beginning of February, the Air Ministry, which hitherto had kept the Defiant under wraps by designating it an aircraft on the 'secret list', decided the time was right to release carefully selected details to the national press. A media briefing led to a series of newspaper reports of how the RAF's new secret fighter would be the scourge of the Nazi bombers. One Press Association report, carried by titles up and down the country, ran: 'The new Boulton Paul Defiant low-wing two-seater fighter monoplane, believed to be the fastest warplane of its category yet to go into production, is now being turned out in large numbers for the Royal Air Force. Details of its trial flights are secret, but it has a very high performance and the plane is scheduled to replace older aircraft in Home Defence squadrons.' The report added: 'Exceptionally powerful armament, carried in a power-operated gun turret amidships, is an outstanding feature of the new machine.'[13]

The Air Ministry was keen to promote the modern design of the Defiant, telling air correspondents that the new aircraft was built entirely of metal, chiefly light alloy, and the wings and fuselage had 'stressed skin coverings which carry much of the loads and stresses imposed on the structure in flight'. Reporters were reminded of the Defiant's 'excellent streamline shape and the smoothness of its external surfaces'. Its 'high performance,' said the Air Ministry, is to be attributed to this combination of 'good shape and high surface finish' and a Rolls-Royce Merlin liquid-cooled twelve-cylinder engine, fitted with three-bladed Havilland controllable pitch metal airscrew.

The reports even quoted the Society of British Aircraft Constructors which claimed the Defiant's design 'was largely governed by the importance of speed in production and the company's factory at Wolverhampton is laid out for rapid achievement of a high rate of output'.[14]

But if this was true there was little to show for it. In February 1939 Boulton Paul was still testing its prototype which was yet to be fully kitted out with a turret, gunner and all the ammunition for the four .303 machine guns. The Defiant was now half a ton heavier than a Hurricane,[15] and this added weight of 330 kg would impede the plane's flat speed and climb. But in the first week of April, Kingsley Wood, the Secretary of State for Air, outlined the capabilities of all three of the RAF fighters, telling fellow MPs: 'We are satisfied that they are capable of shooting down any type of bomber.'

This prompted yet further media eulogies for the Defiant. One report said: 'To obtain the maximum cleanness of contour even the rivets of the wings and fuselage are sunk flush with their surrounds. Performance of this new fighter is kept secret, but eyewitnesses have been astonished by its remarkable swiftness on the wing. It looks, and probably is, a veritable hornet of the air.'[16]

So confident was the Air Ministry in their new fighter that it was decided to give the Defiant its first public outing at the annual Empire Air Display in May. That year's aircraft pageant held at RAF Northolt in Middlesex was attended by a record crowd of 1.1 million. Among them were three hundred members of parliament who had come to inspect the new generation of fighter whose revolutionary design was now so vital to the air defence of the realm. According to reports of the event the MPs clustered around the two turret fighters on display – the Defiant and the Royal Navy's Blackburn Roc

– although neither took part in the afternoon's fly-past of twenty-four Wellington bombers followed by six Hurricane squadrons and one Spitfire squadron.

The fly-past finale was reserved for the RAF's newly developed light bomber, the Fairey Battle. In flights of three, they dived at and bombed a flag target, only a few hundred feet from the applauding MPs. Almost exactly twelve months later the ill-fated Battles would be almost wiped out as they flew suicide missions against real targets in France where the German anti-aircraft fire and fighters pulled them out of the sky for fun.

Through the summer of 1939 Dowding continued to step-up Fighter Command preparations. He ensured that his fighter planes had the most powerful engines, ran on high-octane fuel and the pilots were protected by bullet-proof cockpits, reminding the Air Ministry if 'Chicago gangsters have them in their cars my pilots will have them in their planes'.[17] Dowding also introduced a system for identifying friendly aircraft so that British aircraft would not be attacked by Fighter Defence, although more work was needed to stop airborne pilots from misidentifying fellow fighters.

These preparations had not come a moment too soon. Germany's hostility towards its neighbours, and indirectly their British and French protectors, was about to come to a head.

In a heightened war of words Hitler used a number of staged speeches to accuse Britain of conspiring with Jewish 'warmongers' and in January 1939 secretly ordered a major build-up of German warships to challenge British naval supremacy. In March 1939, Germany invaded the remainder of Czechoslovakia, creating the German Protectorate of Bohemia and Moravia and a pro-German client state, the Slovak Republic.

War now seemed unavoidable. Dowding, watching on with interest from his headquarters at Bentley Priory, continued to focus his attention on building a fighter defence system which could repel a large German air attack. Correspondence between the Air Ministry and Fighter Command showed the air marshals remained fixated by the threat of the bomber and the means to neutralise it.

The job of developing and testing modern bomber destroyer tactics was given to Professor Bennett Melvill Jones, another veteran pilot of the First World War who had served as a gunner in a Bristol fighter. After ending his war service with the RAF in 1919 he had sought solace in the Lake District where he wrote a treatise on aerial gunnery. He later forged a career in aeronautical engineering which he combined with his expertise in gunnery development, overseeing trials on siting machine guns in twin-seat fighter planes. His work lay dormant in the Air Ministry files until just before the start of the Second World War when it was retrieved and used to support the idea of free-gun fighter tactics.[18]

When the first Defiants were finally handed over to the RAF by the Boulton Paul company the Air Ministry asked Melvill Jones to assess their feasibility. The initial results convinced him that the German bomber formations could be best defeated using free-gun fighter aircraft.[19] In July 1939 Wing Commander Colin Brown, instructed by the Air Ministry, wrote to Dowding informing him of Melvill Jones' progress in developing free-gun fighter tactics. Brown explained that Melvill Jones had been experimenting with overtaking manoeuvres that would allow Defiants to use the 'windage' to help bring overwhelming firepower to bear on the enemy from the flanks.[20]

Suddenly Dowding, who hitherto had done all in his power to rid his fighter force of the Defiant, became very interested in this idea and wrote to the Air Ministry with tentative enthusiasm for the new free-gun fighter tactics being developed by Melvill Jones, saying 'I think the idea is an excellent one and well worth following up.'

He followed this with a memo to Augustus Orlebar,[21] Director of Flying Training at the Air Fighting Development Establishment (AFDE) at RAF Northolt. Dowding told Orlebar: 'The idea is that we shall make overtaking speed and windage cancel out so far as we are concerned and add themselves together for the enemy. It is a distinctly attractive idea so long as the enemy will allow us to overtake on a parallel course and engage in a broadside battle (I think he will soon learn better). I have made a note at the end with a rough diagram pointing out the advantages of enfilade or raking fire when it can be attained. This will not only give us a good chance of getting useful effects from our "overs" but will also, to some extent, mask the fire of other aircraft in the enemy formation. Will you make some trials with the Defiant and let me know how they work out?'[22]

The reason for Dowding's apparent change in attitude towards the Defiant is not obvious. Perhaps he had finally accepted the thinking behind the concept of the turret fighter, or perhaps he was worried that the Nazi bombers would be too well armoured against his fixed-gun rear attacks. Whatever the reason Dowding, who placed his trust in scientific experiment, was at last able to subject the Defiant to rigorous trials, the results of which the Air Ministry would have to be bound by.

Of course the Defiant was only a small part of Dowding's

overall concern. He urgently needed to test his entire fighter defence system against a dummy attack of invading bombers. But the head of Bomber Command, Ludlow-Hewitt, had demonstrated a marked reluctance to fully cooperate with exercises run by Fighter Command. Dowding was rarely informed of RAF bomber movements, and when they did show up to role-play in an attack on a fighter base Ludlow-Hewitt insisted on flying out of the same aerodrome, rendering the exercise hopelessly unrealistic.[23] The head of Bomber Command also refused to allow his bombers to fly in from more than 10 miles out to sea as he did not believe his crews had the requisite navigational skills. Later when Fighter Command requested a formation of bombers to test their defences Ludlow-Hewitt sent just one bomber.[24]

Dowding's official complaints about Hewitt, aided and abetted by Keith Park, eventually forced Bomber Command to engage in meaningful cooperation. In August 1939, five hundred bombers were flown against Dowding's fighter defences, covering a third of the country, in the biggest air exercise since the end of the First World War. It ran for four days and nights, although complete blackouts were impossible.[25]

Dowding learnt valuable lessons from the operation enabling him to test and then tighten his defences. His filtering system, based at Bentley Priory, was tweaked so that Observer Corps reports could be fully coordinated with radar tracking which were directly fed into radio communication with the squadrons and onto the individual fighters in the air. It was a system that Dowding had spent almost six years perfecting.

Throughout all these exercises and preparations it was accepted without question that the bombers would be flying from bases in Germany and would be unprotected by fighters. Given the known range of fighters at this time, that was a reasonable assumption. However, it meant that the Air Ministry need only focus on tactics for sending up fighters to shoot down bombers and not draw up contingency plans for tackling escorts. Nor had Fighter Command done enough to prepare for German night raids. In fact Britain was in no better position to defend itself against night-bombing operations than it had been when the Kaiser had sent over Gothas and Giants in the last war.

After the August dress rehearsal Dowding was sufficiently satisfied to make his first public broadcast, reassuring the nation that the exercise proved Britain was well prepared for a German air assault, proclaiming: 'I confidently believe that a serious air attack on these islands would be brought to a standstill in a short period of time.'[26] In a confidential report of the operation Dowding reaffirmed this confidence, informing the Air Ministry: 'While I am far from implying that the present system is perfect, I feel that a very great advance has been made during the past year in the mechanism of intercepting raids in daylight.'[27]

Dowding's confidence was predicated on the meaningful number and performance of the Hurricane and the critical arrival of a few Spitfires with the promise of more to come. As to his third fighter, Dowding remained at best ambivalent. The Air Ministry had also been forced to rethink its position. In June 1939 Stevenson had quietly informed Dowding that the Air Ministry was scaling down its turret fighter requirement so that Fighter Command was to have six, not nine, Defiant squadrons.[28] This merely reflected the reality of the retarded development of the Defiant. But as soon as Boulton Paul was able to restore its production targets these squadron figures were to be upgraded.

Dowding's constant undermining of the Air Staff and his downbeat assessment of aircraft for which his superiors held such high hopes continued to arouse antagonism at the Air Ministry. It was not just his opposition to their ideas but the unyielding manner in which he expressed it.

After the war Dowding offered a valuable insight to his attitude when he told his biographer Robert Wright: 'I've always been against all governments. Wherever I have been and whatever I have tried to do, it seemed there was always somebody in government who was hampering my efforts. I do not mean, of course, I am against governments as such. I am against people whose minds have got into a groove about existing practices . . . I have always been against those whose first inclination, because of those grooves, is to resist any suggestion about modification or change in the existing state of affairs, and to go on causing further obstruction merely because of existing practice.'[29]

Dowding was due to step down from Fighter Command in July 1939 to be replaced by Sir Christopher Courtney, the head of Reserve Command. To many in the Air Ministry this transfer of power could not come a moment too soon. But Sir Cyril Newall, realising that while Germany looked so belligerent this was the worst time to replace an experienced leader of Fighter Command, decided to postpone Dowding's retirement and wrote to him telling him to hang on for a few more months. Then on 28 June 1939 a plane in which Courtney was flying as a passenger crashed, leaving him with severe leg injuries. Dowding was now told he would be able to keep his job until October 1940. In customary gruff irritation, Dowding wrote to the Air Ministry to say that his treatment at their hands was 'cavalier' and that if he was to carry on he wanted to have in writing the support of the Air Council, which had previously backed Courtney for his job.[30]

The Defiant remained stuck in its test phase and its early promise limited to the results of trials before its turret had been fitted. The introduction of the heavy turret with the gunner and ammunition left a serious question mark hanging over the new fighter's performance.

A second Defiant prototype had been designed to meet the weight and drag issues which Boulton Paul knew must be addressed before the Air Ministry and, more importantly, Dowding would be able to declare it fit for combat operations. This second prototype, which had flown for the first time on 18 May 1939, incorporated a number of key design changes. The chief improvement was the introduction of the more powerful Merlin II engine, and later the Merlin III, which helped to compensate for the weight and drag of the turret so that the aircraft's performance was now more in line with pre-turret tests. The first production Defiant finally flew on 30 July, but by the start of September only one Defiant had been delivered to the RAF.[31]

The Air Ministry, disappointed by the slow progress of its secret fighter, was determined Dowding should make full use of the small number of Defiants which were with the RAF.

And once the production hold-up was eased, ministers fully expected Fighter Command to begin filling its squadrons with the Defiant.

On 10 August 1939 Harold Balfour, the Under Secretary of State for Air, wrote to Dowding asking him for a progress report on the Defiant fighter. Balfour, a First World War ace who had flown Sopwith Camels, and, like Stevenson and Douglas, could see the merits of a bomber destroyer, was seriously concerned that not enough effort was being made to bring the Defiant to operational readiness.[32]

But Dowding would not be rushed into equipping his squadrons with a third fighter that had not been fully combat tested. He waited almost a month before he replied to Balfour's letter, by which time Britain was at war.

# Chapter 6

# STATE OF WAR

THE ALLIES' CONSPICUOUS failure to prevent the Nazi invasion of Czechoslovakia allowed Hitler to set his sights on the conquest of Poland.

In April 1939 the German leader unilaterally withdrew from both the German-Polish Non-Aggression Pact of 1934 and the London Naval Agreement of 1935 which restricted the number of German warships. Adopting the same strategy he had used so effectively against the Czechs, Hitler stirred up anti-Polish feeling by falsely accusing Poland of crimes against the German-speaking minorities. The Führer told the German people that just as the Treaty of Versailles had deprived Germany of the Sudetenland, it had also given away the city of Danzig, where many ethnic Germans resided.

In May 1939 Hitler gathered his generals and air commanders to make preparations for the Poland campaign. His secret pact with the Russians meant he didn't have to worry about Soviet aggression from the east, and he gambled that France and Britain lacked the political will to back the Poles.

Just after midday on 31 August Hitler signed directive number one for the 'conduct of the war'. It began: 'Since the situation on Germany's eastern front has become intolerable and all political possibilities of a peaceful settlement have been exhausted, I have decided upon a solution by force.'[1]

Hitler's directive precisely identified the key targets for the Luftwaffe which included airfields, factories and civilian populations living in the cities. To carry out these orders Göring could call upon 1180 fighters, 290 Ju 87 Stuka dive-bombers, 1100 conventional bombers (mainly He 111s and Do 17s), and an assortment of 550 transport and 350 reconnaissance aircraft.

Despite emergency diplomacy by the British and French Governments, Hitler resisted all efforts for a peaceful resolution. This would turn out to be the German leader's first serious miscalculation. Instead of backing down and allowing Germany to once again roll over an inconvenient neighbour, Neville Chamberlain and the British Cabinet decided to stand by their undertaking to the Poles.

Germany invaded Poland on 1 September 1939. Britain did not issue a formal declaration of war until the French had a chance to recall its parliament on the evening of 2 September.

At 11.15 a.m. on the following morning Chamberlain addressed the nation by radio, declaring that a state of war now existed between the United Kingdom and Germany: 'This morning, the British ambassador in Berlin, handed the German Government, the final note, stating that unless we heard from them, by 11 o'clock, that they were prepared at once, to withdraw their troops from Poland, a state of war would exist between us. I have to tell you now, that no such undertaking has been received, and that consequently, this country is now at war with Germany . . . We have a clear conscience; we have done all that any country could do to establish peace. The situation in which no word given by Germany's ruler could be trusted, and no people or country could feel itself safe had become intolerable . . . Now may God bless you all. May He defend the right. It is the evil things we shall be fighting against – brute force, bad faith, injustice, oppression, and persecution – and against them I am certain that the right will prevail.'[2]

Britain's declaration of war hastened Hitler's contingency plans for an air assault against the UK economy and armed forces. 'Attacks on the English Homeland are to be prepared,' Hitler said, adding the caveat, 'but the decision regarding attacks on London is reserved for me.'[3]

Meanwhile the German war machine began the business of crushing Poland. Captain Adolf Galland, one of the Luftwaffe's leading fighter aces, recalled: 'It was still dark on the morning of the 1st of September as we climbed into our cockpits. Blue flames spurted from the exhausts of our engines as they warmed up and at the first signs of dawn the fireworks started.'[4]

Galland was joined by the battled-hardened Hannes Trautloft who commanded 2./JG 77, stationed at Juliusburg airfield, tasked with spearheading the fighter attacks against the Polish air force. Poland could muster only six hundred aircraft, none of which was a match for the state-of-the-art Luftwaffe fighters. Poland's two fighters, the PZL P.11 and PZL P.7, resembled the RAF's high-wing Gladiator with a top speed barely reaching 230 mph. The ease with which these aircraft were swept aside must have come as both a salutary warning and a relief to the British Air Staff who only a few years earlier had placed its faith in the Gladiator as the RAF's front-line fighter. The Polish pilots put up a brave fight, but it was never a fair contest and they quickly succumbed to faster and heavily armed Me 109s.

Trautloft, in his personalised Emil Red '1', three stripes on its fuselage identifying it as the commanding officer's, added one more to his growing number of conquests. He claimed a Polish light bomber and reconnaissance aircraft, known as the PZL.23 Karaś ('crucian carp'), of which he made short work over Warta nine miles north-west of Sieradz on 5 September. The PZL.23, with a crew of three, had been designed in the early 1930s and was powered by a Bristol Pegasus engine. By 1939 it was easy meat for the Luftwaffe pilots. Nevertheless, this short engagement with the Luftwaffe gave the surviving Polish pilots, flying slower but more agile fighters, invaluable experience trying to outmanoeuvre the faster and more heavily gunned 109s. Some escaped to Britain where they flew Spitfires, Hurricanes and Defiants. Their aggression and hatred of the Germans meant the RAF Polish squadrons were extremely effective in pressing home their attacks.

Britain's response to the invasion of Poland was to prepare for immediate air raids. Chamberlain instituted a War Cabinet and restored Churchill to the Cabinet as First Lord of the Admiralty.

On 3 September, Fighter Command totalled thirty-five squadrons: twenty-one piloted by regular crew, fourteen by auxiliaries in what Dowding considered, 'various states of efficiency'. Only twenty-two were equipped with Hurricanes or Spitfires. The remaining thirteen comprised Blenheims, Gladiators and Defiants.[5] The Air Ministry expected the Germans to begin bombing almost immediately and the RAF was put on standby.

Once again PO John Banham, now attached to 611 Squadron at Duxford, was sitting in his Spitfire waiting for the order to scramble. But this time Banham's Spitfire's eight machine guns

George Heseltine, the author's great uncle, who, after recovering from wounds sustained in the Gallipoli campaign, volunteered for the Royal Flying Corps and flew two-seater fighter bombers with 20 Squadron during the First World War. Twenty years later he joined up with the RAF. *(author's collection)*

n the Battle of Britain, George Heseltine (second from left) was serving with RAF intelligence. *uthor's collection)*

George Heseltine piloted an Fe2d, known as a 'pusher' because the propeller was behind the pilot. It was one of hundreds built by Boulton Paul. On May 5 1917 George's Fe2d was set ablaze when attacked by a superior number of single seat German fighters. He managed to crash-land the aircraft without any serious injury to himself or his observer. *(WW1 forum)*

The observer in the Fe2d had to stand up to operate the rear machine gun. He also had a forward-firing machine gun. *(author's collection)*

Less than 20 years later the Air Ministry and Boulton Paul had adapted a state-of-the-art electro-hydraulic powered turret which housed four Browning .303 machine guns. The Defiant turret was situated behind the pilot's cockpit and gave the RAF fighter extraordinarily destructive and concentrated fire power. *(RAF in Combat)*

he prototype Boulton Paul Defiant K8310, as originally rolled out at the factory in Pendeford, Volverhampton, without gun turret and with a single-seat cockpit. On its first flight on 11 August 937, the aircraft was found to have excellent performance and agility. The addition of the turret and ir gunner had a negative impact on this. *(RAF in Combat)*

efiant N1650, seen here during a test flight, was delivered to the RAF on 5 August 1940, just as the attle of Britain got going. The Defiant was affectionately referred to as 'Daffy' by the aircrews. *AF in Combat)*

A heroicised depiction of the Defiant, which was seen as a key weapon in Britain's armoury against the Nazi onslaught. *(The Aeroplane, December 15 1939)*

he Air Ministry wanted Fighter Command to equip a third of its squadrons with Defiants but Hugh owding resisted, so only two Defiant squadrons took part in the Battle of Britain. Chronic hold ups t the factory also thwarted the Air Ministry's ambitions. *(RAF in Combat)*

A tale of derring-do. How the *RAF Flying Review* tried to rehabilitate the combat reputation of the Defiant. *(RAF Flying Review, August 1963)*

Defiant pilots and gunners after their day of greatest success over Dunkirk, shooting down a record 37 (later upgraded to 38) German aircraft in one day. It remains a record for the number of enemy planes shot down by a single RAF squadron in one day of combat.
Back row: Pilot Officer G. L. Hickman, Flight Lieutenant N. G. Cooke, Squadron Leader P. A. Hunter, Pilot Officers M. H. Young, G. H. Hackwood, E. G. Barwell, S. R. Thomas and D. Whitley.
Front row: Sergeant E. R. Thorn, Pilot Officer D. H. S. Kay, Sergeant A. J. Lauder, Pilot Officer R. W. Stokes. *(IWM CH197)*

From left to right: The lucky three. PO Hugh Tamblyn, Sq Ld William 'Dickie' Richardson, PO Ian MacDougall. The only 141 Squadron pilots to have returned safely after the July 19th 'slaughter'.
*(Richardson family)*

q Ldr Philip Hunter, now a decorated and experienced fighter commander, leading a section of efiants in the summer of 1940. *(RAF in Combat)*

unter, addressing his crews after another successful action in 1940. *WM/Air Historical Branch CH196)*

Sgt Fred Barker with his teddy bear mascot. Barker and pilot Sgt Ted Thorn were the most successful Defiant crew in WW2 with thirteen kills. Barker could also claim to be the highest scoring air gunner of the war. *(IWM CH2526)*

264 Squadron was recalled to the frontline of the Battle of Britain in August 1940. *(RAF in Combat)*

were all properly sighted and instead of three aircraft, the squadron was at full strength. 'The squadron,' recalled Banham, 'was in camp and we were sitting, in turns of three aircraft at the end of the airfield. We sat there for two hours at a time ready for dispersal. I remember it was very boring sitting for so long in the hot sun all day.'

Another pilot, the more rookie Eric Barwell, remembers an overwhelming feeling of excitement: 'We were on parade by 11 a.m. when the voice of the Prime Minister, Neville Chamberlain, was heard on the radio saying that a state of war existed between us and Germany. That fateful Sunday, 3 September 1939, had some clear memories for me. Having been told positively that we were now at war the order was given: "Fall out those with Wings!".'[6]

These fresh pilots, still waiting to join squadrons, fully expected to take to the skies in whatever aircraft were available, but were instead loaded into trucks and driven to the perimeter fence of the airfield where they were ordered to man the Lewis guns. Barwell and Banham would soon meet as brother pilots attached to the RAF's most famous Defiant squadron. In the coming air battles they would both see much action. And Banham, who also flew Hurricanes, would make RAF history – the only Battle of Britain pilot to fly all three front-line fighters.[7] William 'Dickie' Richardson, about to take command of a Defiant squadron, typified the older pilots' response to the outbreak of war. He sent his wife and two young children to Cardiff so that they would be out of harm's way, allowing him to get on with the business of shooting down Germans.

The immediate prospect of enemy bombers over British cities brought the Air Ministry to a state of buttoned-up panic. They now looked to Fighter Command and its tricky commander-in-chief for reassurance that his fighter squadrons would be able to defeat the bombers and keep the cities safe. Of particular concern was the state of readiness of the RAF's bomber destroyer. Over the summer months Dowding had been in receipt of a number of increasingly urgent enquiries about the promised Defiant squadrons. Two days after the declaration of war, Dowding finally decided to answer the Air Ministry.

In a letter marked secret and headed 'free-gun fighter tactics' the head of Fighter Command wrote to Harold Balfour, Under Secretary of State for Air, explaining: 'The first two "Defiants" have been allotted to Northolt [for testing] and as soon as they arrive I will see that the tactical and performance tests are undertaken on high priority. In the meantime we are at war and I must ask that no squadron shall be rearmed with "Defiants" until I have satisfied myself an improvement in fighting efficiency will be thereby affected. The nature of the trials carried out will depend upon the results of the performance and handling tests,' signing off, 'I have the honour to be, sir, your obedient servant, H. G. T. Dowding.'[8]

Dowding was determined not to be railroaded into sending up Defiants before the aircraft had been fully tested and the pilots experienced enough to fly them. It made no difference to him that the Air Ministry, and just about everybody else in Britain, believed the German bombers would soon be on their way.

Certainly the Air Ministry wasn't taking any chances and, anticipating a heavy aerial bombardment, had moved Sholto Douglas and a shadow Air Staff to Garston, north of Watford, which was to be the reserve operations and intelligence centre. Recalled Douglas: 'I was in charge of the whole show and I was to exercise operational control over the RAF should the Air Ministry in London be blown to smithereens . . . we seriously thought that would happen, through the heavy bombing that we expected from the Germans.'[9]

The Air Ministry estimated that the RAF faced in the region of 1650 Nazi bombers, rising to two thousand by mid-1940. But the reality was that the Luftwaffe's commitment to Poland, where it had lost 285 planes, meant the Germans could only call upon one thousand serviceable bombers. And Luftwaffe high command was by no means convinced that it was capable of bombing Britain into submission. The Luftwaffe's intelligence chief Beppo Schmid warned in July that Britain could not be defeated by air attack alone and that a decisive invasion would be necessary. Hans Geisler, who had been given the task of devising a plan for attacking England from the air, argued for at least another year of rearmament before the job could be accomplished.[10]

The expedited production of Britain's new fighter aircraft was now in full swing. But Britain badly needed pilots as well. All leave was cancelled and the Auxiliary Air Force and Volunteer Reserves were mobilised so that peacetime pilots were soon wearing the sea-grey uniform of the RAF.

Jim Bailey was one of many RAFVRs who had been pressed into service and posted to RAF Cranwell where he trained on Hart and Hind biplanes. He recalled: 'When they divided us into those who would fly single-engined aircraft and those to fly twins, I applied for the single-engined aircraft. I hoped to become a fighter pilot for I was of too independent a nature, I feared, to belong to a larger crew and too fastidious to bomb civilians. In the event the bomber pilots on our course were all killed or made prisoner in the early stages of the war.'[11]

Bailey was sadly referring to the pilots and gunners of the twin-engined Fairey Battles and Bristol Blenheims which were obsolete by the start of the war. But because the RAF had nothing else, they were flung at the Nazis in the first weeks of the coming campaign in France in support of the BEF (British Expeditionary Force).

Back in Germany, Trautloft's exploits during the Poland campaign had won him promotion to the rank of Hauptmann, and on 19 September 1939 he was made Gruppen Kommandeur of I./JG 20.

In those first nervous hours of war, the Air Ministry and Fighter Command waited patiently for the Germans to play their hand. But apart from a false alarm over a French aircraft misidentified on radar, the first twenty-four hours passed without incident. The Cabinet decided to seize the initiative. That night ten RAF Whitley bombers flew over the Ruhr region dropping millions of leaflets informing the Germans that their leader's wishes could have been settled peacefully but instead their government had 'condemned you to mass murder, starvation and the hardships of war which you can never hope to win. Hitler has cheated not us but you'.[12]

Douglas urged the Cabinet to take further advantage of the German paralysis and send bombers against industrial targets in the heart of the Third Reich. He argued that the Luftwaffe was still fully occupied with defeating the Poles which left them exposed to bombing runs on a second front. 'I had expected,' he later said, 'the RAF would be given instructions to start attacking Germany immediately and I still feel that that was what we should have done.'

Instead the next day, on 4 September, fifteen Blenheims and fourteen Wellingtons carried out a bombing raid on German warships at Wilhelmshaven and Brunsbüttel. The German cruiser *Emden* was damaged but the RAF paid a heavy price with seven bombers shot down, mostly from anti-aircraft fire, but at least one by an Me 109. This was the first Luftwaffe victory against the RAF.[13]

It was now obvious to Douglas and the rest of the gung-ho Air Staff that attack was not going to be the best form of defence. Both sides backed off, and the state of war was in name only as hostilities entered the phase known as the Phoney War.

For the next five months the RAF and the Luftwaffe went about the business of building up their respective strengths for the full-scale battles to come. However, that did not mean there was no contact between the two air forces. Instead of launching all-out air attacks, the RAF and the Luftwaffe probed each other's defences. The Germans tended to launch single aircraft reconnaissance missions while the British maintained sea patrols to combat the growing U-boat threat.

But on 6 September, Fighter Command's much-trumpeted defence system contributed to a shameful tragedy.

A technical fault at the Chain Home Radio Direction Finding (radar) station at Canewdon, near Rochford, compounded by a series of mistakes within RAF Fighter Command's fighter control system, resulted in the false alarm of an incoming air raid over Essex.

No. 56 Squadron scrambled fourteen Hurricanes from North Weald to intercept the 'German' raiders. The Hurricanes had not all taken off together and became further separated in their hunt for the 'enemy' aircraft. In turn, the inexperienced ground plotters marked some of these Hurricanes as 'hostile' and soon the operations room table in Uxbridge became cluttered with 'enemy' aircraft. To meet the growing 'threat' more squadrons, including 151 Hurricanes from North Weald, as well as the Spitfires of 54, 65 and 74 squadrons from Hornchurch, were called into the 'battle'. None of the RAF pilots had been in action before and few had even seen a German aircraft. In the confusion three Spitfires from 74 Squadron mistook three Hurricanes from 54 Squadron for German fighters and their leader, Adolph 'Sailor' Malan, who later became one of the most decorated Battle of Britain aces, ordered an attack. Two of the three, Flying Officer Vincent 'Paddy' Byrne and PO John Freeborn, opened fire. POs Frank Rose and Montague Hulton-Harrop were shot down. Rose managed to bail out but Hulton-Harrop was shot through the back of the head and killed. He has the tragic honour of being the first British fighter pilot to lose his life in 'combat' in the Second World War.[14]

This friendly fire incident (which became known as the Battle of Barking Creek) took place on the third day of the war and exposed dangerous weaknesses in the Fighter Command home defence system. Dowding, who was especially concerned about the lessons to be learned, had another reason to take a keen interest in the tragedy. His son, Derek, was a pilot serving with 74 Squadron, the unit which had shot down the two Hurricanes.

Barking Creek was a serious failure and the two Spitfire pilots faced charges at a court martial hearing.

What a relief it must have been for the Commander-in-Chief of Fighter Command to discover that his own son had not been one of the Spitfire pilots to face any blame. Derek Dowding continued to serve bravely throughout the war, distinguishing himself at Dunkirk and the Battle of Britain.

But his father made sure lessons were learnt. Urgent action was taken to ensure that the RAF had a workable 'friend or foe' radio signal system fitted to each RAF fighter which was recognisable to ground controllers. The system, already in use, was called 'pip-squeak' and relied on an aircraft's voice radio set to periodically send out a 1 kHz tone which was picked up by ground-based high-frequency direction finding (HFDF) receivers. Using three HFDF measurements, observers could determine the location of friendly aircraft using triangulation.

Further training was given to controllers, plotters and radar operators so that the fighter pilots scrambled to intercept the enemy aircraft 'pilots' were given much more accurate information. Aircraft recognition, both on the ground and in the air, was also worked on and while the friendly fire problem was never completely remedied, it had greatly improved by the time of the Battle of Britain.[15]

A combination of jumpy RAF pilots and the almost complete absence of the Luftwaffe over southern England skies had contributed to Barking Creek. But further north, in closer striking range from the Luftwaffe bases, real German coastal and sea operations triggered the first aerial combats of the Second World War. In fact the first aircraft operating from Britain to be credited with shooting down an enemy plane was the American-built Lockheed Hudson flying with 224 Squadron at RAF Leuchars, near Edinburgh.

The Air Staff had commissioned Lockheed to convert the civil passenger Hudson to a light bomber and reconnaissance aircraft. It was fitted with four .303 Browning machine guns, two at the front and two in a dorsal turret designed and manufactured by Boulton Paul. These were to be fitted in Britain at the same time the company was already undertaking orders for the Defiant and the Blackburn Roc. This greatly added to the production demands on Boulton Paul's factory capacity and no doubt contributed to hold-ups in the roll out of the Defiant. But the RAF and the Air Ministry also had high hopes for the Hudson.

The Hudson Mk.I was nearly 60 mph faster than the RAF's staple coastal command aircraft, the Anson, able to carry four times the bomb load and had twice the range of nearly 2000 miles. On 23 June 1938 Lockheed was given a contract for two hundred aircraft, and in February 1939 the first aircraft arrived at No. 224 Squadron.[16] It was the job of the Hudsons to search out enemy shipping and U-boats operating in the North Sea as well as carry out coastal reconnaissance missions. It wasn't long before they made contact with the enemy.

After the cancellation of the Nazis super-bomber project, the enemy had precious few long-range aircraft and so the Do18, a seaplane, was given the job of working with the U-boats to target British shipping. The Do18 had a huge range, exceeding 4000 miles, but was relatively defenceless against even lightly armed RAF machines.

At the start of the war my great uncle, Lt Albert 'Leslie' Womersley, was a pilot with 224 Squadron. He was of solid Yorkshire stock, educated at Sedbergh School in Cumbria and had been working for the family's Bradford-based oil- and grease-manufacturing business, Andrew Womersley and Son. In 1935, twenty-four-year-old Leslie Womersley took a commission in the RAF and was assigned to the RAF Intelligence Corps. In early 1939 he was promoted to Flight

Lieutenant and given command of a flight of three Hudsons based at RAF Leuchars.

Just after 7 a.m. on 8 October 1939 Womersley's three Hudsons took off from Leuchars on a patrol over the North Sea. His co-pilot was Sgt Morrison, and Cpl Daniel Turner[17] was in charge of radio and navigation. Leading Aircraftman (LAC) William Appleby[18] was positioned in the newly fitted Boulton Paul turret armed with two Browning machine guns and a thousand rounds of ammunition. Access to the turret was tight, through a very small underside entrance. But once in position the gunner had excellent views above the aircraft. The turret was powered by a Boulton Paul electro-hydraulic system, the same unit as used on the Defiant. A reflector gunsight was fitted to a beam, and the gunner used a central control stick to swivel his turret to wherever he needed to direct the fire. The turret had two speeds, and in the event of an electrical failure the gunner used a manual 'coffee-grinder-style' traversing handle.[19]

Womersley led the three Hudsons 100 miles out to sea at an altitude of 1000 feet. Shortly after 8 a.m. Morrison sighted a Do 18 flying low across the sea close to Skagerrak, Jutland, Denmark. The Dornier was flying reconnaissance in support of a German naval task force which had sailed from Kiel to operate off the south coast of Norway. The German battle cruiser *Gneisenau*, light cruiser *Köln*, and nine destroyers had orders to sink Allied shipping and entice the British Home Fleet into within range of Luftwaffe bombers. But the Hudsons had already sighted the German ships and reported their location to the Royal Navy.

When Womersley encountered the Dornier he immediately alerted the Hudson piloted by Flying Officer Frederick Burton (the third Hudson had gone to investigate a reported sighting of a U-boat) and then took his machine on a diving attack against the German seaplane. The Hudson's front machine guns scored direct hits but the Dornier gunner was able to return fire, hitting Burton's Hudson in the tail. However once the Hudsons were able to bring their turret guns to bear, the German aircraft had no answer and was forced to make a crash landing in the North Sea. After seeing the German crew escape in a dinghy from their stricken aircraft, Womersley ordered the Hudsons to use their guns to blast the Dornier until it was sunk. He then radioed a Danish fishing ship, *Teddy*, to alert it to the whereabouts of the German crew. They were all safely picked up and, after a short internment in Denmark, soon back home in Germany. The incident became the subject of a German radio broadcast by Lord Haw-Haw, the Irish-American Nazi collaborator William Joyce, who thanked the British pilots for their efforts to save the German crew. The Irish traitor said their actions typified the chivalric code in which he said the air war was to be fought between the 'knights of the sky'. This code was not always honoured and during the desperate fighting of the Battle of Britain there were plenty of examples of far less chivalric conduct committed by both sides. The German fighters would shoot RAF pilots as they floated down to earth in their parachutes and Dowding ordered that the Red Cross-marked rescue planes of the Luftwaffe, used to retrieve airmen from the channel, were legitimate targets.[20]

The Dornier was the first enemy aircraft to be shot down by British aircraft flying from bases on the British mainland.

The Hudsons' first blood handed the RAF a small propaganda victory. Great Uncle Leslie was awarded the DFC and later photographed attending Buckingham Palace with the rest of the family who had come down from Yorkshire to proudly witness the event. I still have a copy of the *Daily Mirror* which covers the story of how the 'war hero' gave the waiting paparazzi the slip so he could head off to the Savoy for a secret rendezvous with some girlfriends.

The *Mirror* reported: 'Womersley was so shy that he would not face the newspaper cameraman and begged him to "cut it out", refusing to come out. Lieutenant Womersley, however, made his exit by another gateway, and thus evaded all the efforts of the photographers. Even his parents were left in the lurch, for after waiting for some time for his reappearance they were informed that he had left some time ago.'[21]

Back at the Boulton Paul factory in Wolverhampton they were jumping for joy. John Dudley North's hydraulic turret had passed its first combat test and proved that in the right hands it could shoot down enemy planes. The fact that the Dornier seaplane was practically obsolete by the start of the war, and hardly representative of the heavily armoured Luftwaffe bombers and the much faster Messerschmitt fighters, was not something that was going to spoil the celebrations.

# Chapter 7

# COMBAT READINESS

GERMANY'S RELUCTANCE TO mount a bombing campaign against Britain in the closing months of 1939 gifted the RAF valuable time to make vital preparations before the start of the Battle of Britain.

But while Dowding made good use of the winter weeks, fine-tuning his home defence system, the armchair air marshals spent it wrangling with each other over the best tactics for defeating a German air armada. Fighter Command still favoured the fixed-wing fighters with their forward-firing machine guns. Sholto Douglas, the Deputy Air Chief, and Donald Stevenson, the Deputy Head of Home Operations, wanted to be able to utilise the 650 free-gun fighters which they hoped would soon come on stream.

The longer the Phoney War dragged on, the greater chance the air marshals had of bringing the Defiants into the war.

Professor Bennett Melvill Jones, the scientist in charge of the turret trials, had based himself at the Aeroplane and Armament Experimental Establishment at Boscombe Down, Wiltshire, where he set up home in a caravan with his family.[1] Eight weeks after the start of the war he reported back to Dowding and the

Air Ministry. In his letter to Dowding of 7 November he outlined the tactical advantage the Defiant would have over the German bombers. 'The enemy,' wrote Melvill Jones, 'apparently have not so far taken adequate steps against crossfire attacks so if we can develop them we should for a while be in a very strong position.'

'This advantage,' continued the weapons scientist chief, 'is fundamental and cannot be eliminated by any action that the enemy may take. I put forward these arguments not to show that the turret fighter is a better weapon than the fixed-gun fighter and should replace it, but to urge the importance of giving the Defiant a thorough trial in action in order to throw as much light as possible on the potentialities of the turret type for future use. Success will depend to a very large extent on the careful training of the crews to work together and the use of correct methods of attack and of aiming, and it is for this reason that we are pushing on as fast as we can with the development of tracer bullet . . .'[2]

On 19 November 1939 Dowding replied to Melville Jones agreeing with him that the Defiant's combat future would not be decided by academic argument but by RAF trials of the aircraft in exacting flying conditions.[3] In a memo marked secret Dowding said: 'I have chosen a specially good squadron commander to get ready the Defiants, and we will settle all the outstanding points by practical trial which is so much more satisfactory than argument.'

Dowding was careful to give the impression that he retained an open mind on the Defiant as a military advance in the theory and practice of destroying bombers. But he also let it be known he remained of the view that the fixed-gun fighter was the best machine for the job. He told Melvill Jones: 'The dog-fighting qualities of a Home Defence Defiant are comparatively unimportant. Its job is to shoot down bombers. The point is, unless and until the enemy arm themselves from astern, the eight-gun fighter is a very deadly weapon and better than the turret fighter on account of its extra speed and firepower. Let us say the time comes when the enemy is completely armoured from attacks from behind and the fixed-gun fighter has to resort to deflection shooting [firing ahead of the moving target]. In theory the Defiant overtakes to one side and engages with lateral fire. In practice (except with surprises) the bomber will be able to turn its stern to the Defiant before the latter gets into a position to open fire.'

Dowding then offered a solution to his own conundrum: 'Some form of tactics may be evolved where the Defiant hunts in couples so that one or other always gets a shot, but I think the single bomber will always be able to evade the single Defiant. However, as I say, those things are better decided by experiment rather than argument.'[4]

But just as there appeared to be consensus on the value of an RAF free-gun fighter the production problems which had beset the Defiant from the outset threatened to end its chances of ever playing a leading role in the defence of the realm. The Air Ministry's blueprint for a large number of RAF squadrons to be equipped with Defiants had always looked a remote prospect. Britain was already more than three months into the war and not a single RAF squadron had been equipped with Defiants. In March 1940 only thirty-seven of the updated 650 Defiant order had been delivered.[5]

In contrast, the first Supermarine Spitfire, which had only been handed over to the RAF in August, was now on stream, well ahead of the Defiant. By 3 September, at the start of the war, eight Spitfire squadrons (187 aircraft from an order for three hundred) had been fully equipped with the fighter.[6] Yet at the start of the year the Air Ministry had more Defiants on order than Spitfires.

An Air Ministry report concluded: 'The failure of Boulton Paul to deliver Defiants in accordance with planning has been noticeable for a long time . . . No attempt has been made to enquire further into the causes of the failure as it is already realised that the organisation of the firm is considered not to have been capable of meeting the demands made upon it.'[7]

However, this was not the whole story. The government had over-burdened the company's factories with other aircraft and turret orders. The Air Ministry's insistence that the firm must first complete the order for the naval turret fighter, the Blackburn Roc, severely hampered the company's ability to meet the deadline for the Defiant contract.

There were also serious problems concerning the fractious working relationship between Boulton Paul and some of the contractors who had been called in to take up half of the production. An internal memo between exasperated officials at the Directorate of Aeroplane Production reveals just how fraught relations had become between Boulton Paul and its two subcontractors, Aero Engines and General Aircraft. One official complained to another: 'I entirely agree that [Aero Engine's director] Mr Gordon England's attitude in each of these cases as and when they arise is almost always quite unreasonable, but, on the other hand, Boulton and Paul's attitude is seldom better and often worse. I am quite certain that we are just making trouble for ourselves by agreeing to any further orders of any sort between these two parties. In fact my own ambition in this connection is to see the present orders cleared up and to be shot of these continual squabbles of which the only things that are clear are that production does not eventuate but that neither party is in any way to blame. In future, therefore will you please whenever possible do all you can to prevent Boulton and Paul placing any further orders of any sort with either General Aircraft or Aero Engines Limited.'[8]

A subsequent Air Ministry 'special investigation into the production of the Defiant' went further concluding Boulton Paul to be 'very lackadaisical'.[9]

There was one further, perhaps more significant, factor that ensured Spitfires and Hurricanes would reach Fighter Command squadrons ahead of the Defiant. Lord Beaverbrook, the Minister of Aircraft Production, had deliberately omitted the Defiant from a list of five key aircraft, including the Spitfire and the Hurricane, which had been accorded 'absolute priority' status. In practice it meant that whenever a subcontractor was working on a contract for a Hurricane and a Defiant, the Hurricane would always have priority.[10]

Douglas and Stevenson had no choice but to acknowledge the economic reality of the situation – the Boulton Paul factories had demonstrably failed to deliver the Defiant in the numbers the Air Ministry had desired. But if Beaverbrook was still dragging his heels, Douglas and Stevenson had not given up on the turret fighter. They ordered Dowding to carry on equipping his squadrons with Defiants as soon as they became available.

Faced with the imminent threat of an air invasion which might throw up many unknown challenges, Dowding agreed to nominate a squadron and commander for the first RAF Defiant fighter unit. That squadron was 264 under the command of Squadron Leader Stephen Haistwell Hardy.

No. 264 Squadron's motto was 'We Defy' and its emblem was a knight's helmet, signifying the squadron's readiness to fight. It was formed in the First World War when it was equipped with Short 184 seaplanes stationed at Souda Bay, Crete, and at Siros on the Greek mainland. In the last months of the war 264 was ordered to patrol the shipping routes and defend the convoys on their way to Salonika. But the squadron saw very little action and was disbanded a few weeks after the armistice.

Born in 1905 Stephen Hardy, the married son of a family of Anglo-Indian colonialists, joined the RAF in 1923 and the following year was commissioned as a pilot attached to No. 100 Squadron, flying Fairey Fawn single-seat light bomber biplanes.

In 1926 he was transferred to No. 84 Squadron equipped with Westland Wapitis, a two-man fighter bomber armed with one forward-firing Vickers machine gun and one Lewis gun and capable of carrying up to 582 lb of bombs under the wings and fuselage. Hardy spent several years with the squadron in Basra in southern Iraq. But he returned to Britain in 1929 to start an aircraft engineering course so he could qualify as a specialist engineer officer. In 1934 he married the daughter of another Anglo-Indian family and in January 1937 was posted to HQ Fighter Command as an Engineering Staff Officer, where his understanding of aeronautical technology had brought him to the attention of Dowding.[11]

At the end of the first week of October, Germany wound up its campaign in Poland and Hitler was able to turn his full attention to Britain and France. Unshackled, the German Stukas, Heinkels and Dorniers carried out a series of successful attacks on shipping in the Thames Estuary and the Straits of Dover. In November more than thirty ships were sunk or damaged. To halt the rising loss in shipping the Cabinet asked Fighter Command to provide standing patrols to protect the convoys from the Luftwaffe raiders. But Dowding was reluctant to get drawn into wasteful combat with the German fighters and resisted the Air Ministry approaches by arguing it was not strictly Fighter Command's responsibility. Instead he urged Coastal Command and the Fleet Air Arm to bear the burden, although neither had the aircraft to do the job properly. At this early stage of the war Dowding was still focused on building up his fighter squadron forces.

On 30 October 264 Squadron was re-established at Sutton Bridge, Lincolnshire, adopting the name Madras Presidency Squadron, in honour of a financial donation by the Presidency of Madras.

Hardy was now joined by Flt Lt George Skelton, the experienced Boulton Paul test pilot. Between them they had the job of bringing the aircraft and the crew to combat readiness. The pilots were mostly newly trained volunteers with a sprinkling of old hands, including Flt Lt Bill Toyne from 213 Squadron and Flt Lt Nicholas Cooke from 611 Squadron. All of the squadron's gunners were volunteer reservists with an average of just two hours' flying experience. After arriving at Sutton Bridge these green gunner boys were immediately sent on a one-month course at the Air Gunnery School at Penrhos in north Wales where they were instructed in the new tracer bullet method of targeting, which Professor Melvill Jones had been so enthusiastically championing.[12]

Yet two months after the start of the war Hardy still hadn't received his Defiants, leaving his pilots to train on Miles Magisters and Fairey Battles.[13]

On 7 December the squadron was moved to Martlesham Heath, near Ipswich, where flying trials of the Defiant were already taking place under the stewardship of Augustus Orlebar. Two days later three Defiants were officially handed over to Hardy and his virgin crews. At the close of the year 264 had received a total of nine Defiants. Now Hardy hoped to have a few weeks either side of the New Year to prepare his unit for combat missions.

But there was renewed urgency from the Air Ministry to try out the Defiant against the enemy before the end of the year. On 5 December 1939 Donald Stevenson, who was now Director of Home Operations as well as aide-de-camp to the King, wrote to Dowding: 'We are most anxious, as well I know you are too, to discover as early as possible what the Defiant is capable of doing against the enemy bomber. We would be glad if arrangements could be made for a Defiant to be sent to an area in which an encounter is most likely to occur in the near future. We suggest Drem [an RAF station in East Lothian, Scotland] as a possibility.'[14]

Dowding however was unwilling to release the Defiants for combat until the crews had undergone proper training. He was fully aware that some of the pilots were still waiting to be assigned to the novice squadron.

Eric Barwell wasn't posted to 264 until just before Christmas 1939. He had been transferred directly from 266 Squadron which was flying Spitfires at Sutton Bridge where his brother

Philip was wing commander. However, it was thought 'bad show' that 'a brand-new Pilot Officer should serve under my Wing Commander brother'.[15] Wing Commander Philip Barwell was already a war hero, having been involved in one of the first combats when on 21 October 1939, as commanding officer of 46 Squadron at Digby, he was sent up with a flight of Hurricanes to intercept enemy raiders far out to sea. They found nine Nazi floatplanes, twin-engined He 115s, of which Barwell destroyed at least one and shared in the destruction of another. Altogether the squadron shot down six of the German machines. This was the first occasion radar had been successfully employed by Fighter Command to intercept and destroy enemy aircraft.

It was decided to separate the brothers and induct Eric into 264 Defiant squadron. 'I drove to Martlesham on about the 20th December,' Eric Barwell recalled, 'but on reporting to the 264 Squadron CO, S/Ldr Stephen Hardy, was told I must have more training first; quite likely he was suspicious of me, the first RAFVR pilot he had seen. Anyway, home I went for Christmas and reported to 12 Group Fighter Pool on New Year's Day, at Aston Down on a Cotswold hilltop. Here I had a month flying Harvard aircraft, American trainers of which those first ones were almost impossible to recover from a spin, but were good fighter training machines. The training there was for fixed-gun fighter tactics, not relevant to the Defiant, but the formation flying practice was very useful. That month of January 1940 was a very cold one and the Aston Down hilltop was bitter. At one time we had the sort of icing conditions which break telegraph wires under the weight of an inch or more of ice forming on them. That condition was blamed for a Harvard crashing, with both instructor and pupil being killed.'[16] Barwell didn't rejoin 264 until early February.

On 7 December Dowding officially responded to Stevenson's request to send a Defiant into combat, telling him: 'I consider this step would be premature and should be liable to get misleading information about the capabilities of the Defiant. I have had a long talk with Hardy and have given him a programme of work for the Defiants, the crews of which must be trained on lines somewhat different to our normal fighting methods. I think it probable that the Defiants can best be employed in pairs, but in any case I should be reluctant to send a single aircraft into action until the pilot and the gunner have had plenty of practice together and until the air gunner has had experience in operating the turret and firing his guns at a flag or drogue target. If it is necessary that a single aircraft shall go into action as soon as possible I will press on with this preliminary training, but I should prefer to wait and undertake the experiment rather more methodically.'[17]

The Air Ministry's anxiety about the fighting quality of its aircraft was heightened by the inconclusive nature of a number of skirmishes between German bombers and Spitfires. On the same day that Dowding had written to his Whitehall bosses urging patience a small group of Heinkels had flown a reconnaissance mission over Scotland. Spitfires flying with the local squadrons had been sent up to engage the enemy but the German planes had got away without a single shot being fired in anger.

This rather unsatisfactory encounter prompted Stevenson to write once again to Dowding: 'Thank you for your letter dated 7th of December in respect of trying a Defiant out as soon as possible against an enemy bomber. We are quite ready to agree to your suggestion that a pair of Defiants should be given the opportunity of adequate practice together and air gunnery experience before this takes place. We hope however that this will take place in the very near future as it is most desirable to discover as early as possible the fighting qualities of the movable gunfighter in view of the inconclusive combat between the Spitfire and the Heinkel formation on the 7th of December.'

Dowding, complying with Stevenson's entreaty, drafted a memo to his commanders at No. 12 Group which had responsibility for the 264 Defiants, telling them: 'The Air Ministry require two Defiants to be used against the enemy as soon as possible. Several crews should therefore be selected for this purpose from the very beginning and the best crew will be selected when the Squadron commander considers that their training has reached a point which justifies the employment on service.'[18]

He also issued an order that no gunner should enter a Defiant turret without a 'parasuit' which had been adapted as a padded back part of the seat. This was in response to reports that the tight confines of the Defiant turret made wearing a normal parachute impractical. This in turn prompted concerns about the possible difficulty 'padded out' gunners might encounter escaping from the narrow turret doors in the heat of combat.

Nevertheless the hydraulic-powered turrets were proving very popular with new gunners who had great fun using the 'arcade' joystick to swing the guns from side to side. Among the controls was a boost button to swivel the inner turret at double speed. Most of all, the gunners spoke of the thrill of sitting back in the turret and blasting away with the four powerful machine guns during gunnery practice.

Encouraged by the results of gunners' target practice using the four .303 machine guns taking place at Penrhos, Stevenson wrote again to Dowding: 'By the time all the crews return to Martlesham the pilots should have begun to settle down on their new aircraft and the squadron can be sent on operational training. Given reasonable weather conditions some pilots and crews might be ready to undertake operational duties by the middle of January.'[19]

But this was very wishful thinking on Stevenson's part. The truth was the new Defiants now being trialled by Hardy and his crews had run into mechanical problems and equipment supply delays. On 1 April 1940 the Directorate of Technical Development of the Air Ministry was forced to write to Boulton Paul about the hold up in providing new handles for the Defiant's troublesome turret doors.

The supply problems had become so desperate that Hardy drafted a memo to Wing Commander David Carnegie at Bentley Priory complaining about the lack of technical support from Fighter Command. 'Many thanks for your letter of 23rd of December 1939. I have received a copy of No. 12 Group's letter and we are trying to do the best we can. We have got so far fourteen pilots in the Squadron off on Defiants, but we are receiving no help at all in the matter of equipment or transport. We have no tankers, oil browsers, tool kits or starter batteries and the time is fast approaching when training will be completely stopped on account of these deficiencies. Please do not think that I am trying to appear helpless, but it is not fair to expect a completely new show to achieve the best results without normal help . . . I should very much like you to come down one day in the new year to see it as being a practical man you'll be able to appreciate our difficulties . . . we will also have a Defiant ready for you to fly. With best wishes for the New Year yours sincerely Stephen Hardy.'[20] Shortly afterwards 264 Squadron was grounded until the mechanical and supply problems had been resolved.

Dowding's reluctance to commit to the RAF's newest aircraft was not merely based on mechanical and supply problems. He had become seriously concerned about new reports of the Defiant's lack of speed and therefore its ability to catch German bombers.

Dowding had already shared some of these reservations with Melvill Jones who was also pressing Fighter Command to give the Defiant a chance against the German bombers. In a memo from the previous month Dowding wrote: 'It is all very well if the enemy keeps in formation and limits himself to such evasive manoeuvres as are then possible. But our experience on the few occasions hitherto we have intercepted enemy formations is that they break up to single aircraft which dive down to the surface of the land or sea and fly away on a zigzag course. In such circumstances the Defiant would be quite useless.'

Dowding even suggested to Melvill Jones: 'If the Defiant is no value to Home Defence fighting it might nevertheless be useful with the Field Force where enemy formations may be expected to be more cohesive. Failing this we can always find a use for the type in Group Pools and Advance Training Establishments. Another possibility might be to use the Defiant as an escort fighter, but this is not a recognised practice and the Defiant is terribly handicapped if attacked from below by the fact that its gun cannot fire downwards . . . Almost all of their time at AFDE has been taken up in remedying engine defects.'[21]

It was left to Keith Park, head of No. 11 Group and Dowding's most trusted aide, to try to get the Defiant deployment programme back on track. In the New Year, he told his boss: 'I suggest we would get quicker and better results if the tactical trials of two or more Defiants against formations of bombers are undertaken by the AFDU [Air Fighting Development

Unit]. One section and later a complete section of 264 Squadron could be attached to AFDU whilst No. 111 Squadron is still away in the North. If the above suggestion is adopted the employment of Defiants in combination with Spitfires could also be tried out at AFDU. These trials are so important as to justify relieving the Northolt Squadron for a few days from investigation Patrols.'[22]

On 17 January 1940, 264 Squadron began undertaking operational training involving tactical beam attacks on Blenheims, which played the role of the German bombers.

Events of the New Year wrenched the British from the false security of the Phoney War. On 10 January 1940 Major Erich Hoenmann crash-landed his Messerschmitt Bf 108 Taifun in neutral Belgium near Vucht. On board were the plans for the German attack on the Low Countries, a discovery which put the Belgium and British military on immediate full alert.

In the mind of the Air Ministry, the prospect of a German all-out attack on the Low Countries made the case for the RAF's flagship bomber destroyer stronger than ever. But if Dowding wouldn't be hurried along by the coaxing and exhortations of the government, perhaps public pressure might change his mind. So it was decided to place a number of articles in the press characterising the threat posed by Germany's new generation of bombers, the Ju 88 and the Me BF 110 fighter bomber, while at the same time unveiling the fighting potential of the RAF's secret weapon, the Boulton Paul Defiant.

Several newspapers carried suspiciously similar reports which began: 'There is evidence that the Germans are pressing on with the construction of fast, long-range bombers designed for use other than in close co-operation with military or naval forces. With this weapon still in his hands, it seems unlikely that the enemy will capitulate without attempting a desperate onslaught on Britain's vital targets.'

After extolling the virtues of the Spitfire and the Hurricane, the newspapers then suggested: 'The fixed-gun fighter, however, has certain limitations. One of these is the inability to make a broadside attack on its quarry. A new type of British fighter, the two-seat Boulton Paul Defiant, which has been developed for the Royal Air Force, overcomes this difficulty by the use of the power-driven gun turret. The turret houses a battery of guns, and is operated by a trained air gunner. In an attack upon an enemy aircraft the pilot of the turret fighter could place his aircraft in such a position that his bullets would strike the enemy at an angle favourable to penetration of the vulnerable parts. Flying alongside a formation of hostile bombers the Defiant gunner would be able to rake them with gunfire from nose to tail.'[23] One over-zealous report even suggested that the Defiant was faster than the Spitfire. If it was supposed to be Britain's top-secret weapon, it was a secret no more.

Dowding, however, remained unmoved and unbothered by the growing interest in the RAF's untested fighter. On 19 January he wrote to Harold Balfour, the under secretary of state for Air, setting out his own less-than-rosy assessment of the Defiant. He attached three secret reports compiled by the Air Fighting Development Unit (AFDU), Aeroplane and Armament Experimental Establishment (A&AEE) and Hardy's own squadron analysis which had all been finalised in the last three days.

Dowding began by saying: 'These three reports contain certain inconsistencies, the most important of which refers to the speed of the Defiant. It will be seen from paragraph 4 of No. 264 Squadron report that the speed of the Defiant is considered inadequate for overtaking even against a Fairey Battle flying at 180 miles an hour. Professor Melvill Jones also expresses some doubt on this score in a personal letter to me whereas AFDU appear to have had no particular difficulty in operating against Blenheims. This of course is a crucial point which can only be settled by further experience.'[24] In fact the Defiant lost up to 15 mph when the guns were held in the 'broadside position' which Dowding told Balfour 'lent colour to the theory that the Defiant may prove to be too slow for modern purposes'.

Dowding wasn't finished, pointing out further drawbacks with the elevation and depression of the guns, the restricted view of the air gunner, and the lack of the necessary electrical charge to operate the cine camera guns.[25] But he reserved his deepest skepticism for the suggestion that the Defiant may need to be protected by Hurricanes or Spitfires. 'If this proved to be necessary,' he warned, 'it will constitute a serious handicap to the Defence.'[26] In understated Dowding speak, 'serious handicap to the Defence' was about as bleak an assessment as he could give.

He was however more sanguine about the air gunners' poor shooting results which Hardy, who appeared more and more negative of the fighter by the day, said was 'disappointing'. Dowding remarked: 'Nevertheless they will have learnt something about the new method of shooting with tracer ammunition which they could not have learnt in the Squadron.'

He reserved his final comments for the hold ups in Defiant production, saying: 'Serious progress cannot be made in the unit until the proper equipment is provided. The Defiant itself is more than a year late in delivery and the fact that microphones, earphone plugs and leads have not yet been received by the unit shows up our supply system in a melancholy light.'[27]

Keith Park echoed Dowding's reservations about the Defiant's performance. On 19 February 1940 he wrote to Dowding telling him he found it difficult to reconcile claims of the Defiant's speed with the official test results. And he urged him to continue with the Blenheim trials to 'calm any doubts about inadequate speed of the Defiant'.[28]

Despite everything, Hardy had worked wonders with the squadron and on 20 March No. 12 Group told Dowding that two sections of Defiants had been declared operational. The following day six Defiants, led by Flt Lt Nick Cooke, flew to West Wittering from where they carried out convoy patrols over the Channel.

However, on 24 March without warning the Air Ministry transferred Squadron Leader Hardy to another command. It was a strange decision. Hardy had brought the squadron to readiness, building up an excellent rapport and loyalty with the crews. No other commanding officer in the country was more familiar with the strengths and weaknesses of the Defiant than Hardy. Perhaps his downbeat reports had found disfavour with the ministry. Whatever the reason for Hardy's transfer his successor would need to be an exceptional leader and gifted pilot if the squadron was to be ready in time to intercept the first wave of German bombers expected to be soon sent against Britain.

The crews of 264 didn't have to wait long for Hardy's replacement. On 1 April Squadron Leader Philip Algernon Hunter arrived at Martlesham Heath. Events would later show that Dowding and the Air Ministry could not have chosen a better commanding officer to take the Defiants into battle.

Hunter was born in 1913 in Frimley, Surrey, and then educated at three public schools: King's School, Canterbury; Rosalyn House, Felixstowe and The School, Bishops Stortford. He completed his training at the Royal Air Force College Cranwell, passing out as a probationary pilot officer on 11 September 1931. But Philip Hunter lived in the shadow of his father. Squadron Leader Albert Hunter[29] was a pioneer aviator who had served with the Royal Flying Corps on the Western Front. He left the war with the unique and special honour of being awarded both the OBE and the French Croix de Guerre.

Philip Hunter was determined to emulate his father and pushed himself hard to make his parents proud. On 29 August 1932 he joined No. 25 Squadron based at RAF Hawkinge in Kent, flying Hawker Furies. The following year he was sent to Ismailia in Egypt where he flew Fairey Gordon light bombers with No. 6 Squadron. Later he was promoted to Flight Lieutenant and returned to England, joining the staff of the Royal Air Force College Cranwell.

At the start of the war he had been the commanding officer of 254 Squadron, flying Bristol Blenheim twin-engine fighter bombers. His transfer to Defiants in March 1940 was the challenge he had been waiting for. He knew a great deal was expected of the turret fighter. In Hunter the Air Ministry had a squadron leader who was prepared to believe that the Defiant aircraft was a revolutionary breakthrough in fighter design. Now all he had to do was to prove it.

The contradictory reports concerning the speed and performance of the Defiant as a bomber destroyer left Hunter much to do in a short period of time. Yet very soon after joining the squadron he was so sure of the Defiant's attributes that he persuaded Fighter Command to arrange a dogfight trial with the fastest and most agile fighter of its day, the Supermarine Spitfire.

It was agreed that Hunter would fly a Defiant against a Spitfire piloted by Squadron Leader Stanford Tuck, a skilled and experienced pilot who was destined to become one of the highest-scoring aces of the Battle of Britain.

The trial took place on 6 April 1940 at the Air Fighting Development Unit, RAF Northolt. Both aircraft were fitted with cine guns. For the purpose of the trial Hunter was to fly a patrol between Northolt and White Waltham, giving Tuck 'full initiative' to commence his attack.

Throughout the 'combat' Hunter twisted and turned his aircraft, trying to keep it out of the range of Tuck's guns. The official AFDU report read: 'After some preliminary practice engagements the Defiant was placed on a patrol line and a Spitfire instructed to attack when he desired . . . As the Spitfire approached, the air gunner of the Defiant was able to open fire. The Defiant then went into a steep turn and was followed by the Spitfire. The engagement lasted about ten minutes and the air gunner after the first five minutes had used up all his film. During the whole engagement the Spitfire was unable to bring his guns to bear and finally landed having failed to use his cine gun.'[30]

In Hunter's own notes of the trial (adopted by the AFDU report) he said it was 'imperative [for the Defiant] to turn at an air speed of at least 160 miles an hour because in a vertical turn the aircraft stalls at the much greater speed than when flying straight . . . By losing height slowly it is possible to maintain a rate for turn and keep up the speed. At one time of the encounter the Defiant was on the tail of the Spitfire but below it. At no time did "g" force affect the pilot or gunner.'

It was a remarkable result for the Defiant, an aircraft 50 mph slower than the Spitfire. The trial had shown that, in the right hands, the RAF's newest fighter would be able to hold its own against the German Me 109. The report was widely circulated among the Air Staff who used it to further press Dowding for the Defiant to have a front-line role.

Hunter's next job was to settle the question of the Defiant's speed and its ability to catch the German bombers.

On 14 April, Fighter Command arranged for the Defiants to be flown against Blenheims, the same aircraft Hunter had commanded in his previous squadron. The results of the trial showed that with the Blenheims flying at 220 mph, all the Defiants, with a height advantage of 1000 feet, had successfully driven home their attacks.

News of the success of the trials was greeted enthusiastically at the Air Ministry. Two days earlier a force of eighty-three Blenheims, Hampdens and Wellingtons took part in a bombing raid against German shipping at Stavanger, Norway. The RAF lost three Wellingtons and six Hampdens mostly to attacks from BF 110s. Intelligence reports showed that the German fighters were able to draw alongside the British aircraft and use the rear gun to pour fire into the sides of the bombers.[31]

Hunter set to work carefully drawing up complex attack patterns against enemy bomber formations, offering six different combat approaches with guidance on optimum altitude, gun positions and action to be taken if the leader is hit.[32]

Despite his great efforts to get the squadron ready for its first combat mission the old supply problems continued to impair progress. In memos to Fighter Command dated 6 and 30 April 1940[33] Hunter complained that the situation was so dire he was having to strip some of his Defiants for spare parts. He asked for a 'large reserve' to be made available immediately or the 'robbed aircraft would be reduced to bare airframe and engine'. Among the vital equipment in short supply were radio components, oxygen regulators, cowling brackets and insulator glass.

Mechanical problems included a repeated failure of the downward aerial masts to retract with the undercarriage, so that they were breaking at a rate of one a day. To rectify the faults as quickly as possible Hunter flew down to Boulton Paul's Wolverhampton factory to pay North a personal visit so that he could explain exactly what was needed. Hunter also told North that it was vital all his Defiants were fitted with constant airscrew propellers and were able to use the newly available 100-octane fuel. Both would help address the Defiant's slow rate of climb, but not its maximum speed.

No. 264 Squadron's preparations were further hampered by the Air Ministry's insistence that the Defiant was to be both a day and night fighter. As a result, Hunter had to ensure enough pilots were available for night-flying exercises while also meeting the pressures of readying the squadron for day combat missions. Through April crews from 264 carried out thirteen hours of night flying. Hunter's pilots were also involved in supporting the second Defiant squadron, 141, by ferrying Defiants from the RAF maintenance depots to Turnhouse in Scotland where the newly established unit was stationed.

None of this was ideal preparation for a front-line fighter squadron. Time was running out for Hunter and his crews. Very soon the German advance across Europe would bring the Nazi bombers in close striking range of Britain.

# Chapter 8

# BAPTISM OF FIRE

THE ARRIVAL OF 264 Squadron and Britain's secret air weapon at Duxford aerodrome, one of the RAF's key fighter bases, caused something of a stir.

Guy Mayfield, the Duxford chaplain, wrote in his diary on 7 May: 'A Defiant with the new squadron leader and herald of the new squadron (all very secret) arrived here this morning. CO's name is Hunter. I spent a long time going over it with the air gunner. The intensely secret part of it all is that it looks like a conventional fighter from the air, but it carries an air gunner who can shoot forward and backward, as well as the fighter guns.[1] We suppose that the Germans don't know that we have any aircraft like this. It has come here because of the battles that are expected to come later this month. I like the gadgets which prevent the air gunner from shooting his own air crew. I can just squeeze into the air gunner's turret.'[2] It appears that from his diary entry even the Duxford chaplain wrongly believed, or was allowed to believe, that the Defiant could fire forwards.

Two days later Hugh Dowding called his senior staff and both commanding officers of the two Defiant Squadrons 264 and 141 to Bentley Priory for a 'conference' on fighting tactics for the free-gun fighters. Present were Fighter Command heads of 11, 12 and 13 groups: Air Vice-Marshals Keith Park, Trafford Leigh-Mallory and Richard Saul. The Air Ministry was represented by Wing Commander Burns, Assistant Director of War Training and Tactics. However, Squadron Leader William Richardson, the commanding officer of the second Defiant squadron, did not attend, sending in his place PO Ian Donald.

As they gathered in the main hall, Dowding told his commanding officers that the Phoney War would soon be over and that their pilots would be facing the battle-hardened Luftwaffe. Dowding explained the purpose of the conference was to 'deal with the tactics of movable gun fighters before the Defiants get into action'.[3]

Dowding made sure that all those present were given a copy of Hunter's tactical memorandum of Defiant two-seater attacks dated 27 April 1940, as well the conclusions taken from trials carried out by the Air Fighting Development Unit.

The first point of contention was the flying formations of the Defiants. Dowding said he had wanted the Defiants to fight in twos, but Hunter insisted that sections of three aircraft was the most effective deployment which he said was central to his six tactical attacks, each very detailed and requiring close cooperation between all the pilots.[4] The diagrams drawn up by Hunter resembled naval battle plans rather than aerial combat tactics for modern fighters.[5] Leigh-Mallory and Wing Commander Burns backed the commander-in-chief, favouring fighter sections of two. Park agreed, arguing that with 'one in the box' a section of two was just as manoeuvrable as three. Nevertheless, Hunter's view prevailed, saying his trials had proved the tactical advantages of 'twos' over 'threes'.

It left Dowding to remind his commanders that, 'We must never lose sight of the main advantage of a turret fighter, which is a number of aircraft can fly in formation on parallel course and get converging fire on the enemy.' He stressed that what the Defiant had over the Hurricane and Spitfire was its capacity for 'enfilading fire when it comes to attacking large formations'. Dubious of Hunter's complex tactical attack formations he recommended that after sighting the enemy, the Defiants should form up behind the target and choose the simplest and easiest approach: 'As the pilots acquire skill in this method they can start taking shortcuts and perform more complicated manoeuvres.'

Dowding said it was a 'fallacy' to think the bomber would not deviate from its course and therefore it would be 'unwise' for the Defiants to 'get too far ahead of the enemy aircraft'. And he confidently predicted that the bomber might find it impossible to throw off a section of Defiants that was directly behind and below, arguing that although the bombers would have defensive machine guns these 'would not nearly be as effective as a fighter'. And so, he urged, more consideration should be given to Defiant crews to get into a position 'where we can do things to the enemy rather than a position where he cannot do anything to us'.[6]

Whatever reservations Dowding had held about the Defiant he had been careful not to voice them in the company of his subordinate officers who had the task of taking the Defiant into battle. Hunter left Bentley Priory greatly boosted by the confidence his commander-in-chief had placed in the new turret fighter.

No. 264 Squadron would not have long to wait before they experienced their first taste of combat. Just hours after Dowding had called his commanders together and prophetically warned of the coming air battle, Adolph Hitler gave the final order to launch his decisive offensive. At 9 p.m. on 9 May 1940 the fragility of Europe's Phoney War was broken by the rumble of German armour on the streets of Luxembourg. The Luxembourg defences, such as they were, offered little resistance and the Germans' Army Group B rolled on into Holland, supported by paratrooper landings at The Hague and on the road to Rotterdam.

Waves of Stukas launched ceaseless dive-bombing attacks on the Dutch units opposing the German armour columns, while medium bombers were used to terrorise the civilian population. To exploit their early victories and maintain momentum the Luftwaffe ferried the paratroops and field weapons to forward positions behind the Dutch lines. The Dutch were now in peril of being overrun.

Britain immediately answered the Dutch Government's call for aerial support and the War Cabinet authorised Fighter Command to send fighters to help stem the Nazi air attacks. Within hours of the German advances, British-based fighters were being ordered into battle. Squadrons of Hurricanes and Spitfires began flying combat missions over the Low Countries, contesting the airspace with the Me 109s and 110s. At the same time Blenheims from 600 Squadron carried out ground-attack operations against the advancing German columns, while the Hudsons provided the top air cover.

Just forty-eight hours after finalising the tactics for his free-gun fighters, Dowding decided to unleash the Defiants. The RAF could call upon a total of fifty-eight aircraft, the majority operational and close to combat status. No. 264 Squadron was placed on standby at their new base at RAF Duxford. No. 141 Squadron would be held back in reserve.

On 10 May at 1 a.m. Flt Lt George Skelton, with twenty-eight-year-old Canadian PO Jack Hatfield as his gunner, flew a night defence mission to meet the expected threat from Luftwaffe raiders against Britain. One hour later the Defiant returned to Duxford without sighting the enemy. The next day Squadron Leader Hunter led a section of Defiants on an equally uneventful daytime convoy patrol near the Happisburgh Lightship off the Norfolk coast.

Then on 12 May the Air Staff finally got what they had been pressing Dowding for, for five months. Six Defiants led by Squadron Leader Hunter and Flt Lt Nicholas Cooke were ordered to Horsham St Faith, near Norwich, where they refuelled and were joined by six Spitfires from 66 Squadron, commanded by Squadron Leader Rupert Leigh. Just after 1 p.m. the Defiants, accompanied by the high-flying Spitfires, were ordered to patrol over the Hague. Hunter and Leigh were briefed that the Defiants were to attack enemy bombers and troop transporters while the Spitfires would take care of the faster Me 109s and Me 110s. The combined patrol reached the Hague just before 2 p.m. but without one of the six Defiants which had to turn back with engine trouble.

Two miles west of The Hague the British force caught sight of a Ju 88 attacking a British destroyer, its bombs clearly visible as they plopped into the water close to the ship. Seeing the closing British fighters, the Ju 88 turned to escape but Hunter ordered his section of three Defiants to cut it off. The pilots commenced their overtaking attack, flying below and then over the top of the bomber, giving the gunners plenty of chance to sight their guns.

Red 3, the third Defiant in the section, flown by PO Michael J. Young, was in striking distance. Young's gunner, LAC Stanley

Johnson, thirty-seven, had now locked onto the target and he patiently held his nerve as Young closed on the enemy. When they got to within 100 yards, Johnson let him have it, firing two bursts of five hundred rounds from the four .303 Browning machine guns. Smoke immediately started billowing from the Ju 88's port engine.

Young's report of the action read: 'Sighted enemy at 14.10, 2 miles west of The Hague at 3000 feet. Enemy turned inland and was attacked from port side about 3 miles inland. Enemy dived to left and was attacked by three Defiants. Two crossing over from the right and the third from the left. The Ju 88 flew low over three fields . . . and had smoke pouring from his port engine. He crashed in the middle of a field and his port airscrew flew into the air.' Young reported back that all the crew were dead.[7] The Defiants had their first kill.

But that wasn't the end of the combat. Shortly after they had downed the German bomber, the two Defiants of Yellow section and three accompanying Spitfires spotted an He 111. Cooke and Eric Barwell both used their newly fitted 12 lb engine booster to increase speed,[8] closing in on their quarry to within 100 yards. Cooke's gunner, Cpl Lippett, got in the first two short bursts firing between four and five hundred rounds which peppered the metal-plated side of the German bomber. Cooke's eager 'wingman' Barwell had also been closing in for the same kill, recalling later: 'I was about to attack a Ju 88 when my flight commander got in front of me and shot it down himself, which annoyed me.'[9]

Two of the four He 111 crew were killed in the attack, a third died of his wounds a few days later and the fourth was captured by Allied ground troops.[10] Three Spitfires from No. 66 also claimed a share of the kill. The Defiants and Spitfires still weren't quite finished. Shortly after the first attack Cooke sighted another He 111 at about 3000 feet, which also dived for cover. The three Spitfires peeled off and attacked the enemy machine from the rear while Cooke and Barwell carried out crossover attacks making clean hits. The Heinkel 'smoke issuing from both engines' rapidly lost height and crashed in a field resting up against a hedge.[11]

The Defiants and Spitfires broke off their attacks and returned to Duxford, Hunter's section landing ten minutes before Cooke and Barwell. It was a momentous day for Hunter and 264 Squadron who had proved that the RAF's secret fighter was capable of doing precisely what it was designed for – shooting down bombers. News of 264's successful maiden combat was warmly applauded by the Air Staff.

It was now the turn of the other half of the squadron to show what they could do. The next day (13 May) B Flight was ordered back to Martlesham Heath to take part in a second combat patrol over Dutch territory. At 04.15 hours the experienced Flt Lt George Skelton led the six Defiants over the North Sea towards the Dutch coast. Once again they were accompanied by a flight of six Spitfires from 66 Squadron. They had orders to seek out the Ju 52 transport planes which were helping the German forces to leapfrog the Dutch defences and complete the final phase of the assault on The Hague.

The two squadrons, a section of Defiants each following a section of Spitfires, reached the Dutch coast just after 5 a.m. about 10 miles north of The Hague. But the British fighters ran into intense Dutch anti-aircraft (AA) fire which had failed to distinguish the RAF planes from the more plentiful Luftwaffe. The British fighters encountered more AA over Maassluis, this time German, forcing them to take evasive action, flying back inland. It was the Spitfires who first sighted hostile aircraft – a group of seven Ju 87 Stukas, which were returning to their airfield after completing a bombing run on Dutch defensive positions. The Spitfires dived on their slow-moving prey and the Defiants followed them down in line astern. Soon the six Defiants had the enemy in their sights.

PO Samuel Thomas and his gunner John Bromley were the first to bring their guns to bear. Recalled Thomas: 'The aircraft [Stukas] were immediately formed in line astern and kept turning. I got into position on one Ju 87 and my air gunner (LAC J. Bromley) shot it down. I saw this aircraft go down. Then, afterwards, another Ju 87, which was coming up behind us, was also shot down apparently out of control.'

But the Stukas were not alone. The lead German had fired off a red flare summoning fighters from the Luftwaffe's most advanced fighter wing, Jagdgeschwader (JG) 26.[12]

Very soon twenty-five Me 109s were diving down on the battling Defiants. The first Defiant to be hit was Thomas's, who was still pressing home his attack on the Stukas and so hadn't noticed the new threat. Then Thomas heard John Bromley give out a cheer, signifying he had hit one of the German fighters as it attempted to get on the Defiant's tail. It was to be the Liverpool gunner's last mortal utterance.

Another 109, following on, unleashed a hail of bullets into the Defiant's rear, tearing apart the British machine. Recalled Thomas: 'My starboard tank caught fire and a stream of bullets came from the rear and shot away the dashboard and part of the control column. I lost control for some time but eventually managed to turn the aircraft on its back, as had been prearranged with the air gunner in order to facilitate bailing out. I could get no reply from the air gunner. I bailed out when the flames were coming up right into the cockpit.' The stricken Defiant plunged to earth with Bromley either already dead or too badly wounded to escape from his turret.[13]

The next Defiant in trouble was Skelton's, attacked by a combination of two Stukas and an Me 109. Skelton's gunner PO Jack Hatfield shot down one of the attacking Stukas but the incoming machine gun and cannon fire had badly damaged the Defiant. Hatfield desperately tried to contact Skelton on the radio transmitter (RT) but he got no reply.

Recalled Hatfield: 'By this time our own aircraft was in a steep spiral turn and the second Ju 87 continued to follow us. I could not get in touch with Skelton so I think he was probably killed in the first encounter. Our aircraft started to spin and I managed to escape from the top of the turret with only one door open. I must have pulled my parachute automatically because I was not conscious until I landed in some water.'[14] But Hatfield was not out of danger. One of the Stukas wanted to make sure of his kill and continued firing incendiary bullets at the escaping British pilot, badly injuring his elbow.

Meanwhile PO Sam Thomas had safely landed on an island among some tall reeds, south-east of Dordrecht. Lying on his back, and out of the battle, he traced the contrails of the continuing dogfights in the clear blue sky above. And then just as he was reflecting upon his good fortune he saw one of the Defiants explode in the sky above him. This third Defiant was crewed by PO Gordon Chandler, from East Horsley in Surrey, and his gunner LAC Duncan McLeish, both aged twenty. Their bodies were later recovered by the Dutch and given church burials. Chandler's remains, not discovered for almost a year, were partly identified by a membership card to the Leander

Club, the most exclusive and prestigious male-only rowing club in the world.[15]

There were still three Defiants left in the fight which had developed into a series of individual dogfights between the 109s, Stukas, Defiants and Spitfires.

In the melee the Defiant crewed by PO Patrick Greenhous and Sgt Rupert 'Harry' Greenhalgh[16] claimed two 109s before they were hit. Bullets ripped into the Defiant's starboard petrol tank which caught fire and a cannon shell lodged in the cockpit, injuring Greenhous. The pilot tried to contact his gunner: 'I then found that the intercom was unserviceable so, as prearranged, I rocked the aircraft as a signal for my gunner to bail out. As this produced no response, I thought he must have been wounded so decided to make a crash landing.'

But Greenhalgh had already clambered out of his turret and left the aircraft. Greenhous managed to put the Defiant down in a meadow adjoining the Rijsdijk dyke in the Willemspolder at Oosteind, part of Oosterhout, just as Greenhalgh was descending by parachute. Neither man was badly injured but they had landed in the middle of a German infantry unit. The two friends, now separated, decided to make a run for it, only to be caught by a German motorbike and machine gun sidecar. They remained in captivity for the rest of the war. Neither of Greenhous's infantry officer brothers survived the war.[17]

The Defiant of PO Alex McLeod chased after an escaping Stuka and his gunner LAC Walter Cox, firing into the belly of the German, caught it with several short bursts from his four machine guns. Flames jetted from the Stuka's wings as it dived out of range. But quickly the British hunter became the quarry when bullets from a 109 started ripping into the aft of the RAF fighter. 'I tried to bring my aircraft in position for my gunner to shoot at the Me 109 by turning steeply to starboard,' recalled McLeod. 'After an exchange of bursts from either side my gunner reported that all four guns were out of action.'[18]

McLeod managed to evade the Messerschmitt's guns by turning sharply, giving Cox time to clear and re-cock his guns. The British pilot, seeing the other remaining Defiant under attack, tried to offer assistance but was again attacked by a 109 with which Cox exchanged fire. He repeated the same manoeuvre as before, but this time turned so quickly that the Defiant stalled. Cox's guns were now out of ammunition and the starboard and port petrol tanks were on fire.

McLeod decided to head south-west and make a forced landing near Zevenbergen. The Defiant landed safely but Zevenbergen had been overrun by the Germans and so McLeod and Cox set to work burning their aircraft. The two RAF men then sought refuge in the cellar of a local farmhouse which proved an ideal hideout. After a perilous game of cat-and-mouse with German ground forces the British crew slipped out of the village the next day, eventually making their way to Folkestone on board a destroyer.

The final Defiant in action that day was crewed by PO Desmond Kay and LAC Evan Jones. This was supposed to be the flight spare and had been a last-minute call-up to the day's sortie which meant the crew had been unable to properly test their RT. As the combined Defiant and Spitfire flights reached the Dutch coast and came under AA fire, Kay lost contact with the rest of the flight. Kay had fallen 100 yards behind the second Defiant in his section and was unable to pick up radio signals from his leader and he now found himself detached. Unperturbed, the Defiant pressed on, and, after sighting Stukas dive-bombing the main railway line between Rotterdam and

Dordrecht, launched a single aircraft attack, shooting down at least one of the enemy.

Recalled Kay: 'I climbed to 4000 feet when I saw a Spitfire and watched for further activity below me.' Dropping down to 2000 feet the isolated Defiant found twelve Ju 87s circling and bombing a village. 'I singled out one which I again attempted to get into range on my port rear quarter. To do this, I had to lose speed considerably with the result that I was soon being chased off by the Ju 87s further astern. I slowed, turned and climbed away from them, my gunner having difficulty in rotating the turret owing to the hydraulic motor being damaged, and forced the boost control cut-out for more speed.'[19]

By now Kay realised he had just 30 gallons of fuel left, not enough to get the plane back to base, so he set a course for Knokke in Belgium. On route he was overtaken by a Spitfire flown by Flight Officer Brown of No. 66 Squadron who had had the same idea. Recalled Kay: 'I saw Brown land on the bombed aerodrome at Aalter [some 15 miles from Knokke] and then turn completely over owing to a burst tyre. I then followed him in and managed to land successfully with 8 gallons to spare. After some repairs and refuelling we took off and returned safely to England.'

Hunter, waiting anxiously at Duxford for news of the squadron's second combat, soon came to the grim realisation that Kay was the only surviving pilot from the day's action. It appeared that five of the six Defiants and ten crew had been lost in their first combat. This was not just devastating news for the squadron, it was also a serious setback for the development of the Defiant.

On Tuesday 14 May the performance of all the British fighters was directly brought to the attention of the War Cabinet, chaired by Winston Churchill. The new British Prime Minister had been in office for just two days. Churchill was informed that on Saturday 12 May one Hudson was lost on a reconnaissance to the Frisian Islands while a Blenheim had destroyed a Heinkel on a reconnaissance of Holland. The RAF had also shot down two German fighters but at the cost of two more of their own fighters.

But what of the first Defiant operations?

Sitting with Churchill, Chamberlain, Lord Halifax, Clement Attlee and Archibald Sinclair MP, the Secretary of State for Air, was Cyril Newall, Chief of the Air Staff. Newall solemnly informed the politicians that after a successful first combat mission, the following day only five of the six Defiants had returned home.

These first missions were recorded in the Cabinet papers as follows: 'A composite patrol of six Spitfires and six Defiants shot down two enemy aircraft in The Hague area and all returned safely. Waalhaven Aerodrome was attacked in the evening by five Beauforts and eight Swordfish with the loss of one aircraft. On 13 May the composite patrol of Spitfires and Defiants was again sent out; at least eight enemy aircraft were shot down but five Defiants failed to return and another forced landed.'[20]

The next two days brought brighter news about the fate of the missing five Defiant crews.

PO Thomas had left the safety of his temporary island hideout and found a rowing boat which he used to contact a friendly Dutch family. The father of the household took him to a nearby Dutch military unit where he was reunited with Hatfield. But because the German units had penetrated so far into Dutch territory the two airmen were questioned for hours by Dutch intelligence officers who suspected them of being Nazi saboteurs. The men were finally released and ended up on a destroyer bound for Britain. They turned up at Duxford at 7.30 p.m., the day after they had left on their fateful mission.[21]

It was Hatfield's sombre task to give George Skelton's family the news they had been dreading most. Skelton's wife Karin was seven months' pregnant and carrying their third daughter. When she opened the door she must have known what her husband's gunner was about to say. Hatfield told her the last time he had seen George was after he had bailed out of their Defiant as it plunged towards the earth.[22] Officially Skelton was now reported missing in action and, judging from Hatfield's dark demeanour, no one had any hope of him being alive.

But the Boulton Paul Defiant test pilot had not died in a Dutch dyke.

Skelton had recovered consciousness in the nick of time and battled to regain control of his spiralling aircraft. The experienced pilot somehow managed to glide down, using the long reeds to break the impact, and made a perfect emergency landing at the edge of the Donge River south of the town of Geertruidenberg. Badly injured in both arms and legs, he was found by a Dutch skipper who took him ashore in a rowing boat and then brought him to the St Theresa Hospital at Raamsdonksveer, where he was secretly treated by Dutch doctors. When the Germans found him they transferred him to Germany. News of Skelton's miraculous escape reached his wife on 6 June 1940 in a letter conveyed to her via the Red Cross. In it, Skelton told his wife that although he had 'been shot up quite badly' with canon splinters the German doctors 'have been exceedingly kind'. He advised her that now that she knew he was alive to make sure she was drawing his pay again and then suggested 'why not have some driving lessons in the old car?'. The money couldn't have come a moment too soon for Karin Skelton as she had been forced to make a claim on the RAF Benevolent Fund. Skelton added: 'Enough now darling please don't worry yourself overmuch, things were never as bad as they appear.' Because of his injuries, he was repatriated to Britain via Sweden in 1943.

Thanks to the treatment he received from German doctors, Skelton was later able to fly again. In the winter of 1944, after France had been liberated, he spent some time in Cannes with his wife and family to help hasten his recovery. At the end of the war he was promoted to wing commander and, from December 1948 to December 1950, served as Air Attaché in Prague, before ending his career as Chief of the Air Staff. He died peacefully in King Edward Hospital in London on 18 October 1985, aged seventy-six.[23]

The day after the fateful mission of 13 May A Flight was ordered back over Holland but were recalled just before they reached the coast. The Dutch Army was close to capitulation.

By the late evening Fighter Command was in a position to chalk up the scores of the day's fighting. No. 264 Squadron claimed four Stukas and one Me 109 for the loss of five of their own. Only one of No. 66's Spitfires was lost, but the Spitfire squadron claimed just one kill, a Stuka. In turn, the Luftwaffe claimed nine British fighters, although only one was identified as a Defiant. The actual German losses were four Stukas.

These first combat figures from an early air battle involving British fighters tell us three things about the fighting qualities of the crews of the Boulton Paul Defiant. The first is that in an air war of propaganda that would become characterised by overclaiming on both sides, the Defiant gunners' accounts of how many enemy they had shot down were honestly held and often accurate. The second is that the Defiant appeared to be more than capable of doing what it was designed to do – shooting down enemy bombers, perhaps even better than the fixed-gun Spitfires. But pitted against overwhelming numbers of German fighters, attacking with a height advantage, the Defiant was as vulnerable as any other fighter. And thirdly, and most importantly, the crews of 264 Squadron had shown they were among the bravest serving in the RAF.

Their valour was recognised on 15 May when the head of No. 12 Group, Trafford Leigh-Mallory, wrote a personal message to 264 Squadron which Hunter proudly read out to his men: 'I want to congratulate No. 264 Squadron most heartily on the success of their operations over Holland which have proved the success of the Defiant as a fighter. I much regret the loss B flight suffered in the second operation. The courage and determination displayed were of the highest order and create for No. 264 Squadron a tradition that any squadron might well be proud of.'[24]

This was followed by a message from Cyril Newall, Chief of the Air Staff: 'You have done magnificent work during the last forty-eight hours in Holland and Belgium and fully justify the confidence placed in you. Keep it up.' John Dudley North, the Bouton Paul chairman, sent his own personal message to Hunter which simply read: 'Congratulations on first blood.'[25]

But with five Defiants in enemy hands, the RAF turret fighter and its tactical advantage was no longer a secret.

For Hatfield, Kay, Jones, Thomas, McLeod, Cox and the rest of the 'blooded' Defiant crews of 264 Squadron the air battle over the continent was about to enter its most intense phase.

# Chapter 9

# DUNKIRK MISSION

THE AERIAL BATTLES over Holland gave the Luftwaffe its first serious test against an equally matched offensive fighter force. The Stuka and Messerschmitt crews, who had effortlessly brushed aside the Polish, Czech, Dutch and Belgian air forces, quickly discovered that the famous Spitfires of the RAF were not going to be so easily rolled over. They also now knew the name of another rather less familiar RAF fighter, one that represented a wholly different threat.

The Defiants' participation in these early combats was only a small part of a complex, fast-moving bigger picture in which a number of British aircraft types were being tested for the first time. But the five captured Defiants which had fallen on Dutch territory seriously perplexed Luftwaffe intelligence – a free-gun turret fighter was a wholly British contribution to aerial combat completely alien to Göring and his Staffel leaders.

By mid-May Churchill and his military advisers were confronted by the second, and more dangerous, thrust of the German advance. After allowing their forces to be sucked into the Low Countries to meet the initial German push, the Allies were caught on the second prong of Hitler's daring Blitzkrieg plan. Bypassing France's 'impregnable' Maginot Line, which fortified its border with Germany, the bulk of the German forces was being rapidly funnelled through the Ardennes. The speed of the advance of the Panzer armoured divisions, supported by nearly two thousand bombers and fighters, caught the Allies by almost total surprise, threatening to split their forces and cut off their supply lines.[1]

The RAF had already committed a significant proportion of its fighters in support of the BEF – ten Hurricane squadrons and an assortment of reconnaissance aircraft. A second force of light bomber squadrons of mostly Fairey Battles, based near Reims in France, awaited orders to launch attacks on the heart of Germany's industrial Ruhr. But now, several days after the German assault, the Air Staff appeared reluctant to commit them.

On 14 May 1940 Dowding wrote to Richard Peirse, the newly appointed Vice Chief of the Air Staff, urging him to launch the British bombers against the 'enemy's oil reserves'. The Commander-in-Chief of Fighter Command believed the last few days of fighting had demonstrated how important it was to destabilise the German advance. Dowding argued that a night-time offensive bomber operation would 'slow down the intensity of the enemy's air operations and the activity of his mechanised columns'. But he also hoped that the attack would provoke the Luftwaffe into launching air attacks on Britain: 'We should bring the German bombers to a position where Fighter Command could operate with maximum effect instead of with minimum efficiency as is now the case,' wrote Dowding, adding, 'if you're ever going to bomb their oil stores we should do it when they are full and not when their contents have been used in attacks on us.'[2]

It was a bold strategy which might have helped the Allies take back the initiative. But events were moving fast, and the British and French bomber forces were already committed to urgently stemming the flow of the German break-out across France. On 14 May, in a desperate attempt to stop German forces crossing the Meuse, the Advanced Air Striking Force (ASS) launched an 'all-out' attack by all available bombers against the German forward units and pontoon bridges at Sedan. Leading the operation was the RAF's state-of-the-art light bomber.

The Fairey Battle was powered by the same high-performance Rolls-Royce Merlin fitted to the Spitfire, Hurricane and Defiant. However the British light bomber, with its three-man crew and bomb load, was significantly heavier than even the 3½-ton Defiant, restricting it to a top speed of just 257 mph. Its defensive armament of two .303 machine guns was shamefully inadequate.

When the sixty-three Battles and eight Bristol Blenheims arrived over their target they were cut to pieces by the Germany fighters and Army flak units. Out of the total strike force of seventy-one light bombers only twenty-eight Battles and five Blenheims returned after what was likened to an aerial Charge of the Light Brigade. The engagement marked the last throw of the dice of the Allied bomber air forces and ended the Fairey Battle's front-line service role. All that now stood in the way of the Luftwaffe was a motley collection of Allied fighter units – 81 Belgian, 261 British and 764 French fighters of various types. Ranged against them were 836 German Me 109s.

The French and Belgian fighter force was mostly obsolete, poorly organised and badly led. Only the British Hawker Hurricane, the United States-built Curtiss Hawk 75 and Dewoitine D.520 could compete on the same terms as the Me 109. Like the Hurricane the French D.520 had better manoeuvrability than its German opponent. But on 10 May 1940, only thirty-six D.520s had been dispatched, all to one squadron.[3] Dowding had been careful to hold back his prized Spitfires.

That left ten Hurricane squadrons in theatre carrying out escort, defence and bomber destroyer roles. The French and Belgian fighter force was quickly eliminated from the battle, suffering terrible losses in the air and on the ground. The Hurricanes took up the strain, often bravely confronting superior numbers and exposing themselves to heavy ground fire.

On 14 May RAF Hurricanes shot down thirty German planes at the expense of twenty-seven of their own, including the loss of fifteen pilots. Over the next three days (15–17 May), fifty-one Hurricanes were destroyed, in both combat or in accidents.[4] The Luftwaffe losses were greater but, crucially, sustainable. By 17 May, the end of the first week of fighting, only three of the Hurricane squadrons were near operational strength, hopelessly inadequate to impede the rapidly advancing Germans who were threatening to overrun RAF airfields.

Of the 261 Hurricanes sent to France only sixty-six returned; 120 of the lost planes were repairable but had to be left behind.[5] By 20 May Fighter Command was reduced to just 247 Spitfires, ninety-nine Hurricanes and eighteen Defiants.[6]

Dowding realised that in terms of the air war in France the tide had turned decisively in favour of the Luftwaffe. He now firmly fixed his energies on husbanding his dwindling squadrons for the defence of the home country.

Dowding wrote to Peirse again, warning him of the catastrophe that would befall Britain if his fighter force was 'bled dry' of Hurricanes, something he had foreseen the previous autumn: 'The "Hurricane tap",' Dowding wrote, 'is now turned full on (if you remember my metaphor when I had an interview with the Air Council early last autumn) and you will not be able to resist the pressure to send Hurricanes to France until I have been bled white and I'm in no condition to withstand the bombing attack which will inevitably be made on this country . . .'

By coincidence, on the same day the French Government made a formal approach to the British Cabinet requesting another ten squadrons. Heeding Dowding's advice, the Committee of the Chief of Staff and the War Cabinet both declined to take any immediate action. However, Churchill wanted to do as much as he could to bolster French resolve and so overruled his advisers by agreeing to the French request. Churchill later said he felt able to acquiesce to the French because Dowding had told him that Fighter Command required a minimum of twenty-five squadrons to defend Britain from a Luftwaffe onslaught.[7] Dowding strongly refuted this claim, saying that he always maintained he needed fifty-two.

When Dowding found out he was about to lose ten more squadrons he became incensed and on 15 May wrote another letter, this time to the new Air Minister, Archibald Sinclair, requesting permission to address the Cabinet in person. Although a very unusual request it was granted. That evening Dowding was among thirty other ministers and chiefs of staff crowded around the Cabinet table. Churchill made Dowding wait before calling him forward. The Prime Minister sat in silence as Dowding purposefully presented his case against the release of any more fighter squadrons to the doomed fate of France. To emphasise his point he produced a piece of paper upon which the night before he had sketched a graph showing the steady increase in Hurricane losses. Pointing at the graph he told Churchill: 'This red line shows the wastage of Hurricanes in the last ten days. If the line goes on at the same rate for the next ten days there won't be a single Hurricane left either in France or in England.' The Commander-in-Chief of Fighter Command then withdrew. Churchill, who did not respond, sat back scowling at the air chief, the tense silence tacit recognition of the desperate state of the Hurricane reserves.[8]

Churchill was not a man who liked to be crossed, especially by military experts who often did not understand the wider political picture. Dowding would later pay a high price for speaking so plainly in opposition to the expressed resolve of the Prime Minister.

The next morning, 16 May, the Allies received the news that the Dutch had signed their terms of surrender. With the situation across the Channel looking bleaker by the hour, Dowding decided to replead his case by writing to Harold Balfour, the Under Secretary for Air, warning him of the dire consequences for the nation if the Cabinet changed its mind. It was a letter that may have helped change the course of the war.

He beseeched Balfour: 'I hope and believe that our armies may yet be victorious in France and Belgium but we have to face the possibility that they may be defeated. In this case I presume that there is no one who will deny that England should fight on, even though the remainder of the continent of Europe is dominated by the Germans. For this purpose it is necessary to retain some minimum fighter strength in this country and I must request that the Air Council will inform me what they consider this minimum strength to be. I would remind the Air Council that the last estimate which they made as to the force necessary to defend this country was fifty-two squadrons and my strength has now been reduced to the equivalent of thirty-six squadrons . . . I must point out that within the last few days the equivalent of ten squadrons have been sent to France, that the Hurricanes in this country are seriously depleted . . . I must therefore request as a matter of paramount urgency the Air Ministry will consider and decide what level of strength is to be left to Fighter Command for the defences of this country, and will assure me that when the level had been reached, no one fighter will be sent across the Channel . . . if the Home Defence Force is drained away in a desperate attempt to remedy the situation in France, defeat in France will involve the final, complete and irremediable defeat of this country.'[9]

Dowding was right to be suspicious about the government's true intention. That morning the War Cabinet ordered the Air Staff to send four more Hurricane squadrons to France.

Sholto Douglas, unwilling to confront the Cabinet head-on, thought he could soften the blow to Fighter Command by modifying the order to eight flights of six aircraft each, rather than four complete squadrons. He reasoned that by splitting up the units in this way no squadrons would be lost to France because Dowding would be able to build on the stump that remained in England. But Dowding regarded this as yet more evidence of Whitehall's woolly thinking. No matter how the Air Ministry cut the cloth he was losing the same number of fighter aircraft.[10]

It was left to the Chief of the Air Staff, Cyril Newall, to salvage the situation. Instead of sending six more squadrons to

France, Newall suggested sending three squadrons in the morning and another three to relieve them in the afternoon. This way Dowding's precious Hurricanes would return to their fighter bases in southern England and be spared the debacle unfolding on the continent. By 20 May the fighter crisis had run its course. In the face of the German advance towards the Channel coast, the Air Ministry ordered the withdrawal of the remainder of the Hurricane squadrons.[11]

During the first weeks of the conflict in Europe seventy-five Hurricanes had been shot down and nearly twice that number damaged.[12] These were losses Fighter Command could ill afford. But if things looked bad for the RAF it was much worse for the Army, which was on the brink of its biggest defeat since the First World War.

On 21 May the Allies failed in their last-ditch attempt to cut through the German spearhead at Aras. The British, French and Belgian armies were now trapped between the German Panzers and the sea. The only hope was a mass evacuation from one of the Channel ports. The long and shallow beaches of Dunkirk were the most obvious location from where to launch the rescue operation. But the German Army was racing onwards, threatening to catch the retreating Allies before they could reach the ships which were to carry them to safety.

Then Hitler and his all-conquering generals made their first mistake of the war. Generaloberst Gerd von Rundstedt, commander of Army Group A, was worried about his stretched supply lines and the risk of another Allied counter attack. Late on 23 May von Rundstedt asked and was granted permission to halt his Panzers. Hitler had gifted the British a narrow window of opportunity.

While the German Panzer divisions rested, the job of

annihilating the British Army was left to Hermann Göring and his much-vaunted Luftwaffe. Göring, whose childish excitement at the prospect was palpable among his own senior Air Staff, told Hitler: 'Leave it to me and the Luftwaffe. I guarantee unconditionally not a British soldier will escape.'[13] At his disposal were 2750 aircraft; 1180 bombers, 340 dive-bombers, 970 single-engined fighters and 270 twin-engined fighters.[14]

The Führer gave Göring his blessing, adding one further task. The small number of bombing raids that the British had managed to execute against targets in the Ruhr had infuriated Hitler. On 24 May he issued directive number 30: 'The Luftwaffe is authorised to attack the English Homeland in the fullest manner . . . this attack will be opened with an annihilation in reprisal for the English attacks on the Ruhr.'[15]

At last Dowding would get what he had asked for when he first urged Peirse to order the attacks against Germany's industrial heartland. But his most immediate concern was how best to support Operation Dynamo, the evacuation of nearly four hundred thousand troops now making their way across northern France to Dunkirk.

On 26 May General Wolfram von Richthofen, the commander of Fliegerkorps VIII and cousin of the 'Red Baron' Manfred von Richthofen, sent in his Stukas and bombers. The British soldiers, waiting on the beaches of Dunkirk, were at the mercy of the Luftwaffe onslaught as wave after wave of German dive-bombers headed for the French town. One of the Tommies desperately trying to get back to England was the brother of Patrick Greenhous, the Defiant pilot who had been shot down just days earlier and was now a prisoner of war. Patrick Greenhous' brother was part of the British Expeditionary Force

(BEF) and had somehow managed to reach Dunkirk. He now waited patiently on the beach with the tens of thousands of Allied troops hoping to be rescued.

The task of protecting the soldiers from the Luftwaffe fell to Keith Park, head of No. 11 Group. Dowding gave him sixteen squadrons, around two hundred aircraft, from the thirty-six squadrons of Fighter Command. The other twenty were to provide the backbone of a very stretched home defence against the possibility of an impromptu German invasion and mass bombing campaign, both of which the War Cabinet expected.

In the coming days Fighter Command's depleted resources were to be tested to the full. The hour flight to the French coast was close to the RAF fighters' operational limit, giving them only a short time over the combat zone. There would be neither radar to warn them of enemy aircraft nor ground control to guide them to their targets. They would also have to endure heavy anti-aircraft fire from both German and British batteries. The most dangerous would be the defensive and indiscriminate guns of the British destroyers desperately firing at everything that came in range.

Dunkirk was to be the first major air battle of the war – the seasoned Luftwaffe pilots, who ruled the skies of Europe, pitched against the untried aircraft and rookie aircrew of the RAF. And in the thick of the action would be the Defiants of 264 Squadron.

If Dowding and Park were concerned about the loss of the five Defiants on 13 May they did not let it influence the forward fighting role they gave 264 in the coming battle. With so few fighters to call upon perhaps they had no choice. But in Squadron Leader Philip Hunter, who was absent from the second fateful operation over The Hague, Dowding could rely on a leader of exceptional quality. Eric Barwell later recalled that the loss of the five Defiants and a number of aircrew on their second combat was a 'black' period for the squadron but Hunter, 'a rattling good man', had kept morale high.

And 264 was not the only squadron to have suffered losses. The day the Defiants were being readied for combat four Hurricanes from 605 squadron had been shot down by Me 109s near Arras and Doullens, in twenty-six patrols carried out by the RAF.[16]

On 22 May Hunter and 264 Squadron were ordered from their Duxford base to Manston, the RAF's front-line airfield during the battle of Dunkirk. There had been a military airport at Manston ever since the First World War. Its strategic value as a fighter base in the cockpit of Kent was to prove vital to combat operations over northern France. Fourteen Defiants, including two reserves, arrived at Manston at 9.45 a.m., half an hour after taking off from Duxford.

Manston was already busy when the Defiants touched down, with ground crews working hard to prepare the fighters for the day's operations. Spitfire and Hurricane squadrons were lined up side by side on the roads throughout the camp. When Hunter and his Defiants flew in there was only one vacant pitch. But within twenty minutes after touchdown petrol bowsers arrived to refuel the aircraft. Hunter was immediately briefed to be ready to fly to France – 'patrol Abbeville, Doullens, Arras' – where they could expect to face accurate AA fire. But in the chaotic urgency of the new mission that order was quickly cancelled, as was another to escort a civil flight to Merville.

Hunter recorded in the squadron's log: 'There was no telephone communication nearer than the other end of the aerodrome almost a mile away and so I stationed a reserve pilot at this telephone to pass any messages. At about 14.40 I received the following message "264 Patrol Dunkirk Calais Boulogne. Relieving 54 Squadron from Hornchurch who are at present patrolling that area".'

So it was well after 3 p.m. that the twelve Defiants were heading out to sea, flying in sections of three in line astern, feeling their way towards the French coast near Cap Gris Nez. En route they passed a small number of Royal Navy ships which they gave a wide berth. Approaching Dunkirk, Hunter spotted seven Me 110s in front and high above them. The squadron leader gave the order to engage and the Defiants, in tight formation, climbed towards the enemy fighters. Hunter recalled the encounter in his combat report: 'The enemy had a height advantage of at least 1000 feet. We manoeuvred for position for at least ten minutes but at 10,000 feet the enemy disappeared into the cloud. I kept my formation below the clouds and waited. Eventually one Me 110 came down, throttled right back, and just out of range obviously intended to commit me to a stern chase, treating us as Hurricanes because obviously from the previous manoeuvres they appeared to be trying to get on our tails. I refused to be drawn and shortly afterwards six Me 110s came out of the clouds but when they found us still in formation they sheared off and climbed back into the clouds in the direction of Germany.'[17]

This inconsequential tentative encounter, so familiar to George Heseltine and the fighter pilots of the First World War, was the first time the RAF's newest fighter had engaged the Luftwaffe's own much-heralded fighter bomber. The futures of both aircraft would be emphatically decided in the ferocious air battles of the coming summer.

The Defiants returned to base, but later that evening were

ordered back over the French coast to escort a flight of Blenheims on a bombing mission against forts in Boulogne which had fallen into German hands. When the Defiants arrived they found three Ju 88s attacking up to twelve Royal Navy vessels which were defending themselves with heavy AA fire. When the German bombers saw the Defiants they broke off their attack and fled, but not before sinking one of the cruisers. The Defiants returned to base without firing their guns in anger.

A Spitfire squadron and two Hurricane squadrons operating in the same area had been engaged in bitter dogfights after encountering a large formation of Me 109s. In the first action eight Hurricanes of 242 squadron and seven Hurricanes of 32 Squadron left Manston at 12.45 p.m. to escort a single Blenheim from Hawkinge to Courtrai. Two Hurricanes returned with engine trouble, leaving a force of thirteen aircraft. After crossing the French coast they ran into a thundercloud and lost sight of the Blenheims around Courtrai. Shortly afterwards the British machines were set upon by eighteen Me 110s and twelve Me 109s. During the dogfights four of the seven Hurricanes from 242 Squadron and one Hurricane from 32 Squadron were lost. They claimed seven enemy fighters, but the official Luftwaffe loss was only two Me 109s shot down in the battle.

Later that evening the Spitfires of 92 Squadron took on thirty Me 110s protecting a smaller group of Ju 87s and Ju 88s which were bombing Boulogne harbour (92 had already lost one Spitfire that morning in dogfights with twelve Me 109s newly fitted with canon armament). It was to be the first significant encounter between the Me 110s and the Spitfires.

The RAF fighters climbed to 4000 feet to engage the German force. But it was the slower Me 110s, each painted with a yellow shark jaw, which came off best. In a series of dogfights the front and rear guns of the 110s accounted for three Spitfires, including one piloted by Squadron Leader Roger Bushell who was taken prisoner near Boulogne (later executed by the Gestapo for his part in the Great Escape). Another pilot was 'badly wounded in the thigh' but managed to land at Hawkinge.

The squadron's intelligence report must have made grim reading for the Air Chiefs and Fighter Command who had been anxiously waiting for a combat which would allow them to assess the fighter capabilities of the Me 110. It concluded: 'Most of our aircraft were hit many times. Pilots state that the Me 110 evasive tactics are steep turns towards Spitfire's tail to enable the rear gun to fire. About twenty Me 110s were seen flying in line astern in a tight circle around the bombers which was very difficult to attack. The Me 110 is not so fast as a Spitfire on the level but very good in a fast turn and a steep dive, although the Spitfire can hold it on a turn. They appear to use the stall turn a great deal. During the first ten minutes of the combat continuous transmission in German was heard on the RT. Squadron Leader Bushell, Flt Lt Gillies and Sgt Klipsch are missing. One Spitfire seen crash to the ground. Flt Lt Green landed at Hawkinge with bullet in leg.'[18]

Most worrying of all for Fighter Command was 92 Squadron's claim to have 'definitely shot down' seven Me 110s. In fact Luftwaffe records show that all the Me 110s returned safely, although two had suffered damage.

For one of the surviving RAF Spitfire pilots that day the encounter with the rear-firing German fighter was all too familiar. Just six weeks earlier[19] Robert Stanford Tuck had experienced the distinct disadvantage of being in a dogfight with a tight-turning rear-firing fighter. On that occasion the aircraft was a RAF Defiant flown by Philip Hunter who had helped develop very similar defensive tactics now being deployed to great effect by the Me 110s.

On 24 May Stanford Tuck, in temporary charge of the squadron, was back in action over the French coast between Calais and Dunkirk. The losses of the day before meant that the squadron fielded just eight aircraft. At 11,000 feet they sighted a formation of thirty Do 17s flying in four vics in echelon (a vic comprises three aircraft: standard flying formation for RAF fighters at the start of the war). Above them were fifteen Me 110s. Tuck led the Spitfires in an attack on the German bombers, raking them with crossfiring machine guns. Tuck closed to 50 yards on the enemy bombers and claimed two Dorniers shot down. But despite the ferocious assault by the British planes the Dorniers maintained their formation. Now the Me 110s, which had hesitated in going to the aid of the bombers, joined the fight. Once again it was the Spitfires which came off worse. Flying Officer Peter Cazenove was shot down and forced to belly-land on a beach near Calais where he was taken prisoner. (Three times he had tried to board a British destroyer and each time he was refused.[20]) Tuck was wounded in the leg but managed to fly his damaged fighter, minus his cockpit, back to Kent. Two other Spitfires were also badly damaged but the pilots returned safely.

In two days of fighting, 92 Squadron had lost six Spitfires and the remainder badly damaged. Two pilots were dead, two were seriously wounded and three, including their squadron leader, were prisoners of war. Fighter Command decided to withdraw 92 Squadron from the front line.

On the same day, 24 May, 264 Squadron returned to the fray. All of Hunter's twelve Defiants left Manston at 12.30 p.m. to patrol between Calais and Boulogne. But over Boulogne at about 6500 feet three British destroyers mistook them for enemy planes and opened up with heavy AA fire. The Defiants were forced to take evasive action even though they had signalled with two-star cartridges that they were friendly. (Friendly fire from British ships was to be a continuous problem for the RAF throughout Operation Dynamo.)

As the 264 Defiants approached Calais, Hunter spotted a lone Me 110 and climbed to deliver an attack. Hunter's gunner got in a short burst, forcing the German fighter to dive away towards the line of Defiants which were waiting below. In a desperate attempt to summon help the German gunner let off a red flare. But it was too late – several of the Defiants had the enemy machine firmly fixed in their sights. It was Flt Lt Edward Whitehouse and his gunner PO Horace Scott who delivered the fatal burst, setting the Me 110 on fire. After breaking from the attack Hunter identified nine more Me 109s flying in vics of three, close enough for the Defiant pilots to pick up the German chatter on the same radio channel. Hunter signalled an immediate attack but the engagement was short-lived and inconclusive as the 109s used the cloud cover to get away.[21]

A second sortie over Dunkirk that afternoon was equally inconclusive, although the Defiants saw several Me 109s and a single Me 110 which appeared to be bravely acting as bait for the British fighters. The squadron carried out a further patrol that afternoon without incident.[22]

As the Germans stepped up their assault on Dunkirk the fighting in the air, sea and on land was being fought in desperate terms and at the highest cost. No one felt this more than the Commander-in-Chief of Fighter Command who had a personal stake in the Dunkirk campaign. His son Derek was flying Spitfires with 74 squadron and on 24 May had shot down a Do 17 and Ju 87.[23] Two days earlier Dowding's nephew was killed fighting with the Tank Regiment in a rear-guard action to protect the British retreat.[24]

After one day's rest the Defiants were in the air again, this time patrolling over Calais where Hunter located a 'concentration of enemy tanks', but when he went down to investigate the Defiants came under aggressive anti-aircraft fire. Another patrol that evening was uneventful.[25]

While the Defiants found the Messerschmitts reluctant to engage them in combat the Spitfires had mixed fortunes during a series of hard-fought tangles. No. 54 Squadron claimed nine 109s shot down on a single offensive patrol between Calais and Dunkirk on 24 May. On the same afternoon 74 Squadron, commanded by the gifted South African fighter pilot, Adolph 'Sailor' Malan, lost four Spitfires when they came off second best after catching a formation of Heinkels before being dived upon by a cluster of 110s.[26]

On the afternoon of 26 May Hitler ordered the Panzer units to resume their advance against the retreating British, French and Belgian forces, but not in time to stop the Allied retreat from Lille or prevent the preparation of the defences vital for the evacuation. Along a string of pinch-points in northern France and Belgium the BEF courageously fought a rear-guard action which would ultimately deliver salvation to hundreds of thousands of their brother soldiers. This left the RAF having to cover a broad range of objectives in support of the ground forces, including the protection of other French ports and bomber escort duty. Spitfires, deployed to neutralise the German fighters, were routinely facing odds of two or three to one during their patrols, but the Hurricanes, used in support of the BEF units further inland, faced even greater perils.

However, after the capture of Boulogne and Calais the objective for both sides became much clearer. The British and French would have to defend Dunkirk to the last man while the German airforce had the simple military goal of bombing the French town to oblivion.

Just before 7 p.m. on 26 May, Churchill ordered the commencement of Operation Dynamo. Initial plans called for the rescue of forty-five thousand British soldiers within the first two days, by which time German stormtroopers were expected to have broken through the Allied defences.

Every hour one thousand more troops were gathering on the embarkation beaches. Göring, with characteristic ruthlessness, unleashed his bombers and fighters with orders to pulverise the British forces. The Dorniers and Heinkels set about demolishing the town while waves of Stukas were sent to sink the ships. German fighters had the job of protecting the bombers from the RAF, but in the absence of enemy fighters the Me 109 pilots found time to strafe the concentrations of soldiers who were lining up on the Dunkirk beaches awaiting deliverance.

Me 109 pilot Paul Temme was one of them. He recalled afterwards: 'I hated Dunkirk. It was just unadulterated killing. The beaches were jammed full of soldiers. I went up and down at 300 feet hose piping.' For Peter Townsend, who flew Hurricanes in the Dunkirk operations, it was simply: 'Cold-blooded, point-blank murder. Defenceless men, fathers, sons and brothers being cruelly massacred by a twenty-four-year-old-boy.'[27]

It was up to Keith Park's No. 11 Group to protect the British troops from these attacks as well as shield the ships during the evacuation. But with fewer than two hundred aircraft it was impossible to provide blanket cover. Instead Park made sure that he had non-stop patrols operating in and around the

Dunkirk pocket in daylight hours between 5 a.m. and 9.30 p.m. With just sixteen squadrons to perform this duty some patrols were very thin, often comprising a single strength squadron.

At 09.15 hours on 27 May, 264 Squadron was ordered back over Dunkirk to take part in one of Park's covering patrols. As they reached the burning town they saw eight Me 109s at 9000 feet just south of the main beaches.[28] Squadron Leader Hunter immediately ordered his Defiants to attack in line astern. The 109s took evasive action, seeking cover in the clouds, from where two emerged and commenced a beam attack. The Defiants broke up but not before Hunter's gunner, LAC Fred King, had fired two fifty-round bursts from about 300 yards which set alight one of the German fighter's engines. Then it was the turn of PO Michael Young, who had claimed 264's first scalp on 12 May over Holland. A 109 had launched a beam attack on the Defiant which his gunner LAC Stanley Johnson quickly blocked. One burst of forty rounds from 200 yards was enough to finish off the 109 which started billowing smoke. This is how Young recorded the action in his combat report: 'One of the enemy machines turned and did a beam attack from the port and as it broke away in a vertical turn my air gunner got in a short burst of the enemy aircraft's underside. The enemy machine did a half roll and dived vertically with smoke pouring from it.'[29]

When the squadron returned to Manston, Hunter made a curious addition to his report. He and Young had noticed three other 'fighters' close to the Messerschmitts at the start of the engagement. At first they had thought they were He 112s, but as they got closer they could see the aircraft had been camouflaged to look like Spitfires. It was one of a number of similar reports made by RAF pilots who believed the Luftwaffe was using false flag aircraft to try to trick the British fighters into mistaking enemy planes for their own.

In those critical last days of May the RAF's continuous daylight patrols over Dunkirk meant Park's sixteen squadrons were being stretched to their operational limit. Almost as soon as Hunter's Defiants had refuelled and rearmed they were vectored back to France to try to stem the bombing of the town and the attacks on the Royal Navy ships which had begun the evacuation of the first troops.

At 12.30 p.m. the lead Defiant sighted twelve He 111s at 7000 feet, flying over the stricken town. This time Hunter decided to alter his tactics and radioed Green section to take a position above the German bombers so the three Defiants could protect the other sections against any Me 109s or 110s which might be waiting to bounce the British fighters. The remaining nine Defiants flew down onto the Heinkels, scattering them as they broke formation, diving towards the sea or seeking shelter in the clouds. The element of surprise gave Hunter and his machines plenty of time to pick off three of the enemy bombers before they could get away. The Defiants flew below the wings of the Heinkels, a British fighter on each flank, so that the gunners were able to rake the bombers with enfilading fire. Hunter, Red 1 and PO Young, Red 3, carried out a textbook crossfiring attack to claim one of the bombers which was also attracting flak from the Royal Navy ships and Army AA positions as they flew over the town. Young's combat report read: 'Red section flew in line astern and dived to attack. The enemy formation broke up and one machine climbed out to sea. I followed Red leader into position for an overtaking attack. Enemy aircraft then dived across us towards the land. My air gunner put a burst into his port engine which went on fire. His starboard engine was seen to be burning as he dived towards the coast.'[30]

Blue section led by Flt Lt Nicholas Cooke carried out a similar manoeuvre and claimed another Heinkel when it burst into flames. Cooke said the Defiant was so close he could see the German pilot and navigator duck down when Cpl Lippett began opening fire. Cooke recorded in his combat report: 'During the action we followed the enemy aircraft through several cumulus clouds at 4000 feet. Several bursts from each member of blue section in converging attack and crossover attacks. I could see the pilot and navigator duck at each burst. Then the enemy aircraft engines went on fire and stalled. The enemy aircraft burst into flames on landing.'[31]

A third German bomber was attacked by Yellow section, Flt Lt Whitehouse also positioning his Defiant under an enemy bomber's port wing, closing to about 12 feet before delivering the *coup de grâce*.

All twelve Defiants returned safely to Manston. When Hunter made his report to No. 12 Group he emphasised how 'very poor and erratic' the German rear defensive fire had been. Nevertheless Flt Lt Edward Whitehouse discovered later he had had a very lucky escape when ground crew told him that a tracer bullet had passed through his petrol tank.[32] Luftwaffe records indicate that only one of the Heinkels was shot down. The other two sustained damage and casualties but were able to return to their base.

To try to knock out the RAF patrols Göring added more fighter squadrons to the Dunkirk combat theatre, many of them Me 110s which had already enjoyed considerable success against the Spitfires. But on the evening of 27 May forty Me

110s were summoned to the rescue of a group of He 111s over Gravelines being attacked by Spitfires of 610 Squadron, and suffered heavy casualties when they found themselves also grappling with the Hurricanes of 601, 145, 79 and 56 squadrons. The combined claims for the British fighters were fifteen Me 110s shot down with a further nine unconfirmed. However, heavy fighting throughout the day meant 27 May would turn out to be the RAF's most costly day of the Dunkirk campaign. Fighter Command lost fourteen Hurricanes and five Spitfires, the Me 110s accounting for destroying two Spitfires and six Hurricanes.

One of the day's losses caused special concern at the Air Ministry. PO Peter Stevenson, the son of the deputy head of Home Defence Donald Stevenson, was hit by the return fire from a Do 17 and made a forced landing in his Spitfire on the beach at Dunkirk. Donald Stevenson endured an agonising four-day wait before he received news of his son. The young RAF pilot had survived the crash and followed textbook instructions to disable his Spitfire by removing the blind-flying panel, reflector gunsight and radio before setting fire to the aircraft. PO Stevenson then joined the long lines of soldiers waiting for a berth home. He turned up at Hornchurch on 31 May.[33]

On sea and land the gamble of Operation Dynamo was beginning to pay off, and the RAF was making a crucial contribution in providing fighter cover all along the Channel evacuation routes from Dunkirk to the disembarkation ports of Dover, Folkestone and Ramsgate. But the Air Ministry's ceaseless demands on the RAF's finite fighter resources showed that the armchair air marshals had failed to grasp the organisational demands being placed on Fighter Command and its overstretched squadrons.

Park, with Dowding's tacit backing, later wrote: 'The Air Ministry fails to appreciate the difficulties of operating large numbers of squadrons from forward aerodromes, resulting in frequent hasteners for patrol reports and advanced combat. This continual flow of enquiries from higher authority was a great embarrassment throughout the operations and at times so blocked the land lines that urgent operations orders were seriously delayed between the group Headquarters and squadrons at forward aerodromes.'[34]

At the same time the RAF attrition rate in both aircraft and crews was starting to take its toll. Since the start of the German offensive of 10 May, Fighter Command had lost fifty-four pilots during 112 offensive patrols.[35] Thirty of these losses had occurred in the six days between 20 and 26 May. Conversely the pilots and gunners who had survived these first combats were gaining valuable experience and learning lessons which would keep them alive in later combats.

None more so than the Defiant crews, whose chances of survival depended so much on the intuitive relationship between pilot and gunner. The Defiant may have been a slower fighter than the Spitfire and Hurricane but in those ferocious dogfights over Dunkirk, it held one key advantage – four eyes were better than two in scanning the sky for the superior numbers of enemy machines that launched attacks from all directions and from all angles. Together, the pilot and gunner boosted each other's moral fibre so that in the face of enemy fire they were more likely to press home more attacks. And it was the crews who struck up the closest relationships who also recorded the most success against the Luftwaffe.

The pilots tended to be the alumni of England's public schools, inspired by derring-do of fictional pilots like W. E. Johns' Biggles.

Philip Hunter was the most dashing of Battle of Britain pilots. Loved by his fellow officers and crew, he could call upon nearly ten years of flying experience with the RAF. Like many young pilots the prospect of war hastened Hunter's proposal of marriage to his sweetheart Eleanor Margaret Christie,[36] and within a year their first and only son was born.

While the pilots were public school, the gunners came from more humble stock. Hunter had teamed up with his gunner, Frederick Harry King, in early 1940. Like Hunter, King was an old RAF hand. The Leicester airman joined the RAF in 1935 as an ordinary aircrafthand. He then remustered as an airman air gunner before joining 264 Squadron at Martlesham Heath a few weeks after the first Defiants had been transferred to Fighter Command for operational duties.

Yet these two men, from very different backgrounds, formed a strong bond, knowing that their lives depended on a mutual unconditional trust. And this helped to make them a formidable fighting duo.

In the early skirmishes and heat of combat against a range of Luftwaffe bombers and fighters, the pilot and gunner quickly learned how to work together. The pilot's job was to manoeuvre the aircraft so that the gunner had the best chance of hitting the target. To restrict drag to a minimum, the gunner kept his guns in the aeronautical position, flat against the fuselage and pointed forwards, until he was within shooting range of the enemy aircraft. Then he used the joystick to swing the guns into the firing position, his finger hovering over the firing button until he had the German machine in the gunsights. The two crewmen were in contact by inflight intercom but the noise of battle sometimes made it hard to hear one another. To improve their working relationships pilot and gunner would spend hours, often in the pub, rehearsing procedures for every sort of combat contingency.

Another unlikely pairing was Flt Lt Nicholas Gresham Cooke, aged twenty-six, and his gunner Cpl Albert Lippett. Cooke was the son of a distinguished Addenbrookes Hospital surgeon and the great uncle of the *Guardian* journalist and environmentalist George Monbiot. Cooke, born in Blakeney, Norfolk was educated at Marlborough College and Trinity College, Cambridge. At Cambridge Cooke was a keen sailor and member of the British sailing squad. In 1934 he was hand-picked by the yachtsman and ornithologist Sir Peter Scott to be part of the Great Britain sailing team that went to Canada.[37] Scott recalled Cooke in his autobiography *The Eye of the Wind*: 'We used to call him grasshopper partly because of his long legs and partly because of his habit of suddenly jumping up and rushing off to do something different. But for the next two years he was my cheerful hard-working boundlessly optimistic crew.'

After Cambridge Cooke became an aeronautical engineer and learned to fly with Air Service Training Limited, gaining a Civil Pilot's Licence in 1935. The following year he signed up to the Royal Air Force and was commissioned as an acting pilot officer. In January 1937 he was assigned to No. 46 Squadron, a recently reformed fighter squadron, flying Gloster Gauntlet biplanes, from RAF Digby in Lincolnshire. No. 46 had an illustrious history in the First World War with seventeen of its pilots awarded ace status. On 15 August 1938, Cooke was transferred to No. 23 Group RAF Flying Training based at Grantham, Lincolnshire, as personal assistant to the commander, Air Vice Marshal Lawrence Pattinson, also an alumnus of Cambridge and a former Deputy Director of

Organisation at the Air Ministry. Cooke was one of the first to be posted to No. 264 Squadron when it was reformed at RAF Sutton Bridge in October 1939. After the capture of George Skelton in Holland, the young pilot became the second most senior flight commander after Hunter.

His gunner, Albert Lippett, an acting corporal, was another East Anglian, born in Great Yarmouth. He later moved to Dunfermline, Fife, to marry his girlfriend.[38] At thirty-seven he was one of the oldest members of 264 Squadron. Lippett joined the RAF aged seventeen and had spent most of his life learning his trade as an RAF aircrafthand. After 1935 he left the RAF to take a job in an aircraft factory, but in September 1939 he was recalled for service and transferred to the Defiants of 264.

Despite their class differences and age gap the Cambridge-educated pilot and the aircraft mechanic formed a strong bond. As Operation Dynamo reached its climax these newly forged relationships were about to be tested to the extreme.

# Chapter 10

# DAY OF THE DEFIANT

THE BELCHING, BLACK smoke pouring out of the burning oil refinery could be seen clearly from RAF Manston's watch-tower. British pilots didn't need to worry about navigating to Dunkirk. They just followed the smoke that was drifting across the channel. The small fishing port of Dunkirk was now the critical focal point of a six-week battle that would transform the map of Europe for the next four years.

Göring's Luftwaffe had spared nothing and no one from the daily bombing and machine-gunning attacks mounted against the British and French rear-guard defenders. Then on 27 May the German Army advanced to within artillery range of Allied positions and began pounding the town with an array of field guns. Hundreds of soldiers were blown up or lacerated by the flying shrapnel while waiting for rescue on the beaches.

Conditions inside the town were just as desperate. Dunkirk's water supply had been knocked out during the first days of the fighting, preventing any attempt to extinguish the fires. An estimated one thousand civilians had been killed, one third of the remaining population of the town.

All seemed lost. No one expected to survive the merciless onslaught of the Luftwaffe. But 28 May was to prove to be a day to remember for the stranded BEF and RAF squadrons helping to defend the troops and protect the British evacuation.

That morning Sir Cyril Newall, the Chief of the Air Staff, wrote to Donald Stevenson, the new head of home operations: 'Today is likely to be the most critical day ever experienced by the British Army. The extreme gravity of the situation should be explained to all units. I am confident that all ranks will appreciate that it is the duty of the RAF to make their greatest effort today to assist their comrades at both the Army and the Navy . . . to ensure the protection of Dunkirk beaches (three miles on either side) from the first light until darkness by flying continuous fighter patrols in strength . . . and have due regard to the protection of the bomber sorties and the provision of support in the BEF area.'[1]

Just before midday a full squadron of Defiants left Manston to patrol Dunkirk. It was a clear day and a good one for flying. But as soon as the 264 Defiants were over the enemy coast they ran into around thirty Me 109s which had been casually milling over the town, patiently waiting for the morning arrival of the RAF. Hunter immediately ordered his aircraft into line astern in a half-circle formation, so that each Defiant was protecting the other, just as George Heseltine's old 'pushers' had done twenty-three years before. He then radioed to his flight commanders to follow him in as he climbed into an attack. The Messerschmitts needed no further invitation and fell on the British fighters. For the next few minutes the two groups of aircraft turned, stalled and dived to gain advantage over their opponents. Hunter's gunner, Fred King, was the first to shoot down one of the diving German fighters. In his report

Hunter added: 'Immediately on engaging, my air gunner shot down one Me 109 which was slightly above us and a little later another came into range passing over us which he shot down and he went down in flames.'

In all, six 109s were seen to fall to the Defiant guns. But in the course of these ferocious attacks the three trailing Defiants began to lose touch with the leaders. Slightly adrift from the covering fire of the squadron's battery of defensive Brownings, the last three Defiants were picked off by the German machines which blasted them with cannon and machine gun fire. It would have been worse had it not been for the exceptional bravery of Pilot Sgt Ed Thorn and his gunner LAC Fred Barker who single-handedly engaged three of the attacking 109s and managed to shoot down all three.[2]

Then the Germans were gone and the skies were all quiet again.

As Hunter looked down through the now hazy sky he saw five parachutes, of which he believed two were Defiant crew members. But when the remnants of the squadron reassembled at Manston it became clear that they had suffered three machines destroyed and six crewmen killed. Two of the dead were survivors from aircraft shot down over Holland on 13 May who, after bravely slipping through enemy lines, had climbed aboard a British destroyer, reporting for duty with 264 the following day.

One was PO Alexander McLeod and the other was his gunner PO Jack Hatfield. It was Hatfield who, only a few days earlier, had driven to George Skelton's family home to tell them that his old friend would not be coming back. Instead Skelton survived the war and it was Hatfield who never made it back to England or indeed his home country of Canada.

Hatfield's body was later washed ashore and he was buried in Germany, his remains being reinterred after the war in Becklingen War Cemetery at Soltau. McLeod's body was never found. The other 264 crewmen to be killed in the action that day were Flt Lt Edward Whitehouse and his gunner PO Horace Scott and Sgt Lionel Daisley and his gunner LAC Harold Revill.

The Defiant bravely crewed by Thorn and Barker was badly shot up but somehow got home. They claimed three 109s and would live to fight another day, becoming the most successful pilot/gunner crew of the war.

Later that afternoon the weather closed in and low clouds and driving rain reduced visibility to a few yards. The encounter between 264 and the Me 109s of the Lutfwaffe fighter wing of Jagdgeschwader 51 was the last combat engagement of the day.[3] 264 still managed an uneventful patrol in the early evening, although they could muster just nine Defiants.[4]

The bad weather and poor flying conditions came as a welcome respite for the soldiers on the Dunkirk beaches and the sailors who were trying to rescue them. However, the General Staff had less to cheer about. That afternoon Lord Gort, the general commanding the BEF, received the grave news that the Belgian Army, which was holding his eastern flank between the BEF and the sea, had surrendered. He immediately sent the battle-hardened 3rd, 4th and 50th Divisions into the line to fill the gap the Belgians had relinquished.

It fell to King George VI to send Lord Gort a morale-boosting telegram that read: 'All your countrymen have been following with pride and admiration the courageous resistance of the British Expeditionary Force during the continuing fighting of the last fortnight. Faced by circumstances outside their control in a position of extreme difficulty, they are displaying a gallantry which has never been surpassed in the annals of the British Army. The hearts of every one of us at home are with you and your magnificent troops in this hour of peril.'

In turn the Germans dropped leaflets featuring a map detailing the desperate situation now facing the British. It read: 'British soldiers! Look at the map: it gives your true situation! Your troops are entirely surrounded – stop fighting! Put down your arms!'

On 29 May the weather lifted, starkly exposing the precariously balanced military situation – could the Royal Navy rescue the stranded British and French forces before the Luftwaffe sank all its ships? The answer to this question largely depended on whether the RAF could protect the Royal Navy from the Nazi bombers. That day the Luftwaffe mounted five major attacks against the British ships and on two occasions they were met by strong RAF patrols of four fighter squadrons. In both these combats, 264 was there to engage them.

The first came at 14.00 when 264 and three Hurricane squadrons left airfields at Manston and North Weald for Dunkirk. Two of the Hurricane squadrons flew high to guard against enemy fighters while the Defiants and one squadron of Hurricanes sought out the bombers.

It was a bright late spring afternoon with once again good visibility over the French coast. The Luftwaffe commanders knew what to expect and with good binoculars could just about pick out the British fighters leaving their forward airfields 23 miles away in Kent. As the RAF arrived over the beaches, the Hurricanes of 151 and 56 Squadrons were attacked by groups of 109s and 110s who had been patrolling at 25,000 feet. A series of scrappy dogfights ensued, but neither side gained an advantage.

The German fighters regrouped and reset their sights on the second force of more 'vulnerable' lower-flying Defiants and Hurricanes of 213 Squadron. It would prove to be to be a tactical blunder that was to help make RAF history.

Six Me 109s swept down on the Defiants which, now at 10,000 feet, quickly pulled into line giving the gunners a clear line of fire. PO Young and his gunner LAC Johnson were flying as Red 3 towards the stern of the line of Defiants when Young saw the two 109 V-formations, recalling: 'Several Me 109s dived out of the sun on to our tail. The [gun] fire from one passed close under our tail and my air gunner scored hits as he was about to break away. The enemy aircraft fell away out of control to port with heavy smoke pouring from it.'[5]

Precious combat experience over the last few days meant PO Eric Barwell knew exactly what to do when he found one of the Me 109s on his tail. 'I did a hard turn and the gunner had a low deflection shot at the attacking fighter,' recounted Barwell, who claimed one of the German fighters. Another was hit by PO Terry Welsh and LAC Lawrence Hayden as it came into range at about 150 yards flying overhead and into the arc of the Defiant's guns. Cooke and Lippett also got in on the act, with Cooke recording 'a small burst at 300 yards easily sufficed'.[6]

But a Defiant turret manned by LAC Evan Jones had taken a direct hit from a cannon shell fired by one of the 109s. Jones bailed out of what he thought was a crippled aircraft, only to drown in the sea. His body was later washed up on the Dunkirk beaches and he is fittingly buried in the town's cemetery. However, his pilot PO Desmond Kay managed to safely steer the damaged fighter back to Manston.

As soon as the attacking 109s had carried out their first pass, Squadron Leader Hunter got the Defiants back into formation just in time to meet the second wave. This time the Defiants were facing an attack from twenty-one Me 110s. PO Young had a clear view as they 'circled down from the sun . . . and our formation went to line astern and spiralled towards the sea. At the beginning of the spiral an Me 110 passed overhead from starboard to port. My air gunner put two bursts into it and the port wing caught fire. The enemy aircraft fell into the sea.'

Cooke could see the danger as the Me 110s were now 'above and behind, diving on other Defiants in the formation'. His gunner, Cpl Lippett, fired a small burst from 350 yards which caused smoke and flames to issue from an Me 110 fuselage. Young also saw that another of the Me 110s was 'attacking the tail of one of our machines'. His gunner got in a long burst which instantly sent the German into the sea. The rest of the German formation, now scattered by the overwhelming fire-power of the Defiants' guns, broke off the attack and headed for home.

When the victorious Defiants got back to Manston they claimed two Me 109s, one Ju 87 (Thorn and Barker) and, incredibly, fifteen Me 110s. No. 264 hadn't lost a single aircraft.

The combat was the first time the two much-revered 'bomber destroyers' of the opposing air forces had lined up against each other. And it was an encounter which the Defiants had emphatically won.[7] In the glinting sun Hunter drew his jubilant crew around his aircraft so he could debrief them on the day's operation. Each time they went out they learnt something new about the Defiant, the enemy or the effectiveness of their fighter tactics. Hunter made sure it all counted.

But 264 had little time to rest on its laurels. Three hours later at 17.30 they were ordered back to Dunkirk where the Luftwaffe was carrying out round the clock attacks against the Royal

Navy ships. The Defiants were part of another force of four squadrons (610, 56, 151). Once again the Hurricanes of 151 and 56 were given high escort duty allowing the Spitfires of 610 (in place of 213 Squadron) and the 264 Defiants to safely take care of the bombers.

It wasn't long before the high-flying Hurricanes had engaged a group of 109s at 15,000 feet while the remaining British fighters caught a force of forty Stukas and three Ju 88s bombing ships off Dunkirk. As the Defiants arrived, the German bombers were lining up to launch their assault on the British ships. This time the German fighters were unable to protect the dive-bombers.

Hunter ordered the Defiants into the attack. Cooke, Blue leader, who was to the fore of the Defiant formation, led his flight down towards the massing bombers, shooting two into the sea. The Stukas were now 'caught in line astern' almost at sea level. Cooke recorded later in his combat report: 'On being attacked from below and to one side they released bombs but three Ju 87s were shot down in very quick succession as we flew up the line. All five were in flames and crashed into the sea or on the beach.' Cooke and Lippett claimed three of them. Then the British crew turned their attention to the larger twin-engined Ju 88s, launching a converging attack against one at 4000 feet while hitting a second in a crossover manoeuvre. Both were in flames and Cooke and Lippett had five kills, making them the first RAF 'aces in one day' of the Second World War.

Young and Johnson were also raking the sitting-duck Stukas with crossfire: 'We dived to the attack in line astern down to about 500 feet. The Ju 87s levelled out from their dive and turned out to sea as we passed under one of the enemy aircraft.

A short burst was put into him and he was last seen to dive towards the beach in flames. At the end of the attack another Ju 87 was seen to drop his bombs into the sea and approach us from port. My air gunner fired at him and the enemy aircraft dived into the sea. The formation of Defiants was heading out to sea and a Ju 88 was seen astern going out to sea. I turned into position for an overtaking attack and a short burst was delivered from below. The enemy aircraft flew down to sea level and turned towards the land chased by another of our machines.'

Eric Barwell also recalled the slaughter: 'We came across four Ju 87s, Stuka dive-bombers, flying along a line abreast, three of our planes formatted in the gaps and fired into them and they just burst into flames as soon as we hit their exposed fuel tanks. From our point of view they were easy meat. People said after the war we had over-claimed – but we killed thirty-seven planes in one day.'[8]

The engagement lasted less than five minutes. But in that time the Defiants claimed seventeen Stukas and one Ju 88. All twelve Defiants safely returned to Manston at 20.40. Only Sgt Thorn's machine was badly damaged and was forced to land with one wheel down. It was an incredible day's combat. No. 264 claimed a total of thirty-eight[9] enemy aircraft destroyed during both sorties – the highest number of kills in one day by any single RAF squadron. Afterwards Nicholas Cooke, who with Albert Lippett claimed eight victories, told a reporter: 'It was like knocking apples off a tree!'

German records suggest that the actual number of German aircraft destroyed on 29 May was no more than fourteen. Some of the claims made by the Defiants may have been counted twice as two or more aircraft attacked one German. And those that were thought to have been shot down were only badly damaged, able to limp home. Nevertheless, over-claiming was a common feature among the RAF and Luftwaffe during often confused and ferocious combats that took place over northern France in May and June 1940.

To this very day the 264 claims record still stands. Significantly, the Hurricane and Spitfire squadrons which took part in the same combat patrols on 29 May made far fewer claims and lost a number of aircraft. The four squadrons which accompanied 264 in the afternoon and evening patrols notched up nine enemy aircraft destroyed for the loss of six. No.s 56, 610 (Spitfires) and 151 squadrons each lost two aircraft to enemy fire as well as others damaged. Only 213 Squadron (Hurricanes), which claimed three 109 kills, returned to base without any losses.[10] The Luftwaffe's own exaggerated claims amounted to a total of twenty-nine Spitfires and Hurricanes from these two patrols.

Back at Duxford news of 264's success was beginning to filter through the aerodrome. The Duxford chaplain, Guy Mayfield, wrote in his diary: 'The afternoon well spent in Cambridge in getting a steel helmet and trying to get a revolver licence and a revolver. 264 Squadron have shot down thirty-five German planes today. Great exultation. They were badly shot up but no one crashed. One air gunner bailed out, but why is not yet known.'[11]

The squadron's valour was rightly recognised by a clutch of medals. There was a Distinguished Service Order (DSO) for Philip Hunter and a Distinguished Flying Cross (DFC) for Nicholas Cooke, while the non-commissioned pilot, Sgt Thorn, and 264's most successful gunners Lippett, Barker and King, were each awarded Distinguished Flying Medals (DFMs).

A jubilant 264 Squadron remained at Manston that night.

The following morning they received this congratulatory message from Keith Park, head of No. 11 Group: 'The Air Officer Commanding sends sincere congratulations to No. 264 Squadron on their magnificent performance in shooting down over thirty enemy aircraft today without losing a single pilot, one of whom brought back his aeroplane minus both elevators and one aileron [PO Young].[12]

It was followed by a message from Air Marshal Arthur S. Barratt, Air Officer Commanding-in-Chief of the British Air Forces in France, who cabled the squadron to say: 'Good work. Troops in local area much heartened by your excellent show yesterday.' Although whether Barratt's words truly reflected the on-the-ground sentiment among the troops is very doubtful.

The tens of thousands of military personnel still enduring hourly Luftwaffe attacks as they waited on the Dunkirk beaches were mostly oblivious to the valiant combat of the RAF which was taking place out to sea or behind enemy lines. A frequent complaint which echoed across the beaches was 'Where is the bloody RAF?'. And as we have seen there were even instances of downed pilots being refused places on British ships returning to Dover because of the raw anger directed towards the 'absent' RAF.

However, the Navy's debt owed to Fighter Command for its contribution to saving the lives of so many soldiers and seamen was summed up in a personal message written by Vice Admiral Bertram Ramsay, the head of planning for Operation Dynamo, to Dowding that evening. He wrote: 'Your assistance has been invaluable. I'm most grateful for your splendid cooperation. It alone has given us a chance of success and I trust you will be able to keep it up.'[13]

This welcome RAF success gave Britain a huge propaganda

victory at a critical moment at the start of the war and pictures of the new British fighter featured in cinema newsreels all across the country. Seizing the opportunity to capitalise on the victories of its secret fighter, the Air Ministry granted the media access to some of the pilots and gunners.

This Press Association account was typical of the jingoism reportage of the action:

'THEIR SOS – GERMANS FEAR OUR NEW FIGHTER Press Association Air Correspondent. At a forward fighter aerodrome near the coast yesterday I saw the Boulton Paul Defiant squadron, which shot down nearly forty enemy planes without loss to themselves, one day this week take off on patrol over Dunkirk. They were accompanied by Hurricanes. An hour and a quarter later I watched their return after a hectic engagement, in which they dived on forty Me 109s and were in turn attacked by another forty Messerschmitts and Heinkels. In the tremendous battle that followed planes from both sides were sent down. Though the odds were four to one against, the British pilots more than held their own, but the loss had not been definitely checked when I left the aerodrome. I have since heard that they had accounted for twelve enemy aircraft shot down and three damaged. One or two of the British planes showed signs of the action on their return but they were rapidly rearmed and refuelled for their next offensive patrol.'[14]

Britain's newspaper editors, who had become accustomed to reporting military disasters and defeats, were desperate for a simple explanation for this RAF victory. One Press Association reporter duly obliged: 'Earlier I heard from the pilots the full story of the 12 Defiants which shot down the German aeroplanes earlier in the week over Dunkirk. Actually the number of German victims, X learned, was 38. They included nineteen

Ju 87 dive-bombers and 18 Messerschmitts. "The Germans have been surprised by the Defiant, because it resembles the Hurricane except that its fire comes from multi-guns in a turret behind the pilot," the pilots told me. "Before they have got over their surprise they are shot down".'[15]

It was a glib explanation for a series of successful combats which in fact could only be partially explained by ignorance on the part of the Luftwaffe fighter pilots. Hunter himself had acknowledged in his own combat report from 23 May that he thought some of the German fighters were 'treating us as Hurricanes because they tried to get on our tails',[16] but the Defiants had engaged and been engaged by a variety of Luftwaffe aircraft whose pilots had been briefed about the RAF fighter's rear-firing guns. Many of the 109s had in fact been shot down as they carried out beam attacks on the turret fighters.

The source of the quote used by the Press Association was probably Wing Commander Harry Broadhurst, the station commander at RAF Wittering, who had happened to be at Manston when the Defiants returned from their second sortie on 29 May.[17] When asked about the day's success he happily recounted the light-hearted downplaying of the fighting which was so common among British aircrews when they were relaxing in the bar after a day's fighting. But the truth was that most of the victories claimed that day were German bombers, not fighters. The factual inaccuracy of this kind of reporting didn't matter to the directors and workers at the Boulton Paul factory who happily pinned the newspaper articles onto the noticeboards, proudly adding the words 'our work.'

29th May had proved to be as much a triumph for Squadron

Leader Philip Hunter and his tactics as it was for Boulton Paul's designer and chairman J. D. North. North had gambled the company business and his professional reputation on the Defiant. Now the larger-than-life military aircraft mogul could rightly claim the credit.[18]

Neither did Sholto Douglas nor Donald Stevenson care how the Defiant had come to justify their faith.

## Chapter 11

# DELIVERANCE

ON THE SAME day Hunter's Defiants had made their record kills the Royal Navy succeeded in evacuating 47,000 soldiers from Dunkirk, nearly three times as many as the day before. No. 264 Squadron's contribution to the day's deliverance was rewarded with a twenty-four-hour break from combat, which the crews spent at Duxford. In fact low cloud meant visibility was so poor that neither air force was able to engage the other. That night the Defiant crews rightly enjoyed a boisterous and boozy celebration.

On 31 May, a much fairer day, the Defiants were recalled to operations. But one pilot, who had over-indulged the night before, was clearly not fit for duty. Eric Barwell remembers the hungover pilot sitting on his bed with his head in his hands: 'He was in no condition to fly and furthermore to have done so would not have been fair to his gunner.' Barwell decided to report the drunken pilot to his flight commander, Nicholas Cooke, who was rightly livid. Recalled Barwell: '"What?' he said, "drinking on duty? I'll shoot him with this bloody gun", patting his revolver.' The pilot was withdrawn and replaced with a standby flier. Cooke resolved to deal with the officer severely when he returned from the day's operations.[1]

The rest of the squadron, accompanied by ten Hurricanes of 213 Squadron, took off from Manston in the early afternoon and rendezvoused with another squadron of Hurricanes and one of Spitfires before arriving over Dunkirk. No. 213 flew directly behind the Defiants.

As PO Barwell looked down he could see the men sprawled all along the beach and the boats bobbing at the famous Dunkirk harbour mole which the British used to embark the soldiers onto the smaller boats. Among the tired and hungry soldiers would have been recognisable faces, including a young soldier called Greenhalgh, brother of PO Greenhalgh, already captured by the Germans during the Holland campaign. Greenhalgh would not leave the beaches alive, blown to pieces in a dive-bomber attack.[2]

As the Defiants crossed the French coast, Hunter spotted eight He 111s in the distance, approaching from the south-east of the town on the start of a bombing run targeting the beaches. Hunter immediately ordered an attack, but the German bombers, unwilling to hang around to be caught by the faster British fighters, 'turned tail and fled', dropping their bombs harmlessly into the sea as they went. However, the arrival of the RAF had drawn some unwanted attention. A huge force of forty Me 109s patrolling above the Heinkels began diving out of the sun from about 10,000 feet on to the formations of Defiants and Hurricanes. 'I immediately formed a circle,' Hunter recorded in his combat report. 'One Me 109 flew past us from port to starboard just above me and my air gunner engaged it, shooting it down out of control. It dived straight into the sea.'[3]

But the German cannon was starting to find its mark. A Defiant flown by PO Guy Hickman and LAC Alfred Fidler was badly mauled and ended up in the sea. Both crew were reported missing.

The RAF pilots threw their machines from one side to the other in a desperate bid to shake off the German attackers. In the panic and confusion two of the Defiants collided with each other. Hunter watched in horror as he saw one plane 'completely break up, its wings floating down by themselves'.

One of these hapless Defiants was piloted by Michael Young, whose gunner LAC Stanley Johnson had seconds earlier shot down a diving 109. Recalled Young: 'Immediately after this, whilst formatting in line astern, my air gunner shouted to me that a Defiant was coming up fairly close; a second or so later there was a loud crash and my machine seemed to fall to pieces. I shouted to the air gunner to jump but the RT had failed. I jumped out and landed in Dunkirk, having been shot at by the French when floating down.'[4]

But Johnson was less fortunate. He was unable to escape from his turret and went down with the Defiant. At thirty-seven years old, Stanley Johnson was one of the oldest RAF crewmen to take part in the Dunkirk operations. The other colliding Defiant, crewed by PO 'Bull' Whitley and LAC Turner, crash-landed safely in Allied territory. Miraculously Young, Whitley and Turner all survived and were back at Manston the next day.

The 213 Squadron of Hurricanes trailing the Defiants also suffered several losses in the Messerschmitt attack. They had only just reformed after engaging a separate group of 109s when they were bounced by the larger formation of German fighters. The engagement was over in seconds, giving the Hurricanes no time to turn away from the cannon fire. Five of the ten Hurricanes were shot down and two pilots killed.[5]

Hunter, having already lost three of his Defiants, now decided discretion was the better part of valour: 'I decided on seeing another large enemy formation of Me 109s above us to retreat. I ordered my squadron to follow me to sea level . . . followed by the remaining Hurricanes and then made for home.'[6]

The British fighters had been caught by surprise by the German fighters and had every right to ask why their escort hadn't intervened. Hunter caustically noted in his mission report: 'I did not see the squadrons who were defending us at any time.' Combat records show that 264 gunners claimed four more 109s to add to their growing tally.

Four hours after their bruising encounter with the Messerschmitts, Hunter was briefed to join up with 111 and 609 Hurricane squadrons over Deal and then, as the most experienced pilot, lead the Hurricanes into the Dunkirk airspace. No. 111 followed on in line astern while 609 took up a position 3000 feet above. Almost as soon as they reached the beaches they ran into a large formation of He 111s and their fighter escort, who were being engaged by AA fire from the British positions.

The Hurricanes immediately took on the 109s while the Defiants made a beeline for the bombers. Hunter and King shot down two of the German aircraft and the now consistently effective crew of Ted Thorn and Fred Barker bagged another. Barwell had managed to position his Defiant underneath one of the Heinkels, allowing Williams to empty his machine guns into the underbelly of the bomber. The German machine dropped into the sea, with just two of the crew escaping by parachute.

But the Defiants had also suffered losses. Cooke and Lippett, heroes of the 19 May combat and the squadron's leading scorers, were hit by sustained fire from the Me 109s. Both were reported missing, Hunter saying he believed the aircraft had crashed into the sea.[7] Their bodies were never found.

The Defiant flown by PO Richard Stokes had been damaged by the Heinkel's machine guns. His gunner LAC Henry Fairbrother was wounded in the foot and bailed out shortly after the attack. However, Stokes managed to nurse the Defiant back to Manston where he was later reunited with a rather damp and surprised Fairbrother who had been picked up by a passing boat and returned safely.

Barwell's Defiant had also suffered damage in the action.[8] Return fire from one of the Heinkels hit the aircraft's glycol tank (which cooled the Rolls-Royce engine), forcing Barwell to turn for home. His rapidly overheating engine meant he was not going to make the Kent coast so Barwell got on the RT [Radio telephone] to ask Williams whether he would rather 'bail or ditch'. Williams' reply was equivocal and so Barwell decided to put the Defiant down in the channel. It was the first time a Defiant had attempted a sea landing. Barwell drew back the hood, strapped himself tightly into his seat, and when the Defiant was about 15 feet above the waves, stalled it so the aircraft belly-flopped into the calm waters between two British destroyers. The 3½-ton Defiant took just a few seconds to sink. Williams had been knocked unconscious in the crash landing. He was lying face down in the sea, held up by his 'parasuit'. Barwell swam to him and lifted his head onto his shoulder and then tried to make it for one of the destroyers. Once on board HMS *Malcolm* they were met by PO Michael Young who had also been hooked out of the sea. 'When Williams came round on board the ship he could see Young looking at him through the cabin door with the bright red sun setting in the background,' recounted Barwell. 'He thought he had died and gone to hell.'[9]

Barwell suffered bruised knees, a cut lip and an ear injury when his oxygen mask and flying helmet were dragged from his head in the crash. Even so he was back flying within a week. Barwell's bravery was widely reported in the media. Yet all Barwell told the reporters: 'The main thing is how fine the Defiant was.'

During the day's two patrols 264 claimed four 109s in the afternoon and five Heinkels in the second action. These victories had come at a price. No. 264 had lost three aircraft in the afternoon, including the two which collided, and three crewmen were dead – Hickman, Fidler and Johnson. In the evening patrol they had lost two more Defiants and Cooke, an experienced flight commander, and his gunner Lippett were both posted missing. Barwell, Fairbrother and Williams were all wounded. Cooke never did get to discipline the pilot who had been drunk on duty that morning. Like many pilots he died intestate, triggering an expensive legal battle between the family and four life insurance companies which now sought proof of his death before paying out 'many thousands of pounds' under the terms of the policies.[10] Fighter Command also lost ten Hurricanes and seven Spitfires.

That last day of May in 1940 was the busiest and heaviest day's fighting for the RAF during the entire Dunkirk campaign, flying a total of thirty patrols from daybreak to dusk.

There is little doubt that the two patrols involving the Defiants, which met the full force of the Luftwaffe attacks, blunted the enemy's strikes against the Royal Navy ships which had been targeted by more than three hundred enemy aircraft. That day the Navy lost just two ships (both minesweepers) while evacuating nearly sixty-eight thousand men from the

Dunkirk beaches – the greatest number in a single day during the whole of Operation Dynamo.

No. 264 Squadron had served in the front line from 12 to 31 May, shooting down sixty-five enemy aircraft, more than any other RAF squadron. They had shown skill, gallantry and moral fibre when they found themselves greatly outnumbered by the Luftwaffe's superior forces. And they had done all this in an aircraft which had not been fitted with the same bullet-proof cockpits that Dowding had insisted must be used to protect the pilots of the Spitfires and Hurricanes. Nor had they been equipped with the constant speed propellers that they had been promised and which would have improved their rate of climb. Overall, Hunter and his men had paid a high price, losing twelve aircraft and fifteen aircrew killed (plus three prisoners of war), depriving 264 of two very experienced Defiant pilots, George Skelton and Nicholas Cooke. Fighter Command decided it was time to pull 264 back from the front line so the squadron could regroup and replace lost crew and aircraft.

The Duxford chaplain, Guy Mayfield, simply wrote in his diary: '264 Squadron returned victorious yesterday. Sixty planes shot down over three days. I went to meet them at dispersal point and talked a lot to [Fred] King, the remarkable air gunner. The boys were very tired but exalted.'[11] That days headline simply read: 'MAGNIFICENT WORK OF THE NEW "DEFIANT" FIGHTERS'.[12]

The Air Ministry was keen to learn from the Defiants' combat experience of the past few days. So, on the evening of 31 May, Douglas sent down Wing Commander Eric S. Burns, Officer of War Tactics (Air Ministry), to Duxford to prepare a secret report on the future deployment of the RAF's turret fighter.

Burns interviewed both Hunter and the commanding officer of the second Defiant squadron, Sq Ld William Richardson, who had been ordered to Duxford. Hunter told Burns that while he had not been impressed with the fighting qualities of the Me 110, the Me 109 had presented a serious threat to the Defiant, especially 'with a height advantage and diving out of the sun'.

He also passed on his concerns about faulty radio communications between the Defiants and the Spitfires and Hurricanes which he said were making it impossible for the squadron leaders to talk to each other once the fighters were airborne. Hunter's ground crews told Burns that the Defiants low-slung aerials hindered the tuning of the radio sets to the same frequencies used by the two other British fighter types. This explained why the Hurricanes and Spitfires hadn't picked up Hunter's radio calls for assistance and so failed to come to the Defiants' rescue on 31 May.

Burns noted in his report to the Air Ministry: 'All squadrons taking part should be working on the same wavelength and tuned to the Defiant's frequency. Without cohesion and direction from the leader a Defiant squadron loses a very high proportion of its effectiveness. It is essential that the accompanying squadrons [Hurricanes and Spitfires] should act as an upper guard, turning when the Defiant turns and always keeping it in sight. The guard becomes useless if it is at the end of the patrol line and the Defiant at the other. If a large force of Defiants and single seat fighters keep in contact then the German fighters do not attack and the bombers retire without attempting to complete the mission.'

During the meeting Richardson repeated the request for bulletproof cockpit windscreens to make the Defiant 'the perfect aeroplane'. Burns agreed but saw no need for forward machine guns 'owing to the danger that pilots would regard the Defiant primarily as a front gun fighter'.

Reporting directly to Douglas and Stevenson, Burns advised that, despite its success on 31 May, 'the Defiant's proper role is against bombers in home defence, not in offensive patrols against unspecified targets. It has been shown how effective it would be against Ju 87s and He 111s; against fighters however it has not been nearly so effective except when fighting a defensive battle on its own terms. If large formations of bombers attack this country by day, the Defiant should be in its element, provided that Spitfires or Hurricanes are also there to draw off the enemy fighters in the early stages of the encounter.'[13]

For that to happen Fighter Command would have to first solve the radio communications problems which had dogged both the Defiants squadrons. If they didn't the Defiant would be unable to profit from the protection offered by the single seat fighters and would remain vulnerable to attacks from the German 109.

By 1 June the bulk of the BEF had been evacuated off the beaches. Göring had failed to deliver on his promise to annihilate the British Army at Dunkirk. Throughout the eight daytime operations the Luftwaffe had repeatedly tried and failed to sink the British Navy or destroy the key 'moles' which had been so critical to the disembarkation of the Allied soldiers. Had the German bombers been allowed a free hand in these twin objectives, few doubt they would have succeeded in the destruction of the British Land Army. Instead at 23.30 on 2 June the Senior Naval Officer at Dunkirk was able to send the signal to Vice Admiral Dover, Bertram

Ramsay: 'BEF evacuated'. At no time during the operation did the Luftwaffe enjoy air superiority over the combat zone.

That day[14] Dowding sent this message to the brave fighter pilots and gunners of No. 11 Group who had taken part in the operation: 'My Dear fighter boys. I don't send out many congratulatory letters and signals, but I feel that I must take this occasion when the intensive fighting in Northern France is for the time being over, to tell you how proud I am of you and the way in which you have fought since the "Blitzkrieg" started. I wish I could have spent my time visiting you and hearing your account of the fighting but I have occupied myself working for you in other ways. I want you to know that my thoughts are always with you and that it is you and your Fighting Spirit which will crack the morale of the German Air Force and preserve our country through the trials which lie ahead. Good luck to you.'[15]

Dowding paid a special personal tribute to Hunter. According to Fighter Command's official report[16] of the battle, Dowding, in one of his rare complimentary messages, which the report said were 'so rare as to be very precious', the commander-in-chief 'congratulated Squadron Leader Hunter of No. 264 Squadron upon the prowess of his officers and men'.

The Air Ministry claimed, during the thirteen days of fighting, that 260 German aircraft had been destroyed in return for 106 British fighters and only fifty-two pilots killed or captured. In fact the Luftwaffe lost only 132 aircraft, including some shot down by naval AA fire.[17] The actual RAF losses totalled 109 fighters: 56 Hurricanes, 45 Spitfires and 8 Defiants. Sixty-eight RAF pilots were killed, missing or captured.[18]

No. 264 was a single squadron among sixteen which flew the bulk of Fighter Command patrols during the Dunkirk campaign. Yet its success had been strikingly disproportionate to its strength – a fact that would not have gone unnoticed by the Commander-in-Chief of Fighter Command who closely studied the combat reports.

The triumph of the Defiant had also richly vindicated Donald Stevenson and Sholto Douglas and their judgement call on backing the new fighter. How could Dowding now resist their claims for more Defiant squadrons to take their place alongside the Hurricanes and Spitfires?

Once again the Air Ministry fed the media with stories, promoting the campaign for the Defiant and applying pressure on Dowding and Fighter Command. The Defiant's contribution to the aerial battle was typically summed up by BBC correspondent Charles Gardner, who famously gave breathless live radio broadcasts capturing the action of the dogfights later fought over the Kent ports at the start of the Battle of Britain. Gardner was closer to the action than most reporters. He had already spent some time in France with the RAF and a few months later was commissioned into the RAF as a pilot officer. After Dunkirk he reported: 'The Defiant was the weapon Britain produced from up her sleeve just when the world thought the sleeve was empty.' More colourful commentary soon followed, hailing the Defiant as the conqueror of the Luftwaffe and the rightful holder of the title 'bomber destroyer' over the much-feared Nazi twin-engined Me 110.

One opinion piece even claimed: 'There is no other fighter in the world that can fly in front of the machine it is attacking and bring four machine-guns with terrible rates of arc of fire to bear upon the enemy. No other fighter can dive into a formation of enemy aircraft and, while flying a parallel course, pour withering fire into the machines each side of it. No other fighter can fly under a bomber and fire incessantly into its fuselage from beneath . . . The Defiant, in short, can fire at the enemy while doing practically any aerial manoeuvre, including standing on its head. Its chief merit is that it can avoid flak from the most heavily armed section of the bomber – the tail.'

On 15 June, the highly respected aviation expert Charles G. Grey, founder of *The Aeroplane* journal, delivered his verdict on the performance of the Defiant and the concept of the turret fighter: 'The surprise of the later phases of the fight in Flanders has been the Boulton Paul Defiant monoplanes. They were built to a new idea in air tactics conceived by one section of the Air Ministry. Hitherto the pilot has always been the captain of the ship, and has always had guns in front which he has aimed by manoeuvring to suit. The aft gunner has been there to protect his tail, and to get a shot if the pilot thought of putting him where he could get one. Hitherto there has been a theory that one could not fire broadsides from a high-speed aeroplane, because as soon as the bullets leave the muzzle of the gun they are travelling sideways through the air at the same speed as the aeroplane. The spin of the bullet against this side pressure causes it to spin upwards when fired from one side of the aeroplane and to spin downwards on the other side. And as the amount of up or down spin varies with the speed of the aeroplane, no possible sights can allow for such variations. But with four guns firing tracer or incendiary bullets at a rate of 4800 bullets per minute (1200 per gun) the gunners find that they can aim their guns as one aims a hose, by watching where the discharge goes. And, as the German guns have only a slight traverse, the pilot of a Defiant can bring his machine close alongside the beam of a German machine, and a very short burst from the four guns is enough to sink it. This spinning up or down of the bullets is known as the Magnus effect, after the scientist who worked it out theoretically, or as the Cazeau effect, after some gunnery experimental station, I believe in France, where it was tried out. And, as so often happens, theory has been defeated by practice. No doubt, as the result of capturing shot-down British machines, the Germans will soon have power-driven gun turrets. Our job is to produce new types of aeroplanes to beat the new German types.'

On 2 June Harold Balfour, Under Secretary of State for Air, and Colonel Llewellyn W. W. Wakefield MP, minister at the Ministry of Supply, paid a visit to Hunter and 264 Squadron at Duxford. A few days later (8 June) Sir Cyril Newall came to personally congratulate the brave Defiant pilots and gunners.[19] The Whitehall top brass encountered a fighter squadron whose morale was sky-high and who enjoyed complete confidence in their aircraft and commanders.

The Defiants' success meant it was much in demand. On 9 June the intelligence officer of 56 Squadron, whose Hurricanes had flown patrols with 264 during the Dunkirk campaign, wrote urgently to 11 Group HQ asking for a section of Defiants to 'protect the rear of the squadron' from the growing threat of diving attacks from Me 109s.

On 15 June there were further requests for Defiants to take on RAF bomber escort duties over France because their armament made them better suited for the role than the Spitfires and Hurricanes.

Fighter Command denied both requests, saying that 'the supply [of Defiants] alone makes it quite impossible.'

Keith Park was much less diplomatic: 'Other squadrons,' he wrote to 56 Squadron, 'that have had a great deal more experience of air fighting do not consider that they need to be protected by sections of Defiants in order to maintain their morale,' adding: 'The Defiants are not intended to protect the more nimble and faster fixed gun fighters on offensive patrols.'

Park's remarks did not go down very well with 56 Squadron's intelligence officer who wrote back saying that the pilots 'were not impressed by the objection raised' to their request as they frequently saw Me 110s supporting Me 109s over France.[20]

The Defiant was the sort of invention which the British love best – where innovation and eccentric thinking triumph over adversity. It was a novel approach to air warfare which instinctively appealed to Winston Churchill who had spent a political career staking his reputation on high-risk military misadventures from Gallipoli to Antwerp when he was First Lord of the Admiralty. But he had also had the vision to understand how inventions like the tank would transform warfare.

Impressed by the Defiant's success at Dunkirk, Churchill[21] was receptive to the lobbying of Douglas, Stevenson and now Kingsley Wood himself, the Secretary of State for Air. They just wanted more machines to finish the job.

Having won over the public and the Prime Minister to the idea of the Defiant, the Air Ministry desperately looked for ways of bumping up production of the aircraft in time for the coming onslaught.

But it had been clear as early as mid-1939 that Boulton Paul had serious difficulty in keeping pace with technical changes to turret designs as well as meeting general production demands. By the beginning of June 1940 only one hundred Defiants had been delivered to the RAF.[22] Boulton Paul was also building turrets for the Roc, Halifax and Hudson, as well as developing a whole range of new fighter and bomber equipment. Internal industry politics was also holding back production. The company management had fallen out with Lucas, the Birmingham manufacturer called in as a turret subcontractor.[23] Boulton Paul management, according to an Air Ministry report, had 'a genius for upsetting subcontractors'.[24]

Douglas, Stevenson and Wood now turned to Churchill's friend and adviser, Lord Beaverbrook, the new minister for aircraft production, who had a short but proven track record in boosting production for the Hurricane and the Spitfire. The Air Ministry wanted five hundred more Defiants as quickly as possible. Beaverbrook's answer to the production bottleneck was to announce the appointment of Leonard Lord as the new government manager to personally oversee the Defiant production target. Lord had made his reputation as a car-assembly-line specialist at Morris and Austin Motors. The government now hoped he would be able to work his auto-production magic at Boulton Paul. Yet even Lord found himself unable to make any impression on the woeful production rate of the Defiant. His failure is as baffling as it was concerning to the Air Ministry. Lord's biographer, Martyn Nutwood, later wrote: 'He was capable of achieving the most dramatic increases in output along with savings in manpower. Which is why I find it so astonishing that the finest production engineer in the country, possibly in Europe, could apparently bring so little that is positive to this relatively small company.' Lord proved his management credentials after the war when he oversaw the manufacture of the world-beating Mini. Of course the only meaningful measure for ensuring a boost in Defiant production was to give the aircraft 'grade A' priority on par with the Spitfire and the Hurricane. After its success at Dunkirk this upgrade was recommended by the Assistant Director of Aeroplane Production but Beaverbrook rejected the proposal.[25]

* * *

In the aftermath of the bitter fighting of Dunkirk the British and German forces paused to take stock of their relative positions and resources. The RAF and the Luftwaffe had both sustained significant losses. During the six weeks of the entire continent campaign, the RAF had lost more than nine hundred aircraft, half of which were fighters (106 at Dunkirk).[26] The Luftwaffe losses, which had been sustained in spearheading Germany's all-conquering campaigns in Poland, Norway, the Low Countries and France, were even greater.

Yet after Dunkirk and into the summer of 1940 the Luftwaffe still held a significant numerical advantage in aircraft, both bombers and fighters. The Air Staff had already determined that Fighter Command required sixty squadrons to adequately defend Britain from German bomber fleets based in Germany, but to confront the more direct threat from airfields in northern France, it was thought the RAF would require double that number – 120 squadrons. This was based on an estimate of Luftwaffe strength put at 5400 aircraft. In June, Donald Stevenson was given the job of reviewing Britain's defence requirements and assessing the German air force capability. Stevenson reduced Fighter Command's requirement to a more realistic seventy squadrons, moving to eighty as soon as production capacity permitted.

But even Stevenson's down-graded assessment of the enemy's strength was exaggerated. By mid-July the three Air Fleets facing Fighter Command numbered 2800 aircraft. Against them Dowding had seven hundred Spitfires and Hurricanes and two full squadrons of Defiants.[27]

Hitler's crushing victory against the combined French, British, Dutch and Belgian forces raised the expectation in Westminster and across the country that an invasion was imminent. The BEF had been effectively disarmed in France, leaving the Royal Navy and a depleted RAF to defend almost 20,000 miles of unprotected coastline. The Germans could attack at any point at any time.

But the RAF's combat effectiveness, including the much-publicised Defiants' kill-rate, helped convince Hitler and his generals that before they could launch an invasion against Britain the Luftwaffe must achieve total air superiority. Göring and his air marshals spent the next weeks strengthening their air force units before commencing a full-scale air assault. This pause in hostilities bought the RAF and the British military commanders vital time to ready their own fighter force and organise Britain's air defences.

Meanwhile 264 Squadron was close to returning to full operational strength, partly helped by the addition of nine replacement New Zealand air gunners.

Among the officer recruits, was PO John Banham who joined the squadron on 1 June as one of the first pilot replacements: 'I arrived just as the evacuation had been completed when the squadron was regrouping. It had done a marvellous job but had lost a lot of crew.'[28] Three days later Flt Lt Tony Trumble[29] took his place as a flight commander, taking over command of 'B' flight after the death of the experienced Flt Lt Nicholas Cooke. He arrived the same afternoon Hunter was officially presented with his DSO and Cooke was posthumously awarded his DFC. The citation on Hunter's medal not only commended the squadron for shooting down thirty-eight enemy aircraft in one day, it also recognised his 'brilliant leadership as well as his example and courage [being] of the highest order'.[30]

Jim Bailey, another replacement pilot, joined the squadron at Duxford on 19 June. The novice airman was introduced to his new Nissan hut quarters by an elderly batman who had looked after the previous occupant, a Spitfire pilot from 19 Squadron.

'He was a fine Gentleman, Sir, I never looked after a better officer.'[31] The batman had not yet had time to clear the room of the officer's personal effects of family photographs or even, as Bailey noted, his 'soiled clothes, smelling of sweat'. Bailey read the dead officer's log book in which he wrote bumptiously of his flying triumphs: 'gave a much-admired display of aerobatics' and 'did beautiful rolls'. But Bailey wasn't particularly impressed, commenting: 'Its owner must have been a conceited fellow, we thought.' Bailey was teamed up with gunner Jack Scott, one of the Kiwi recruits.[32] Remarked the pilot afterwards: 'He was a young, green and very nice New Zealander, small innocent healthy. If I said anything, he said "Good O, sir".'

The colonial volunteers tended to view Britain's rigid class system with a healthy disrespect. Equally the RAF's strict hierarchical code was slow to accommodate the Commonwealth airmen. When the Anzac airmen arrived at Duxford they discovered that their status as aircraftmen meant they were the bottom of the air force heap, to be assigned to cleaning duties. They even found themselves barred from the sergeants' mess. Since they had travelled halfway around the world to answer the mother country's call to arms this was an indignity too far. One of them, Clifford Emeny, decided to take their case to the squadron leader saying that he hadn't come to Britain to clean up after other airmen. He threatened that unless the situation changed it would be a case of 'no food, no fight'. Although Hunter did not approve of the mutinous language he quietly rang the New Zealand embassy in London and by the end of the day had got all the Kiwi gunners promoted to sergeants.[33]

Jim Bailey remembers how the aircrew spent the next six sunlit weeks: 'Lying lazing on the sward beside our fighters, waiting for the invasion. We practised formation flying and studied toy models of German bombers, and their gun positions and their fields of fire.'[34] There was a scarcity of ammunition for the gunners to practise because so much had been lost in France and they were each reduced to just fifty rounds a month.[35] 'Instead,' said Bailey, 'we dropped practice bombs on imaginary landing barges and laid smoke, smoke which would have become, had the invasion started, mustard gas.'

The Defiants were occasionally scrambled after daybreak when German bombers came racing over the east coast, using the cloud for cover. 'We chased them often,' remembered Bailey, 'but I do not recollect that any of us ever saw one.'

Being the most junior pilot, Bailey's Defiant was the slowest in the squadron. So perhaps it is little wonder that he dreamed of one day piloting the faster and more glamorous Spitfire: 'I was always jealous of these Spitfire pilots for possessing an aircraft more fluent than my own, a single-seater, the last word in nimbleness and power. I think that it was Spitfires from the Aerodrome at Digby that persuaded me, when they took off, a section rising into the air like a spring of teal . . . Then one afternoon, when the air was burdened with big white cumulus with shafts of light splitting the cathedral gloom, a Spitfire dived across the front of me, coming out of one chasm in the trailing cloud, diving to where I could see Digby fighter station camouflaged below. It was entrancing.'[36]

The reality of a dawn scramble was much less 'entrancing' for pilots like Bailey who had been used to the 'deep animal sleep of youth'. On his first 'alert', the squadron was woken at 03.45: 'I turned over and tried to slumber, yet even as I closed my eyes it came to me that all the others were strangely active. Someone was shouting, "Hell and beggary, where are my trousers?" So I woke again, to see in the twilight the last of my fellows strapping on his Mae West [inflated life jacket] and stumbling out. I forced myself out of bed, the air blue cold and it smelt freshly of hay. My clothes were in disorder; so I slipped coat and trousers over my pyjamas. I jumped into the flying boots, grabbed my Mae West and ran through the darkness for the shadow of the aircraft . . . When I reached my old Defiant I tried to be sick. I wasn't sick however so I clambered onto the metal wing and dropped into the cockpit, where my parachute awaited me. Scott slipped into the turret behind. As the prop turned it blew the dew off the rounded Perspex windscreen. I skimped warming the engine, and taxied it out in time to join the second section.'

Bailey's Defiant was soon rolling across the airfield: 'My section leader began to roll forward across the sappy green turf. I opened up and roared over the ground in the chilly twilight of a Cambridgeshire dawn. I had full throttle but Yellow one and Yellow two pulled away from me. It was obviously an emergency so I used the emergency [thrust] handle which gave the engine extra power. Even then I only just cleared the far hedge. Something was wrong, for the engine was only giving 1500 revs. I searched the cockpit. I found that on the previous day they had changed the propeller on this aircraft from a variable pitch to a constant speed airscrew and I had taken off in the full course. I put matters to rights and joined up with John Banham, my section leader. I was cold and excited, indeed I had never been able to fly a decent formation anyway. Then my knees started to knock. Until that moment I had heard of the expression but I always believed it to be figurative, not descriptive. They banged each other inside the pyjamas. I could mock their antics in a detached sort of way but in no way control them. I saw B flight taking off far beneath us and joining up in the formation below. They climbed up towards us.'

As he looked up Bailey saw the 'white bellies' of the three Defiants which he said resembled the 'firm white flesh of fish'. As the morning light began to break though, Bailey reflected: 'I had always been pretty skeptical about the invasion, now I wondered if landings had actually occurred. In a tight formation of twelve Defiants we paraded East Anglia: Cambridge, Thetford, Yarmouth, Southwold, Orford Ness and back, proud of our strength. It was a summer morning and the season for hay making. In summer meadows the grass still rippled sensuously as the wind stirred it, in some the hay was cut and it lay in ripe swathes waiting for the dew on it to dry. The ranks of wheat were yellowing. There had been no other aircraft in the sky, yet Storrs, one of our gunners, swore that as we flew over Norfolk a man, without the parachute, dropped past his turret. He refused to be talked out of it. I, Munchausen-wise, wondered if perhaps an airman from the previous war might have been caught up in an eddy, and had travelled Europe ever since, too high and too cold to disintegrate. When we returned to base, we were told that we had been called out on a false alarm.'[37]

On 21 June the Air Ministry called a conference to evaluate the Defiants' progress. Hunter was given the opportunity to explain in careful detail the attacking formations and defensive descending circles that 264 had so successfully employed against the Luftwaffe the month before. He was able to quell any concern about the vulnerability of the Defiant to the Me 109 and 110 by recalling in great detail how the German fighters were forced to attack on the outside of the 'spiral' (Lufbery Circle) and exposed themselves to the combined concentrated fire of the Defiants' machine guns. During the first patrol of 29 May this had cost the Luftwaffe dearly, losing sixteen aircraft.[38] When they were bounced by 109s out of the sun on 31 May it was the squadron's 'cohesion' that had withstood a determined attack, although Hunter conceded two Defiants were shot down and two collided with one another.

Hunter also suggested improvements. He strongly believed the best way of using the Defiant was in composite patrols with two other squadrons of Hurricanes. But he said that combat missions over Dunkirk had shown that the twin-seat and single-seat fighters could only effectively work together if the RT problems were eradicated and there were pre-ops briefings involving all three squadrons before every combat. Over Dunkirk the Hurricanes had become easily separated from the Defiants so that they ended up fighting as separate units.

The flight commanders and Air Staff, gathered at the conference, were also able to assess the destructive fire power of the Browning machine guns. Dowding had insisted before the Defiants went into battle in May that for maximum results the 'spread' of the bullets should be set so they were as concentrated as possible. There was no doubt that such a focused enfilade of fire had made a vital contribution to the squadron's record victories. But Hunter now said that some of the gunners had reported jamming problems which if corrected might bring even greater results.

Hunter explained that the gunners were forced to use insulating tape to stop the two-pin-plug connections to the guns' solenoid becoming detached. Every vibration from the guns or vibration when a pilot plunged the Defiant into a 'power dive' was shaking the connections apart. Dowding agreed to write to the Air Ministry to ask Boulton Paul to immediately resolve this problem.[39] But it would be a curse that would continue to afflict the performance of the Defiants' machine gunners throughout the coming combats.

The Air Ministry, heeding the advice of Wing Commander

Eric Burns who had visited Duxford and the Defiant crews on May 31, had also raised concerns about the lack of bulletproof-glass cockpits which Dowding had moved heaven and earth to make sure these were fitted as standard to the Spitfire and the Hurricane. Whitehall officials wrote to Fighter Command suggesting that the Defiants should now be equipped with the same. But this was not a view shared by Dowding and Park. Fighter Command replied to the Air Ministry saying that Dowding and Park were unable to 'endorse' the use of bullet-proof windscreens in Defiant aircraft: 'as it is considered that the Defiant should never be in a position from which it could be fired at from directly ahead'.[40] That of course was absolutely no consolation to those pilots who, in the heat of battle, did find themselves facing head on attacks and paid with their lives.

On 16 June Hunter was able to show the air chiefs exactly how the Defiant had beaten off the *schwärmes* of faster Me 109s over Dunkirk.

Quite fortuitously an undamaged Me 109 had fallen into British hands and was being tested at RAF Farnborough. It was arranged that a Defiant flown by Hunter should go head-to-head with the German fighter which was to be flown by the equally experienced fighter pilot, Squadron Leader Hugh 'Willie' Wilson, who tested all captured Luftwaffe aircraft. The Defiant was to have one modification which was missing from the aircraft that had fought over Dunkirk. Hunter's plane was to be fitted with a constant speed airscrew. Air Ministry trials had already shown how much improvement the airscrew made to the performance of the Spitfire and the Hurricane, especially in the rate of climb. The standard propeller speeds offered just 'fine' or 'coarse', whereas the constant speed adapted its revs to suit the condition of the climb.

In a secret memo of the trial written up by Hunter, the Defiant ace explained the outcome of the aerial joust between the two aircraft: 'It was decided that when we reached sufficient height he would allow me to get on his tail and would then endeavour to shake me off. After ten minutes of this practice he was unable to shake me off. When he carried out speed turns it was always very easy for me to follow him: I still had plenty of elevator control and could have tightened the turn considerably. Also in short climbs and dives I was able to maintain a constant position the whole time.'[41]

For the second part of the trial the Defiant and the 109 swapped positions. Hunter continued: 'When he [Wilson] was in position I carried out a very steep turn to the right and aft to complete turns through 360 degrees, I was again on his tail. We then got into formation together and from a 2500-foot dive across the aerodrome, opening up our throttle at approximately the same time. He at first drew approximately 100 yards ahead due to very rapid acceleration and then I maintained station on him some 100 yards behind whilst he dived across the aerodrome very low and then climbed very steeply. For the first 1500 feet I still maintained position on him but after that he drew away rapidly.'

In his report sent to Fighter Command, Hunter set out in detail exactly how a Defiant could defeat a 109. It would prove to be textbook tactics in future combats for the Defiant:

'That should an Me 109 attack a Defiant,' wrote Hunter, 'if the pilot of the latter goes into a really steep turn, he will prevent the pilot of the Me 109 bringing his guns to bear, and will eventually, if the pilot of the Me 109 follows him into the turn, be able to get into a suitable position to deliver his own attack. If conditions are the same for both aircraft, that is to say, if the Me

109 does not have a height advantage, the general manoeuvrability of the Defiant compares very favourably with that of the Me 109, the Defiant being able to turn in a much smaller turning circle and still have full control.' He also noted that at low altitudes the speed of both aircraft 'appear to be about the same'.

In the hands of an experienced and skilful pilot like Hunter, trials had shown how the Defiant could match both the 109 and the Spitfire in a dogfight. But aerial combat in 1940 could never be textbook. Few pilots could fly a Defiant as expertly as Hunter and too many times the RAF fighters would not be trying to outmanoeuvre one enemy aircraft but several, often with a height advantage diving at them out of the sun.

Nevertheless, the Farnborough trials had firmly convinced the Air Staff that the Defiant was capable of outfighting the faster, high-powered Messerschmitt. The Air Ministry, which had been pressing Dowding for more progress in Fighter Command's night defence, were so confident in their new fighter that they now wanted it as the RAF's main night fighter.

On 12 June Air Commodore Sir Christopher Brand visited the squadron so that all pilots and gunners could attend his lecture on night interception and night flying. This meant Hunter and his crews, while conducting daytime patrols, also took part in night sorties throughout June and July. But without in-flight radar units night fighting was like looking for a needle in a haystack and not a single enemy aircraft was engaged, which was very much as Dowding had predicted.

Sometime in June a book had been published which described the current status of the two air powers. It was called *The Sky's the Limit* and its author was James Molony Spaight, until 1937 Principal Assistant Secretary at the Air Ministry. *The Sky's the Limit* represented official Air Ministry thinking of the day. What was so striking about this book was that the front cover did not feature a glamorous Spitfire or a hard-working Hurricane but instead a colour picture of the new Boulton Paul Defiant. Inside the book, Spaight offered the Air Ministry's view of the Defiant by retelling the significance of its success over Dunkirk[42]: 'On 29th May our fighters destroyed at least seventy-seven German aircraft and seriously damaged a number of others. Of the seventy-seven no less than thirty-eight were brought down by a squadron of twelve Defiants without loss to themselves. The success of this new two-seat fighter, equipped with a gun-turret, was the outstanding feature of a wonderful day . . . sixteen of their thirty-eight victims were Me 110s, the others being an Me 109 and twenty-one bombers. It was almost a battue. No single squadron had ever had such a day's hunting, nor had the total bag for the day ever been surpassed.' An Air Staff internal memo written by Wing Commander H.W. Pearson on 25 June, after he had reviewed Burns' own report, confidently predicted that the fighter would continue this success and go on to be 'very effective against bombers once the fighter escort had been engaged'[43]. But he presciently cautioned: 'For this reason it may be advisable never to operate them from forward aerodromes in home defence.' It's not possible to know whether Douglas and Sevenson passed on this instruction to Fighter Command. If they did, then Dowding and Park cannot escape blame for the tactical blunders that led to the combat deployment of the Defiants in the Battle of Britain.

The Air Staff's growing confidence in the Defiant was not wholly shared by Dowding and Park, the commander of No. 11 Group. Both men had kept their counsel after 264 Squadron's success at Dunkirk and had little choice but to go along with the heavily pro-Defiant position taken by Douglas and

Stevenson. Although they applauded Hunter's efforts in public, in private Dowding and Park maintained deep reservations.

Matters came to a head on 21 June when the Air Ministry decided to pass on to Dowding Wing Commander Burns' report[44] of his visit to Duxford on 31 May. Burns' conclusions, which adopted the combat claims made on behalf of 264 Squadron over Dunkirk, infuriated Keith Park who had led Fighter Command's Dunkirk operations. On 29 June he wrote a letter to Dowding[45] setting out for the first time his own evaluation of the Defiant and exploding some of the myths he believed had grown up around the aircraft. He began by discounting some of Burns' 'colourful' exageration contained in his report which he said was based on 'very little fighting experience and should therefore be accepted with reserve'.

Park told Dowding: 'No. 264 Squadron undoubtedly achieved considerable success, particularly on one day, and has been given full credit and a number of distinctions for its share in the fighting.' But the Air Chief Marshal pointed out: 'It should be borne in mind however that this squadron was working under much more favourable conditions than any other of the many fighter squadrons that were employed during the three-week operations over France. Because the Defiants were new and untried equipment, they were given . . . especially favourable treatment, which undoubtedly enabled them to achieve their successes.'

Park said that for several days the Defiants had been placed on defensive patrols off the coast of Dunkirk 'where they were amply screened by Hurricane squadrons who were patrolling in-land and so containing the enemy fighters'. When the Defiants later encountered 'strong patrols' of German fighters, Park said, 264 was given a 'strong protection screen of Spitfires and always with an accompanying Hurricane squadron'.

Park also said that because the Defiant squadron had 'difficulties servicing its aircraft and equipment they were never called on for very early morning patrols as were the eight-gun fighter squadrons who frequently had to be off the ground at dawn'.

According to Park the Defiants were so well protected by the Hurricanes and Spitfires that they 'had rarely to engage vastly superior numbers of fighters, but were afforded ideal opportunities for scoring maximum successes against dive-bombers attacking shipping'. And he claimed that 'on the rare occasions' the Defiants were attacked by German fighters 'they suffered heavy casualties and at their request given a complete day's rest the following day, whereas the eight-gun fighter squadrons carried on from day to day in spite of heavy casualties'. Finally Park asserted: 'Because there was only one Defiant squadron available they were never detailed to patrol in land like the Hurricane squadrons, which were daily subject to enemy AA fire.'

Park's astonishingly partial and self-serving findings reveal for the first time the extraordinary animosity the Air Chief Marshal felt towards the Defiant, and perhaps towards those who in the Air Ministry who supported the new fighter.

He went on to tell Dowding in the same letter that in these 'favourable circumstances it would have been surprising if the Defiant squadron had not achieved outstanding successes, which it did after it had been carefully screened under the umbrella protection of eight-gun fighters.' And he concluded: 'It would be very unwise, now, to assume that Defiant squadrons will always be employed under such favourable conditions now that the enemy can send a strong fighter patrol over our territory. In fact, I would go so far as to say that the Defiants should be developing tactics which did not rely on the protection of eight-gun fighter squadrons.'

This was indeed a serious attack on the combat effectiveness of the Defiant, and the brave aircrew who flew them, by the man in charge of Fighter Command's No. 11 group, which was about to fight the Battle of Britain. It was also a tactical misjudgment as the Defiant had showed that it fought best in concert with eight-gun Spitfires and Hurricanes.

Park's destructive critique of the Defiant was not matched by the reality of the combat and the tactics employed by Fighter Command over Dunkirk. No. 264 often found themselves engaging large groups of German fighters on their own, and Hunter had complained at least once that the Spitfires and Hurricanes were only conspicuous by their absence once the fighting got going. No. 264 shot down just as many fighters as they did 'soft' targets like the slower and more vulnerable Stukas. And when they did confront large *schwärmes* of Me 109s they acquitted themselves no worse than the Hurricanes, often shooting down more of the enemy. Nor is there any evidence to support the suggestion that Hunter asked to be taken out of the front line. Indeed the duration of 264 Squadron's combat operations in Holland and France was longer than any other squadron.

But Park's memo left a serious question mark hanging over the Defiant just as the Luftwaffe was about to launch its air assault on Britain.

Across the channel the Germans were preparing an invasion taskforce of naval ships, troop ships and barges. Before the invasion fleet could set sail the Luftwaffe would need total air superiority. Dowding was determined not to let that happen. To do so he could call upon the greatest air defence system the world had ever seen.

On 3 July Dowding ordered a meeting of his commanders at Bentley Priory to discuss the coming battle and how best to marshall his squadrons.[46] Confronting the Nazi invaders, Fighter Command could call upon forty-two squadrons of Spitfires and Hurricanes and just two squadrons of Defiants.[47] The intractable hold-ups at the Boulton Paul factory meant the RAF would be without significant numbers of its only tried-and-tested bomber destroyer.

On 13 July Dowding dined with Winston Churchill at Chequers.[48] The leader of the nation and the head of Fighter Command enthusiastically discussed the relative strengths and weaknesses of the opposing air forces as well as the RAF's reliance on radar to pick up the attacking bomber formations. But Churchill also wanted to know in detail about each RAF aircraft, including the Defiant. Churchill had long believed, like Stevenson and Douglas, that conventional attacks against bombers from the rear was obsolete. Instead he maintained that 'hostile aircraft can only be engaged with certainty on parallel or near parallel courses'.[49] The successful performance of the 'new' Defiant over Dunkirk, which Churchill had lauded in a speech to Parliament on 4 June,[50] only strengthened his conviction. Dowding was once again being asked to give the Defiant its head. The Commander-in-Chief of Fighter Command had ably outmanoeuvred the Air Staff over the turret fighter but resisting the Prime Minister was out of the question.

Dowding ordered his second squadron of Boulton Paul Defiants to combat readiness.

# Chapter 12

# SLAUGHTER OF THE INNOCENTS

As Britain entered the eleventh month of the war, the government and Fighter Command remained bitterly divided about the combat effectiveness of its third fighter, the Boulton Paul Defiant. The Air Ministry still believed it had a role as a front-line fighter, while Dowding regarded the aircraft much more as the last reserve to face the German bombers after they had crossed British shores.

However, the growing number and scale of attacks being mounted by the Luftwaffe and the prospect of an imminent invasion meant the RAF could ill afford to have one of its fighters, especially one which had already shown considerable promise, sitting out the battle. If there was even the slenderest chance that the Defiant could help bring about victory in the air then it had to be taken. So the pragmatic Dowding agreed to commit to the fight a second squadron of Defiants.

RAF Turnhouse in southern Scotland was more than 400 miles from the English home counties which were to be the backdrop of the Battle of Britain. But the Edinburgh aerodrome was by no means a fighter station backwater. In the weeks after the declaration of war, Hitler and his military commanders had selected this part of the country to test Britain's resolve by sending small groups of bombers to probe the RAF's aerial defences. And it was a Spitfire of No. 603 (City of Edinburgh) Squadron which claimed the first Luftwaffe bomber to be shot down over the British mainland on 16 October 1939.[1] To counter the threat the Air Ministry made Turnhouse a key sector station, equipping it with three concrete runways. Today a Spitfire still stands as gate guard to Turnhouse's successor, Edinburgh Airport.

It was here in October 1939 that Fighter Command chose to bring to readiness a second squadron of Defiants to confront the unescorted Nazi bombers. Yet by the end of June 1940 it was apparent to both the station commander and the crews that the unit was still far from ready for full combat operations. The same shortages and deficiencies which had afflicted No. 264's preparations were also curtailing the progress of 141. Production hold-ups at the Boulton Paul factory in Wolverhampton meant the squadron only had fourteen of its full twenty-four Defiant complement. Some of the pilots and gunners were forced to complete their training on substitute Blenheims and Fairey Battles, undertaking low-flying patrols off the east coast of Scotland. Fighter Command's attention was still firmly fixed on its Hurricane and Spitfire squadrons which were to form the backbone of the country's aerial defences. As a consequence the Defiants were neither given the direction nor equipment they needed. Instead 141 Squadron pilots were left to endlessly practise the attack tactics which had been hard won by Hunter and his crews during the aircraft's first combat missions in May over Holland and France.[2]

By the middle of June not one of the No. 141 pilots had laid eyes on an enemy fighter. The situation had become so desperate that on 19 June Flt Lt Malcolm Loudon and PO Eric Farnes flew down to Farnborough in Hampshire to inspect a crashed Me 109.

Any operational experience under real combat conditions, no matter how slight, was now considered vital for the untested squadron.

Just after 1 p.m. on 3 July one section of Defiants was ordered into the air to intercept an enemy fighter bomber. It was to be the first time the squadron sighted the Luftwaffe.[3] Piloting one of the scrambled Defiants was PO Ian Donald with PO Arthur 'Arch' Hamilton as his gunner – two men from very different backgrounds who had formed a strong bond. Donald, aged twenty-two, was born in Surrey, the son of Air Marshal Sir Grahame Donald, in 1940 the Director of Organisation at the Air Ministry who had won fame in the First World War after miraculously surviving a 6000-foot fall from a Sopwith Camel. Donald like his father was educated at the prestigious public school Dulwich College and entered RAF College Cranwell in January 1936 as an Honorary King's Cadet. After graduation, Donald joined 64 Squadron at Church Fenton. During the 1938 Air Exercises he piloted one of a formation of 64 Squadron Hawker Demons caught in a dense fog which descended suddenly over a wide area of England on 7 August. The conditions made it impossible for the aircraft to land safely so they were routed over RAF Digby, Lincolnshire, where all pilots and air gunners were ordered to bail out, leaving their Demons to crash to the ground. It was an act of RAF incompetence that the young pilot would never forget.

Donald joined 141 Squadron when it was reformed at Turnhouse with Defiants on 4 October 1939. On 29 November he was promoted to acting flight lieutenant and then flight commander.

His gunner, Arthur Hamilton,[4] twenty-eight, educated at the local state school in Harrow, Middlesex, had only joined the RAF in March 1940 as a direct-entry air gunner and, after training, was posted to 141 Squadron in May. Yet in just a few weeks together the two men had formed a close friendship and Hamilton had invited Donald to his impending nuptials which were due to take place on 19 July.[5] Sadly it was a date that would be remembered for other reasons.

As their patrol headed out to sea, the Defiants located the German aircraft and managed to give chase for ten minutes, but the British fighters were too slow and the German raider escaped across the North Sea. The pilots and gunners of 141 Squadron spent the remainder of their days at Turnhouse rehearsing formation flying and patterns of attack for taking on enemy bombers.

On 4 July Squadron Leader William 'Dickie' Richardson took B flight to Prestwick to carry out convoy patrols. The rest of the squadron continued with fighter attack practice. Later that day they were joined by a Hurricane which took on the role of a German fighter, giving the Defiants an opportunity to perform evasive combat drills. The squadron's resources were slightly eased on 7 July when Sgt Peter Dale returned from RAF Duxford with a newly operational Defiant. At the same time a new air gunner, PO James Ritchie, also joined the squadron. While it would soon become apparent that the RAF had too few fully trained pilots there was no shortage of air gunners. Robert McGugan was one of them. He had joined the RAFVR in March 1939 and at the outbreak of hostilities was sent to the Bombing and Gunnery School at Aldergrove, Northern Ireland, before being posted to 141. 'Fighter combat,' recalled McGugan in 1988, 'had become a very regimented thing.

There were a number of attacks which you practised approaching the target from different directions. You cut across in front of the targets so the guns could be brought to bear.'[6] During those early summer days when the squadron was preparing for battle, McGugan said he couldn't recall any of the aircrew complaining about the performance of the Defiant. 'At Turnhouse we practised combats with Spitfires and Hurricanes – we didn't win but we didn't lose ignominiously . . .'

At just twenty years old McGugan was considered the squadron's schoolboy and he remembered 'very few people who served were younger'. Explaining how he viewed the approaching air battles, he candidly remarked: 'I really didn't care if I died or not. I was very immature, a late developer. My morale never seemed to take a tumble. I was cocky and naive.'

No. 141 pilots were just as gung-ho – and accident prone. On 4 July PO Russell Orchard smashed his Defiant into a stationary aircraft injuring himself and his gunner, PO Frank Lanning. Orchard had a reputation for pranging planes. In April he had crashed a Blenheim into the side of a hill at Kippen, west of Stirling, fracturing his skull and injuring two other aircrew.[7]

But accidents were not unusual. Two thirds of Defiant losses during the first two years of the war were caused by pilot error or mechanical failure[8] unrelated to enemy action. Only thirty-seven were actually shot down by the Germans.[9] Orchard[10] and Lanning were treated for their injuries at the airfield hospital. And as the two pilots lay in bed cursing their bad luck they could not have known how fortuitous their incapacitation would turn out to be.

In the first weeks of July the Luftwaffe had largely restricted its efforts to convoy attacks and marauding sweeps across the south of England. Hermann Göring's intention was to lure the RAF fighters into the English skies so that his *schwärmes* of Messerschmitts, which lay in wait at high altitude, could deal a decisive blow to the British fighter forces. Dowding's unwillingness to take the bait and commit his Spitfires and Hurricanes to dogfights with the 109s had helped convince Göring and his all-conquering fighter commanders, who didn't really need much convincing, that the RAF lacked sufficient aircraft to resist the mighty Luftwaffe. However, the first days of July were still worrying ones for Dowding. The superiority of the enemy in numbers of aircraft and personnel meant the RAF pilots would each have to shoot down two opponents. Yet the early skirmishes showed that Fighter Command was barely maintaining equilibrium with the enemy.

Britain feared the worst and the military top brass started making preparations to destroy the Germans on the landing beaches or draw them into fire-traps further inland. Churchill, who had determinedly rebuffed all calls to negotiate with Hitler, knew Britain was facing its gravest hour.

Only Dowding's fighter squadrons stood in Hitler's way. The Air Chief Marshal would need every weapon at his disposal if he was going to succeed in throwing back the Luftwaffe across the Channel. And as he counted the RAF's mounting losses he considered what so many had urged him to do for so long – send for the Defiants.

Keith Park still had deep reservations about the aircraft, believing its initial success had been almost cancelled out by its vulnerability to the much faster German fighters. The Air Ministry triumvirate of Sholto Douglas, Bennett Melvill Jones and Donald Stevenson continued to lobby Dowding with a much more optimistic interpretation of the aircraft's fighting capabilities. They argued that the Defiant had not been given the chance to do the job for which it was intended – shooting down large formations of slower German bombers flying over home territory.

On 9 July (one day before the official starting date of the Battle of Britain) No. 141 was ordered to move down from its base in Scotland to Biggin Hill – the same RAF station where the squadron had last flown its fighters in anger against the German Gothas in 1918. There were local reports that the squadron's new Defiants proudly sported the 'cock' on the side of the aircraft in honour of their victory at the inter-squadron fighter competition just before the end of the last war. But these turned out to be a myth.

The transfer of even a single squadron was a mammoth logistical task. A special train was laid on for 147 airmen, three officers and all their belongings, leaving the nearby Corstorphine station at just after 7.30 p.m. The maintenance ground crews and their equipment travelled separately in two transport planes – a twin-engined Bristol Bombay and the cumbersome Handley Page Hannibal, a large civil passenger biplane which had been requisitioned by the RAF. Five of the pilots chose to drive to Biggin Hill in their own cars while the remaining pilots flew their Defiants to the Kent airfield, arriving in the early evening. From Biggin Hill the squadron decamped 10 miles further south to West Malling, which was to be their operational airfield during the Battle of Britain.

No. 141's Squadron leader, 'Dickie' Richardson, didn't join his unit until much later that evening. He had been ordered to attend a Fighter Command conference at Northolt where he was to report on his squadron's readiness. Richardson was not as enamoured with the Defiant as Philip Hunter, his squadron leader counterpart at 264 Squadron. In fact there is evidence that he harboured serious doubts about the Defiant as a fighter. After giving a perfunctory report in which he declared 141 combat ready, he returned to West Malling. Yet he remained troubled about what was expected of his pilots and gunners in the coming days.

Richardson, a tough commanding officer with particularly piercing blue eyes, was one of the RAF's most experienced pilots. He had enrolled in March 1930 on a short service commission and undertook his training on Airspeed Oxfords at No. 5 Flying Training School at RAF Sealand in north-east Wales. After completing his training he was transferred to 23 Squadron at Kenley in March 1931, when he joined Douglas Bader. Two years later he was granted a permanent commission and being posted to RAF Hal Far in Malta. In 1937 he was heavily involved in the island's Anti-Aircraft Co-operation Unit. Throughout the 1930s carrier-borne aircraft deployed to Hal Far practised attacks against defended harbours and stationary ships so that Malta's Grand Harbour echoed to the drone of low-flying Swordfish performing endless torpedo runs. For an RAF pilot it offered excellent all-round experience in a variety of combat scenarios. But none of these exercises helped prepare the pilots for engagements with the faster German fighters of the day.

Richardson returned to the UK in early 1938 and on 19 March he went to RAF Hullavington as an instructor working with the Hawker Harts, the twin-seat biplane fighter. On 24 July he was promoted to the Air Staff at 13 Group headquarters at Kenton, near Newcastle upon Tyne, and placed in charge of Squadron Leader Operations.

When he was made commanding officer of the newly formed

Defiants race to engage the enemy bombers. *(RAF in Combat)*

By the summer of 1940 the Defiants were well known to the Luftwaffe fighter pilots. Josef Heinzeller, in the foreground, flying his Messerschmitt BF 109E over the Channel during the Battle of Britain. He named all his fighters 'Schnauzl' after his childhood dog, a Scottish terrier. On August 28th he claimed a Defiant kill, one of four shot down in what was to be the aircraft's last frontline daylight combat. The German 'wolf packs' waited in high altitude to pounce on the distracted RAF fighters attacking the enemy bombers below. *(ullstein bild/GRANGER )*

Charismatic fighter ace Sq Ldr Philip Hunter pictured with his 10-month old son, Nigel. Three months later Hunter was dead, missing in action chasing after Nazi bombers on August 24 1940. *(Hunter family)*

Sq Ldr William 'Dickie' Richardson, a friend of Douglas Bader who was flying with him when Bader crashed his biplane in 1931 and had both legs amputated. The brave and experienced Richardson went on to command the second Defiant squadron which was 'slaughtered' on July 19th 1940 just after the start of the Battle of Britain. *(Richardson family)*

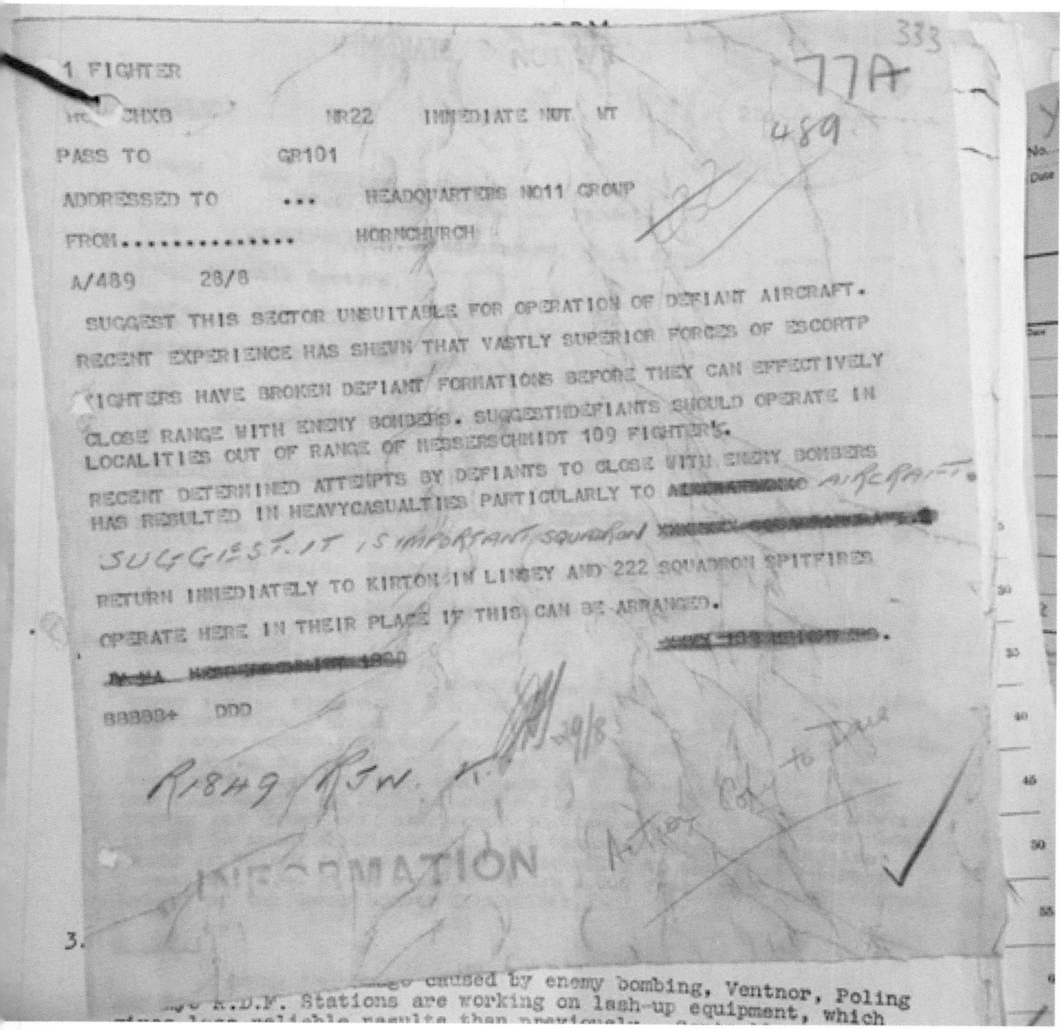

1 FIGHTER

HQ CHXB NR22 IMMEDIATE NOT WT

PASS TO GR101

ADDRESSED TO ... HEADQUARTERS NO11 GROUP

FROM............... HORNCHURCH

A/489 28/8

SUGGEST THIS SECTOR UNSUITABLE FOR OPERATION OF DEFIANT AIRCRAFT. RECENT EXPERIENCE HAS SHEWN THAT VASTLY SUPERIOR FORCES OF ESCORTP FIGHTERS HAVE BROKEN DEFIANT FORMATIONS BEFORE THEY CAN EFFECTIVELY CLOSE RANGE WITH ENEMY BOMBERS. SUGGESTHDEFIANTS SHOULD OPERATE IN LOCALITIES OUT OF RANGE OF MESSERSCHMIDT 109 FIGHTERS. RECENT DETERMINED ATTEMPTS BY DEFIANTS TO CLOSE WITH ENEMY BOMBERS HAS RESULTED IN HEAVYCASUALTIES PARTICULARLY TO AIRCRAFT. SUGGEST IT IS IMPORTANT SQUADRON RETURN IMMEDIATELY TO KIRTON-IN LINDSEY AND 222 SQUADRON SPITFIRES OPERATE HERE IN THEIR PLACE IF THIS CAN BE ARRANGED.

88888+ DDD

333

77A

489

R1849 R3W 29/8

Action Copy to Duty

INFORMATION

3. ... caused by enemy bombing, Ventnor, Poling ... R.D.F. Stations are working on lash-up equipment, which

The urgent telegram written on August 28th 1940 by the station commander of RAF Hornchurch requesting Fighter Command to withdraw 264 Squadron from the frontline after the Defiants had scored highly but suffered badly. *(National Archives, Kew)*

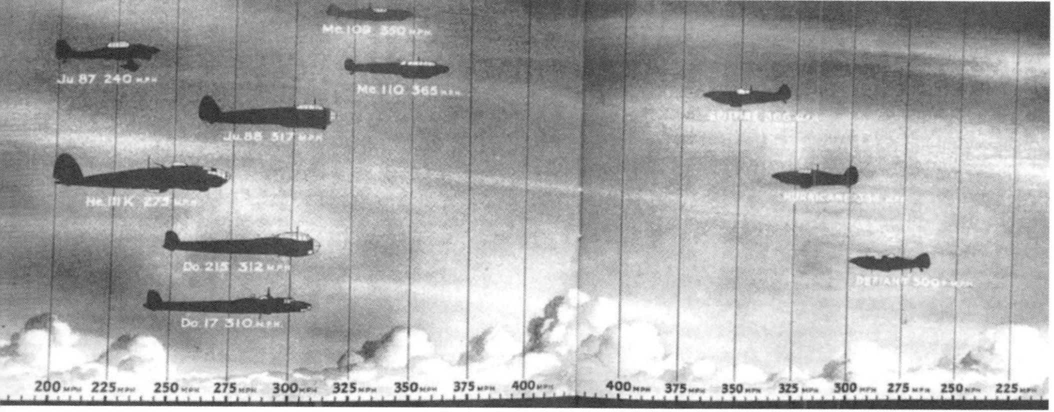


In the Air Ministry's own official report of the Battle of Britain, published shortly after the end of the battle, the Defiant was given equal billing with the Spitfire and the Hurricane. *(Ministry of Information issued on behalf of the Air Ministry 1941)*

Donald Stevenson, Director of Home Operations. He and Sholto Douglas wanted Dowding to equip a third of the RAF fighter force with Defiants. After the success of Dunkirk and the slaughter of July 19th he was told by both Defiant commanders, Sq Ldrs Hunter and Richardson, to fit the Defiant wings with forward-firing machine guns like the Hurricane and Spitfire. In the months after the Battle of Britain Stevenson won the unwelcome soubriquet 'Butcher' because of the reckless missions he ordered over France which cost the lives of many RAF aircrew. *(IWM)*

Sholto Douglas, the Deputy Chief of the Air Staff. Douglas replaced his 'adversary' Dowding as head of Fighter Command after the Battle of Britain. *(Fox Photos/Stringer/Getty Images)*

Air Vice-Marshal Sir Keith Park was unconvinced by the Defiant despite its extraordinary success at Dunkirk. Park was in charge of No11 Group during the battle. He ignored warnings that the Defiants were vulnerable to Bf 109s when they were engaging enemy bombers and he sent them up alone without the protection of Spitfires or Hurricanes. *(IWM/Getty Images)*

Air Chief Marshal Sir Hugh Dowding. The head of Fighter Command gave the Defiants their head after Dunkirk. Should the Germans have added armoured protection to the rear of their bombers Dowding saw how important it would be to have a 'broadside'-firing fighter. *(Hulton Archive/Stringer/Getty Images)*

Harold Balfour, the Under Secretary of State for Air. Balfour urged Dowding to ensure the Defiant was combat ready for the Battle of Britain. *(Hans Wild/Getty Images)*

Sir John Salmond. He headed an inquiry which found Dowding had failed to deploy enough Defiant night fighters in time for the Blitz and he wrote to Churchill asking him to remove Dowding from his post. *(ANL/Shutterstock)*

Gunnery expert Professor Sir Bennet Melvill Jones. He worked hard to develop the Defiant and convinced Dowding that it would achieve great success against German bombers.

*(© National Portrait Gallery, London)*

John D. North had designed the metal frame for the ill-fated British airship the R101 which crashed in France during its maiden overseas voyage on 5 October 1930, killing 48 of the 54 people on board. The Defiant was North's next major project and he set about acquiring the rights for a powered gun turret from the French. But North's factories at Boulton Paul couldn't keep up with demand and, according to the Air Ministry, his company had 'a genius for upsetting subcontractors'.

*(The Turret Fighters/Archives of Boulton Paul Aircraft)*

q Leader (later Group Captain) Peter Townsend (right) flew Defiants at night with 85 Squadron nd was a good friend of Philip Hunter who he described as a 'gentle parfit knight'. After the war he ecame a boyfriend of Princess Margaret. *(IWM/Getty Images)*

Vinston Churchill wrote ) Neville Chamberlain 1 1938 telling him that ne Defiant turret fighter ould be 'paramount' in ne coming battles against ne German bombers. But ord Beaverbrook, who Churchill put in charge of rcraft production in 1940, rioritised manufacturing sources for the Spitfire nd the Hurricane over the efiant. *(Keystone/Hulton Archive/ etty Images)*

Hannes Trautloft: scourge of the Defiant. He led the assault on 141 Squadron on July 19th over Folkestone which cost the lives of ten aircrew and the destruction of six out of the nine British fighters. *(akg-images/ INTERFOTO/HERMANN HISTORICA GmbH)*

PO Sydney 'Timbertoes' Carlin lost a leg fighting in the trenches in WW1 before volunteering for the RFC. He was at least 50 years old when he enlisted with 264 Squadron in 1940, the oldest RAF gunner in the Battle of Britain and probably the whole of the war. He died manning his Defiant turret defending Wittering airfield from an attack by a JU88. *(Find a grave)*

141 Squadron he was thirty-six years old, one of the oldest and most experienced squadron leaders in the RAF.

On 10 July 1940 the Luftwaffe launched its first sustained air attacks against Britain, sending large formations of bombers and fighters to attack shipping in the channel, hoping to lure the RAF into combat. That afternoon, which would turn out to be the opening salvo of the Battle of Britain, Richardson decided to make one more visit to 264 Squadron at RAF Fowlmere in Cambridge, the Duxford satellite airfield. According to Alec Bew, author of *The Turret Fighters,* the meeting did not go well. Hunter once again tried to impress upon Richardson that the only way to defend against a sustained attack of Me 109s was to organise the planes into a descending spiral which offered 360-degree cover with the rear guns. If this was done properly in tight formation, the German fighters would be unable to pick off the Defiants. But Richardson remained unconvinced. He must have known this was the same Lufbery Circle employed by the slower Fe2s, flown by my uncle in the First World War. He told Hunter that in combat conditions, and with rookie pilots, it would be impossible to maintain formation discipline. As far as Richardson was concerned the only way to properly protect the Defiant was by giving it forward-firing machine guns and bulletproof windscreens like the Hurricanes and Spitfires.[11] Nevertheless, whatever misgivings Richardson still held he was careful not to pass them on to his subordinates.

So Richardson got on with the job of preparing Fighter Command's second Defiant squadron for their first combat operation. On 13 July two 141 pilots were ferried to Duxford in a Blenheim to pick up two more Defiants which they flew down to Biggin Hill. Mechanics and armourers busied themselves with last-minute adjustments. Nine air gunners were put through their final paces, ranging and firing the .303 Browning machine guns at the towed targets flown around the Biggin Hill airfield. However, the one modification that would give the Defiants the extra speed and climb that Richardson and his pilots so desperately needed had not been completed.

No. 264's first Defiant squadron leader, Stephen Hardy, had reported to Fighter Command as long ago as April 1940 that it was essential the Defiant was fitted with a higher performance constant speed propeller.[12] Philip Hunter's own trial against an Me 109 had emphatically demonstrated its advantage over the old variable pitch propeller. The Air Ministry knew that most of the German fighters had been equipped with their own version of the constant speed propeller. Yet it wasn't until 22 June that Lord Beaverbrook instructed de Havilland to convert in the field all the remaining Spitfires, Hurricanes and Defiants. Priority was to be given to the Spitfires and then the Hurricanes. The Defiants, once again, were at the end of the queue. No. 141 Squadron's Operations Record Book shows that by 17 July just three Defiants had been fitted with the constant speed airscrew.[13]

The following day the squadron left West Malling for one of Fighter Command's most exposed front-line airfields. Hawkinge aerodrome sits on the top of an escarpment above the town of Folkestone in Kent, just 23 miles from the coast of France. During the First World War it was known as RFC Folkestone and then later RFC Hawkinge, named after the village that lies on the main road to Canterbury. The only squadron stationed there was No. 25 Squadron flying Morane-Saulnier Ls, one of the first fighters fitted with a synchronised machine gun that could fire through the front propellers.

At the outbreak of the Second World War Hawkinge had

been chosen as the liaison station between the RAF and the BEF during operations in France and the Dunkirk evacuation in May/June 1940. From here British bombers and fighters were sent to attack targets selected by the BEF commanders.

On 18 July 1940 Hawkinge was paid a great honour when it played host to a very special visitor.[14] Prince George, Duke of Kent, was the fourth son of King George V and Queen Mary. During his early life he had gained an unwanted reputation as a philandering, bisexual cocaine addict. But he also had a passion for flying, believing Britain's future lay in aviation. In 1937 he was granted a commission in the Royal Air Force as a group captain and promoted to air vice-marshal just before the start of the war. His appearance at the aerodrome, accompanied by a flight of Spitfires, caused a great stir and gave the staff and ground crew stationed there a huge fillip to morale. Although Hawkinge was a front-line airfield at battle stations its commanding officer made great efforts to lay on a first-class reception for its royal guest.

Shortly after lunch the Duke of Kent bid farewell to the senior officers, local dignitaries, airmen and ground crews.[15]

Around the time the Duke flew out of Hawkinge, twelve Defiants of 141 Squadron left West Malling for their own visit. It was the pilots' first experience of Kent's most forward air base. The aircrew would need to acclimatise quickly and get used to the geography and the idiosyncrasies of the landing field. Later that evening three Defiants were ordered on a single patrol over Folkestone. One of the pilots selected to take part was twenty-six-year-old Rudal Kidson,[16] a sheep farmer from Wellington, New Zealand. Three years earlier Kidson, bored with farming life, had joined the Auckland Aero Club and after gaining a full pilot's licence in 1938, sailed to Britain at his own expense where he applied for a short service commission. He was typical of the hundreds of Commonwealth aircrew who had answered the mother nation's call for experienced pilots to meet the Nazi threat in the spring of 1940.

Kidson was teamed up with a British air gunner from Oxford. Peter Atkins was also twenty-six and had been married for three years. After leaving school he too became a keen amateur flyer. A few weeks before the declaration of war he was called up to the RAFVR and was posted to 141 Squadron only a few days before the unit was moved down south.

A second Defiant on the patrol that day was piloted by Dick Howley, a twenty-year-old Canadian who had been sent to school in England. At seventeen he started flying lessons with the Sir Alan Cobham Flying School at Shoreham, Sussex. Like Kidson he was one of the first pilots to join the newly formed 141 Squadron in October 1939. One month afterwards he had had a miraculous escape when he crashed his Blenheim attempting a landing at RAF Sealand. Howley had only recently returned to the squadron after a few days' leave visiting his girlfriend. His family have a cherished picture of the young couple lying on a Kent lawn looking like they hadn't a care in the world. His gunner was a much older Irish-born Englishman from Hertford. Albert Curley, thirty-three, whose father served as an officer in the 6th Dragoons during the First World War, had been called up for service in May the previous year. The evening patrol turned out to be uneventful and the Defiants returned safely to Hawkinge and then flew back to West Malling in the evening.

The morning of 19 July was clear and bright. Twelve Defiants of No. 141 once again set off for Hawkinge, setting down their machines just before 10 a.m. They were joined at the airfield by a battle-hardened squadron of Hurricanes which had flown in from Croydon early the same morning. No. 111 Squadron was the first RAF squadron to be equipped with Hurricanes, which they had been flying since January 1938, already seeing action in the Battle of France and over Dunkirk. They knew the Defiants well, having flown joint missions with Hunter's 264 Squadron. The III pilots were almost exclusively public schoolboys, of whom two were the Old Etonian brothers Basil and Antony Fisher (Basil Fisher died in a dogfight a year later while his brother went on to become an adviser to Margaret Thatcher). No. 111's pilots had a fearsome reputation for flying line abreast when they attacked the German bombers, striking terror into the hearts of the Luftwaffe pilots who were sitting ducks in their glass cockpits.[17] They later reverted to a more orthodox formation when this tactic proved too costly. Flying line abreast presented their own machines as better targets for some of the seasoned German air gunners.

The previous day 111 Squadron together with 615 Squadron (also Hurricanes) had escorted a formation of eighteen Blenheims on a bombing raid which had successfully targeted the jetties and docks of Boulogne, one of the ports the Germans were planning to use for the invasion.[18] In the afternoon they had been scrambled after a Henschel 126, a German reconnaissance plane, that had been sighted near Hawkinge.

Just before 12.30 p.m. on 19 July Biggin Hill picked up reports of German raiders attacking British shipping in the channel. At about the same time Hawkinge air raid sirens were sounded to warn of approaching enemy aircraft. The Hurricanes had been sitting on the airfield since the early morning. But when the telephone rang in the Hawkinge operations room it was the Defiant squadron, none of whose pilots had experienced combat, which was ordered into the air. At the sound of the scramble bell the pilots and gunners rushed from their makeshift tents to the waiting aircraft. The aircrew were already busy starting the Rolls-Royce Merlin engines. Nine sparked into life, but two spluttered and one failed to start at all. So only nine Defiants, flying in three 'vic' sections, left Hawkinge on a flight path to intercept the German bombers believed to be heading for British ships in the Channel. They were ordered to patrol 20 miles south of Folkestone at a height of 5000 feet.

Ten minutes before the Defiants had taken off from Hawkinge, two Staffels of Me 109s, of III/JG 51, left their airfields at Wissant in northern France. Their commanding officer was Hauptmann Hannes Trautloft who, as we have learned, had been flying with the German air force since leaving school. Trautloft and his Messerschmitts had spent the last few weeks harrying the British convoys in the hope of luring the RAF into the channel skies. On 19 July the twenty to twenty-five Me 109s flying in schwärmes of four, each fighter pair protecting the other, were piloted by some of the most experienced aircrew serving with the Luftwaffe. Trautloft was twenty-eight years old and had already chalked up eight years flying and, critically, had fought in the Spanish, Polish and French campaigns where he had shot down a total of ten enemy aircraft. Accompanying him were two more fighter aces who also had enjoyed much combat success in Spain and France. Oberleutnant Arnold Lignitz and Oberleutnant Walter Oesau had also acquired reputations as 'Spitfire killers', shooting down five of the British fighters over Dunkirk in May.

Trautloft rendezvoused with a group of bombers, possibly Stukas, over St Inglevert[21] where his 109s covered the fighter bombers' low-level attacks on Allied shipping. After they had completed a bombing run on a number of trawlers Trautloft escorted the bombers safely to their airfields before leading his fighters on a sweep back across the channel in search of the RAF. They didn't have long to wait before sighting the enemy.

In the far distance, roughly 15,000 feet below, Trautloft could make out the glimmering Defiants, slowly climbing towards their vectored position above the French coast. He glanced at his watch. It was 12.43, thirteen minutes after the British squadron had set off from Hawkinge on their first combat mission. As the two groups of aircraft closed in on each other, Trautloft was sure he was looking at enemy fighters.

He wrote in his diary: 'Suddenly Lieutenant Wehnelt reported over the wireless "down below to the right civil aircraft just crossing the English coast". I looked towards the spot and located the aircraft, counting three, six, nine of them. They seemed to have only just taken off. They climbed rapidly and made a large turn towards the middle of the Channel coming straight for us. They hadn't spotted us yet and so we headed towards them out of the sun. When I was only 800m or so above their formation I noticed the aircraft had turrets behind the cockpit. The aircraft were neither Hurricane nor Spitfire. 'Defiant' suddenly went through my head – heavily armed two-seaters whose back gunner have four heavy machine guns with enormous fire power. They had obviously been sent up to attack the bombers. The enemy formation was still flying tightly together, as if on exercise, when suddenly it turned back toward England. I didn't understand at all what this manoeuvre was for.'

Trautloft checked the sky for any covering fighters and when he was sure it was clear he gave the order to attack: 'I pulled over and dived towards the rearmost Defiant with my *schwarme flieger* [flight leaders] Wenhelt, Kath and Pichon, following behind . . . I aimed for the right-hand Defiant. Suddenly all hell broke loose. The Englishmen had seen us.'

PO H. J. Smith, the Hawkinge station intelligence officer, had come out of the aerodrome flight office to witness the Defiants on their first combat mission. But as he followed the aircraft out over the Channel he could also make out the unmistakable black silhouettes of aircraft diving from the high cirrus clouds. 'I kept them in view with my binoculars and when they were about two thirds of the way across, I saw them bounced by 109s,'[19] he later recalled.

The first to realise the danger was PO Malcolm Loudon, aged twenty-four, who was leading the section behind his squadron leader. He used his radio to try to alert the other Defiants but the Messerschmitts had achieved almost complete surprise and there was little time for the British to react. Even so the gunners still managed to pelt the diving German fighters with some machine gun fire.

Trautloft recalled: 'Defensive fire from a number of turrets flew towards me, fireworks all over the place. I could see the bullets passing by on either side and I felt hits on my machine but pressed on with my attack. 200m, 100m – now was the time to fire, my machine guns and cannon hammered away. The first volley was too high, but the second was right in the middle of the fuselage and parts of the Defiant broke loose and flashed past me. I saw a thin smoke trail appear below the fuselage and suddenly the aircraft exploded in a huge red ball of flames which fell towards the sea. I gained speed in my dive and used it to curve into the attack again to the right. While in the turn I saw another Defiant going down behind me and to my left. By this time all my pilots were attacking.'[22]

PO Ian MacDougall,[23] a privately educated Scot from Crieff, had just turned twenty and was one of the original members of the reformed No. 141 Squadron. When the Defiants received the order to scramble, a few minutes earlier, MacDougall assumed Yellow 2's position after the pilot reported engine trouble and was unable to take off. He recorded the initial moments of the attack in his combat report: 'I never saw any of the enemy aircraft at all, during the first two attacks, but bullets were being fired at me from all angles. After the third attack my engine cut and, believing I had been shot down, ordered the air gunner to jump. But as I got no answer I assumed he was killed.'[24]

With the sun behind them the attacking 109s had caught the Defiants napping. No. 141 Squadron Leader Richardson immediately turned to port, completing a steep turn of 360 degrees. But this proved no defence against the German machines which were now attacking Richardson from below. It was only when the squadron leader, making use of all his aerobatic experience, turned his Defiant towards the attack that he was able to offer any resistance.

But the onslaught was relentless. Loudon's Defiant was caught in the crossfire of two 109s. His gunner, PO Eric Farnes, got in three bursts before bailing out. Loudon bravely grappled for control of his badly damaged machine hoping to get clear of his tormentors.

The next to fall was the Defiant piloted by Rudal Kidson. Bullets and cannon fire had torn into Kidson's engine, sending the aircraft plummeting to sea. Neither Kidson nor his gunner Peter Atkins stood a chance. Kidson and the lost Defiant were never seen again, but Atkins' body was washed up on the French coast and buried in Boulogne's southern cemetery.[25]

The same fate befell another New Zealander, John Kemp, twenty-five, and his British gunner Sgt Robert Crombie, twenty-nine, from Lightwater, Surrey. Crombie had only joined the RAF in September the previous year. Both men were killed instantaneously when their Defiant crashed into the sea, their bodies never found. Their Defiant, serial no L6974, was the same aircraft flown by PO Desmond Kay of 264 Squadron on 13 May and the only one of the six Defiants to get back safely to England after that day's action.

The third Kiwi-piloted Defiant to be hit was flown by PO John Gard'ner: 'My impression was suddenly thud, thud, thudding on the aircraft, which I think probably was my gunner getting a few shots in, but it had coincided with white streaks going under my armpits and out through the front of the aeroplane, a terrible smell of cordite and the cockpit full of smoky stuff. I peeled off rapidly and I went down very, very fast, thinking is that chap still sitting on my tail? I couldn't get any response from my gunner behind me. After the first rush in, as it were, it's bedlam. Nobody knows where anybody is.'[26]

Although Gard'ner's machine had been badly mauled it had not burst into flames like the other three Defiants and he managed to pull off a crash-landing on the sea. The Kiwi pilot, who had temporarily blacked out, struggled to escape from his cockpit as the plane sank into the choppy waters of the Channel: 'I kicked my way out and got myself to the surface just about bursting,' he later recalled. When a Royal Navy torpedo boat approached, his first concern was that they had mistaken him for a Luftwaffe pilot: 'Maybe they thought I was a Kraut but, God bless them, they shouted "We gotcha, we gotcha. Are you all right?" I don't remember much more after that.'[27]

The body of his gunner, PO Dudley Malins Slatter, aged

twenty-six, from Southsea, Hampshire was never found. Slatter had joined the RAF in September 1935 as an aircrafthand. After the outbreak of war he remustered as an air gunner, completed his training, and was posted as a sergeant with No. 141 in June 1940. He had only won his commission on 3 July, sixteen days before his death. Gard'ner believes Slatter was unable to get out of the stricken plane and drowned in his turret.

From his vantage point at the far southern end of Hawkinge aerodrome, PO Smith had witnessed the whole attack. He somberly wrote in his diary: 'They had absolutely no chance against the German fighters and I watched horrified as they were picked off one by one and I saw the spouts of water as they plunged into the sea.' In just five minutes four of the Defiants had crashed into the sea and three others, badly damaged, were desperately trying to get back to base. Only the Defiants piloted by Richardson and Tamblyn were left in the fight. But they now faced impossible odds.

Richardson's combat report read: 'After five minutes Red 2 [Tamblyn] and myself Red 1 were the only two Defiants left, so I decided to break off the combat and returned to base.' Even so both gunners managed to return enough fire to claim one German fighter each. Richardson's gunner PO Anthony Halliwell said in his report, recorded shortly after the attack: 'Me 109s came down out of the sun. As they came in to deliver their attack, I had one in sights until well within range and opened fire whilst still astern. Tracer bullets were seen to hit enemy aircraft which dived down and disappeared into the sea leaving a large round patch of oil and foam.'

Tamblyn's gunner Sydney Powell claimed the second kill. But Trautloft and his 109s could smell blood and pressed home their attack, chasing down the slower, retreating Defiants who were making for the safety of the Kent cliffs.

At Hawkinge the full horror of what was unfolding out to sea had sent panic waves through the aerodrome. The shaken station commander immediately ordered the Hurricanes of 111 Squadron to the Defiants' rescue. Now the race was on to see whether the Hurricanes could reach the fleeing Defiants before the 109s finished them off.

According to the combat reports, the Hurricanes sighted the German fighters at 12.40 p.m. Green section leader Flt Lt Stanley Connors immediately began an attack on a 109 which he shot down in flames. He then made a further attack on another which was carried on by PO Jack Copeman (Green 2) who chased it for five minutes towards France. PO Peter Simpson fired his machine guns into another 109 which Green 1 confirmed had crashed into the sea.

The arrival of 111 had come in the nick of time. Loudon struggled home with his Defiant ablaze and crashed in Hawkinge village, a few hundred yards from the aerodrome. He was taken to Canterbury hospital where five bullets were removed from his arm. His gunner PO Eric Farnes had bailed out after their Defiant was hit but was safely picked up by a British destroyer. The Defiant was a write-off, but miraculously both aircrew survived. Although the medical report said Loudon was suffering from considerable combat shock.[28]

Meanwhile Ian McDougall had managed to regain control of his Defiant after the Merlin engine had spluttered back into life. He successfully landed at Hawkinge. But when he checked the turret there was no sign of his gunner, Sgt John Wise, who had bailed out during the attack and was never seen again[29].

The Defiants of Richardson and Tamblyn were the only two

to return to Hawkinge with both crew alive. It seems they may have been saved by the intervention of one of the Battle of Britain's best-known fighter aces.

South African born Adolph 'Sailor' Malan, who went on to chalk up twenty-seven kills, and PO Peter Stevenson of 74 Squadron had been patrolling in their Spitfires when they were vectored to the battle which had now moved towards Dover.

Stevenson was the son of the head of Home Defence, Donald Stevenson, who had been so instrumental in bringing the Defiants into the Battle of Britain. Stevenson Junior had flown Spitfires during Dunkirk where he had a share of a Ju 88 and a 'probable' 109. More recently on 8 July Stevenson destroyed a Me 109 and two days later claimed another 'probable' and two Me 110s. On 12 July he shared a He 111.

When the two Spitfires appeared Tamblyn's Defiant was being chased over the famous white cliffs by two 109s. Malan and Stevenson arrived just in time to intercept the German fighters, both claiming a 'probable' kill.[30] The Spitfires were too late to help Flt Lt Ian Donald who had managed to steer his blazing machine over the top of Dover's cliffs. But the Defiant was struggling for height and four miles from Hawkinge the engine failed and the aircraft dived into the side of a hill, killing Donald. His gunner, PO 'Arch' Hamilton, was reported missing.[31]

The Hurricanes of 111 had managed to scatter the remaining German fighters who were now heading back to the safety of their French airfields, hotly pursued by some of the British fighters.

Trautloft, had sustained damage to his radiator from the Defiant machine guns and Oberleutnant Kath, his adjutant, had also been hit. Now the hunters became the hunted.

Leading the chase was PO Copeman who carried on the pursuit right to the French coast: 'I waited until my section leader broke away, and then attacked a Me 109 from astern at 250 closing to 150 yards. I fired 800 rounds into him and saw both wings smoking, and he was obviously seriously damaged.' But by now Copeman had lost contact with the rest of his section and so before he reached French territory he broke off and returned to base.[32]

Trautloft wrote in his diary of his desperate race to get his crippled Messerschmitt back to base: 'Suddenly my engine began to run unevenly. I could smell burning oil in the cockpit and my coolant temperature indicated 120 degrees with the oil temperature also rising steadily. For the first time I noticed several hits on my left wing and a trail of smoke beneath it. I felt uneasy – I didn't want to bail out in the middle of the channel. Then Kath appeared on my left. His aircraft was also trailing smoke. "I've got to make an emergency landing," he told me over the WT and like me headed towards the French coast. It is a damned uneasy feeling flying so low over the sea in a shot-up crate, all the more worrying when one's flying height was diminishing steadily and all the while the coast didn't seem to be getting any closer. Luckily there weren't any enemy Fighters about or we would have been easy meat. At last there was land below us and I scraped over Cap Blanc Nez at 200 metres, finally landing at the airstrip of St Inglevert with my prop feathered. I didn't know where Kath had gone. I had my hands full during the forced landing and hadn't been able to follow his progress. During the flight back I'd heard the voices of my pilots over the WT, "I'm attacking", "Abschuss" and then I heard "achtung Spitfires". It was obvious from that that English Fighters had joined in the battle.'[33]

Five of No. 111's Hurricanes landed at Hawkinge at 13.25–13.30 hours and the remaining seven aircraft touched down at their home base at Croydon twenty minutes later. They had sustained no losses and claimed two Me 109s. The only reported damage was to Green 3 whose Hurricane was 'covered with oil from enemy aircraft'.

No. 141's Operations Record Book[34] made less happy reading: 'Six of our aircraft are shot down or disabled, four dived into the sea. POs Kemp, Kidson, Howley are presumed lost. Five air gunners are also presumed lost. Flt Lt Donald crashed at Dover and was killed, his air gunner PO Hamilton who bailed out is missing.' In fact, Hamilton had not left the aircraft. It took a day of digging out the crash site before the recovery crews found Hamilton's body still inside the turret.[35]

The report records that the three surviving Defiants landed at Hawkinge at 1 p.m. – only half an hour after they were scrambled. It also says that the squadron shot down four Messerschmitts, a figure which is confirmed in 111's own Operations Record Book: 'The [German] formation attacked were attacking a squadron of Defiants of 141 Squadron when 111 made their interception. Ten aircraft in all were seen to fall into the sea by Green 1 but out of them four were probably Defiants.'[36] In this account six enemy aircraft were shot down, two by the Hurricanes and four by the Defiants.

Luftwaffe records do not support such a high number of losses. In fact their own records confirm just three 109s badly hit, Trautloft and Kath got home safely but one of the other pilots died of his wounds the next day. The Germans claimed to have shot down eleven Defiants, although of course there were only nine in the air. Lignitz, who sent at least one of the

Defiants into the sea, returned later that day to add a Spitfire to his tally. Walter 'Gulle' Oesau claimed another and also returned to shoot down a Hurricane in the afternoon.

Trautloft's escape may have been a blessing in disguise. He rose through the ranks of the Luftwaffe and was later appointed Inspekteur der Tagjäger, giving him overall responsibilities for all day-fighters. In 1944 he discovered that a number of RAF pilots were being held at Buchenwald concentration camp where orders had been given for their execution. Seven days before the scheduled execution Trautloft, overruling SS officers at the camp, arranged for the Allied prisoner aircrew to be transferred to the safety of a German military prisoner of war camp.

Fighter Command's operations diary for 19 July simply read: 'A force of between 20 to 30 enemy aircraft appeared in the Gris Nez/Calais area at 12.05 hours and proceeded to Dover where an attack developed. Nine dive bombers were reported in action among them and the only news up to 1300 hours is of four of our own fighters down in the sea. SOS action taken.'[37]

The Defiants of 141 Squadron were not the only RAF losses that day.

Among the confirmed kills for that day was a Spitfire from 43 Squadron Tangmere, shot down by a 109 over Selsey Bill. The British casualties followed the loss of three Blenheims and a Spitfire the day before. The cumulative effect on both RAF resources and morale had taken a heavy toll. The 19 July was the greatest loss of life to a fighter squadron since the start of the Battle of Britain. Fighter Command's intelligence log for the day made depressing reading: 'At this time the favourable ratio of the enemy defeats to ours was not being maintained.'[38]

The Air Ministry immediately imposed a media blackout preventing any reporting of the fate of 141[39] Squadron. Dowding quietly ordered the Defiants, who were no longer a fighting force, out of the front line to Prestwick in Scotland. Squadron Leader Richardson was told to urgently report to RAF Northolt, 11 Group Headquarters, 'for a conference.'[40] It was Richardson's thirty-seventh birthday and he knew he was lucky to be alive. For the family of Arthur Hamilton the loss was particularly devastating. The young pilot was to be married that day and his fiancée, Mira Gregory, and family were waiting for him at the local church. A member of the squadron had to drive to the church to inform the families that 'Arch' was missing in action.

There is no official record of what was discussed at RAF Northolt about the day's terrible losses. Indeed there is a paucity of documents relating to the aftermath of the events of 19 July 1940. No. 141 Squadron's archivist was Don F. Aris, an armourer with the squadron during the last three years of the war who prepared aircraft for the ill-fated Raid on Dieppe mission at RAF Ford, Sussex, in August 1942. In his introduction to the archives held at the Imperial War Museum he says: 'The early entries in the Operations Record Books of the squadron are not so complete as they are after 1942. Whether this is due to an official direction at the time or by a change of adjutant is not known.'[41] There are also inconsistencies in the official accounts of the squadrons which took off from Hawkinge that day. The most glaring is the recorded time of 12.20 that the Hurricanes were reported to have been scrambled from Hawkinge to go to the assistance of the Defiants. This was ten minutes before the Defiants took off.

Whatever the record does or doesn't say there is no argument that 19 July represented a disastrous setback for Fighter Command and its third front-line fighter. The death of ten airmen was to be the heaviest loss of life for a single engagement in the Battle of Britain. Dowding and his commanders would have to endure worse days before they could eventually claim victory against the Luftwaffe. But nine days after the start of the Battle of Britain the prospect of defeat looked much more likely. That evening Dowding wrote to Harold Balfour, the Under Secretary of State for Air, warning him that his squadrons were in danger of being 'overwhelmed in the Channel.'[42]

Adolf Hitler also chose 19 July to make one final plea to the British to sue for peace. As he drove to the Reichstag to make his famous speech, the German leader was updated on the air campaign against the RAF and may well have been furnished with details of that day's combat reports, including the 'eleven' Defiants shot down over the Channel. Hitler must have believed himself to be in a strong negotiating position.

In a rousing address Hitler warned the British that unless they listened to reason and 'avert destruction of a great world empire' they would face the overwhelming forces at the command of the Axis powers. 'In this hour and before this body,' the Führer told the Reichstag audience in the presence of Italian Foreign Minister Count Galeazzo Ciano, 'I feel myself obliged to make one more appeal to reason to England.' Hitler warned against interpreting his appeal as weakness and said that 'Churchill may parry my words with the claim that I feel doubt or fear, but in any case I will have my knowledge that I acted rightly, according to my conscience.'[43]

Back at Biggin Hill, 141 Squadron began the cumbersome

business of transporting 150 men, aeroplanes and equipment back to Scotland. Thirteen of the surviving Defiants and one Blenheim reached Prestwick on the evening of 21 July. The squadron's equipment and the bulk of the aircrew travelled by train, van and cargo aircraft, arriving a few hours after the Defiants. However, the loss of four pilots and six gunners left the squadron badly depleted of qualified flying crew. So much so that five more Defiants had to be left behind at Biggin Hill. A rear-guard party of two NCOs and seven airmen were left behind in charge of the remaining aircraft.

At West Malling the task of settling the dead officers' mess bills was given to PO Denis Passadoro, the squadron's intelligence officer. He also represented the squadron at the funeral of PO Arthur Hamilton, the only one of the ten dead aircrew to be buried at Hawkinge. The remains of Hamilton's pilot and friend Flt Lt Donald were sent home to Tilford in Surrey. Both men's funerals took place on 21 July, 100 miles apart. PO Denis Passadoro was one of the lucky ones to have survived 19 July and was later promoted to flight lieutenant. But less than two years later he was dead, fighting in north Africa.[44] Flt Lt Passadoro perished with a number of other officers from 117 Squadron when their Hudson aircraft crashed on take-off just outside Tobruk, where he and the other men are buried.

The air battle of 19 July which pitted the Defiants of the RAF against the German air force's most advanced fighter has been characterised as the tragic failure of a British aircraft design that was more suited to the aerial conflict of the First World War.

But that only tells half the story. Serious questions remain unanswered about why the Defiants were sent unescorted into battle when it was clear by this stage of the war that they needed fighter protection. Park had said so in his memo to Dowding one month before. Of more baffling concern is why a battle-tested squadron of Hurricanes, waiting at Hawkinge, was not scrambled in place of the Defiants or, alternatively, given the job of escorting the Defiants on the mission. That 111's Hurricanes were allowed to sit idly by meant the Defiants of 141 were effectively sent to their deaths. One reason might be that Fighter Command had been unable to solve the Defiant's faulty radio communications. If so, Keith Park might have been reluctant to provide 141 with a protective Hurricane squadron with which 141 could not make radio contact. Battle of Britain history books have called the mismatched encounter between the British and German planes the 'slaughter of the innocents'. Although the pilots and gunners flying the Defiants had chalked up more flying hours than many other squadrons none of those hours included any combat experience. Conversely the German pilots were battle-hardened aces, many of whom went on to survive the war. Hannes Trautloft flew a total of 560 combat sorties and was credited with fifty-eight victories.

For Robert McGugan 19 July turned out to be the luckiest day of his life, which he remembered in an interview forty-eight years later: 'It was the first day that I hadn't been on watch. We had too many air gunners. I would have been flying with Jack Kemp who was shot down and I often wondered if the situation would have been different if I had been up there?' McGugan blames the tactics deployed that day for the heavy loss of life, insisting that the same fate would have befallen a squadron of Hurricanes or Spitfires encountering such a superior number of German fighters diving from higher altitude out of the sun: 'Flying at between 5000 and 10,000 feet was not ideal for any aircraft,' he said. 'It would have been just as easy to shoot down Hurricanes or Spitfires.'

Many believe that by mid-July the Germans had worked out the weakness of the Defiant, specifically that it was defenceless against frontal attacks. But there isn't any hard evidence that Trautloft's Messerschmitts had deployed tactics to avoid the Browning machine guns by launching head-on attacks. In fact Trautloft describes how he flew into a hail of .303 bullets which damaged his fighter. The accounts of gunners Helliwell and Powell also show that the Defiants had clear arcs of fire until they were overwhelmed by the larger number of attacking Messerschmitts.

Even after the battle and tragic loss of life the Defiant aircrew did not criticise their aircraft. McGugan says that while pilots may have wanted more firepower in the front wings, the air gunners 'thought it [the Defiant] was the greatest plane ever'. He also questions Richardson's leadership and suggests that it was significant that he was transferred from 141 Squadron before the end of the Battle of Britain. But such an accusation is not borne out by the records.

The following day, 20 July, Richardson and Tamblyn were both recommended for promotion and continued to bravely serve with the squadron for many more weeks. Dowding later gave Richardson the job of preparing for combat 303 Squadron, the famous Polish Hurricane unit which shot down more enemy aircraft than any other Hurricane squadron during the Battle of Britain. Throughout the war Richardson commanded a number of stations, including Hawkinge, and flew sorties in every fighter type which saw service with the RAF. Towards the end of the war he was made RAF liaison officer to Field Marshal

Bernard Montgomery in the Middle East. He retired from the RAF as an Air Commodore in 1958 but five years later suffered a stroke in his garden. He was rushed to the Atkinson Morley Hospital in London where he died whilst being operated on. His family believe he suffered from an undiagnosed weakened vascular system caused by the enormous strain placed on the body by the G-forces which WW2 fighter pilots had to endure during combat missions. Richardson never talked to his family about his war record. His daughter Meg believes he was terribly affected by the loss of life and the burns suffered by many of the survivors. But his son John remembers secretly listening to his father and his old RAF pals reminiscing about their flying exploits whenever they came to visit. The family met Douglas Bader at an England rugby match at Twickenham just a few weeks before he died. 'He told us that he fondly remembered his friend Dickie and the "slaughter of the innocents",'[45] said John Richardson. The 19 July debacle did not end the Defiant's contribution to the Battle of Britain. In the coming weeks, as the air situation became more and more critical, the pilots and gunners of 264 Squadron would once again have to prove themselves and their fighter.

# Chapter 13

# DEATH OF A HERO

HUGH DOWDING WAS hosting Winston Churchill at Fighter Command headquarters Bentley Priory when he received the grave news about the losses suffered by 141 Squadron. The Prime Minister appeared to take the death of ten aircrew in his stride, and made a remark which indicated he had dispassionately accepted the casualties in terms of the ebb and flow of the fortunes of war. 'That may be so,' replied Dowding, 'but what I am conscious of is that so many of my men have died.'[1]

The same afternoon, Philip Hunter's Defiants were flying patrols over the North Sea protecting British convoys.[2] When they heard of the tragic fate of their sister squadron they were shaken to the core. The loss of half a squadron in a single mission was a serious blow to the morale of all the 264 crews who were still engaged in combat sorties.

For the leaders of Fighter Command it was the kind of tragedy they had feared ever since they agreed to bring the Defiants into the front line. On 23 July it was decided to move Hunter and his men out of harm's way and transfer them to Kirton-in-Lindsay in Lincolnshire where the squadron's former commanding officer, Stephen Hardy, was station commander.[3]

For Hunter the tragedy of 141 only served to stiffen his resolve and prove to Fighter Command that the Defiant deserved its place in the front line. Four days later Hunter and Flt Lt Robert Ash flew to Farnborough to inspect a captured Me 110. Hunter was no more impressed with Germany's Zerstörer (destroyer) on the ground than he had been in the air. However, a genuinely impressive sight greeted the squadron later that month when a fifty-year-old bemedalled airman turned up at the aerodrome claiming he had been posted to 264 for active service. Sydney Carlin, who we encountered at the beginning of the Defiant story flying fighters in the first war, hated missing out on a good fight. In June 1940 the disabled flyer made his way back to Hull from Kenya via a stopover in Malta, just in time for the start of the summer's epic air battle. In Africa he had become close friends with the much younger Squadron Leader Percy Pickard and kept in contact with him when Pickard returned to the UK in 1936 to join the RAF.

With Pickard's help, and some economies of the truth about his real age, Carlin reported to the Air Armaments School at Manby, near Louth in Lincolnshire. The adjutant doubted his sanity in throwing away rank to become a flying officer air gunner but he didn't stand in his way.

Jim Bailey fondly recalled Carlin's arrival at the aerodrome in Lincolnshire: 'About this time we received a small sunburnt gunner, who had a wooden leg and a long history. His proper name was Sid Carlin, but he was known to us all as "Timbertoes". If I remember rightly he was an infantryman in 1914 . . . Anyhow, he passed the inter-war years sailing an Arab dhow along the east coast of Africa. With the resumption of the war, he joined up again; and here he was with us in that noble and dangerous position of a junior air gunner.

His DFC, we were amused to notice, began his second row of medals.[4]

Bailey and the rest of the aircrews also discovered that its latest recruit was no slouch on the dance floor: 'About this time we spent an evening in the officers' club at Grimsby, where a few local popsies were present. By midnight, all, save Timbertoes, had flagged. As he hobbled past one of us he whispered: "I'm dancing with my first white woman for eighteen years".' Fraternising with members of the opposite sex was considered an important part of life for the young RAF pilots and gunners. Indeed one Defiant pilot wrote of his sister complaining that he needed regular 'horizontal refreshment' to retain his 'mental and physical equilibrium'.[5]

Among the other new recruits to join 264 was Frederick 'Freddie' Sutton, twenty-nine, who had been called up to the RAF in April 1940 as a direct-entry commissioned air gunner. After gunnery training, Sutton arrived at 5 Operational Training Unit Aston Down on 14 June and was posted to 264 Squadron at Kirton-in-Lindsey on 9 July 1940. Freddie Sutton was also very taken by Carlin, writing in his diary: 'Timbertoes was a sound chap, a magnificent Hun hater and a permanent object lesson to those men, who half his age and reasonably fit, tuck themselves away in nice safe Admin jobs and call that fighting.'[6]

Following his meeting at Bentley Priory with Churchill, Dowding wrote to the Air Ministry in urgent terms about the scale of the challenge he now faced. He was particularly worried that his sixty squadrons were spread too thinly across the country and that he didn't have enough fighters to protect Allied shipping.[7] He wrote: 'Bearing in mind the fact that enemy bombers are now active almost every night and that units have to be detailed in every sector it appears that three squadrons per sector is about the minimum requirement to safeguard the passage of convoys off the east coast of England and that this number will be inadequate north of the Tay and west of the Isle of Wight where sector frontages are very large.'

He continued: 'In addition to the above I cannot afford to distribute my squadrons evenly along the front but must keep some extra strength in the neighbourhood of London to guard against the possibility of invasion in East Anglia or Kent.' Now coming to the point, Dowding said it was 'obvious' that the Air Ministry must release more squadrons, especially the 'Czechs and Poles'.

The exigent need for more squadrons to meet the broadening threat of invasion meant Fighter Command was also forced to review the status of the Defiant squadrons. Towards the end of July the Air Staff arranged to interview both Philip Hunter and William Richardson about their respective squadron's combat experience with the Defiant. The notes from the meeting made uncompromising reading.

Richardson had told his superiors and just about anyone who cared to listen that he 'would have done better' with forward-firing guns. Given his squadron's experience on 19 July, Richardson's opinion did not come as much of a surprise. But during the briefings it also emerged that Hunter, the key pilot exponent of the turret fighter, had reluctantly come to the same view. Whether it had been 141's mauling on the 19th or his own combat experience which had changed his assessment of the Defiant's armament we don't know.

Donald Stevenson, who was heading the review of the Defiant, wrote to Sholto Douglas on 1 August setting out in frank terms the best approach for the future combat deployment of the turret fighter. He candidly told Douglas: 'Richardson, CC of No. 141 Squadron, who has had short but unfortunate experience with the Defiant in action, was of the opinion that he would have done better with the addition of forward armament. Even if we disregard this opinion as being based on insufficient grounds we should very carefully consider the view of Hunter, the CC of No. 264 Squadron who has proved his ability and leadership and has evolved highly successful tactics for operating his squadron. He too feels that forward guns are necessary.'

But rather than treating the two squadron leaders' recommendations as a rejection of the concept of the turret fighter, Stevenson turned it to the Air Ministry's advantage. 'These conclusions,' he told Douglas, 'bear out the experience we had in the last war when the Bristol Fighter shot down more enemy aircraft with its front than with its rear guns.'[8] He continued: 'The chief argument against the fitting of forward armament in the two-seater fighter is of course that the pilot would try to use his forward guns instead of manoeuvring to enable his turret guns to be brought to bear. Such a distraction would handicap the two-seater fighter in the execution of the role which is the attack of bombers where they are unarmed, avoiding the astern attack which almost every front gun engagement develops. Furthermore, the Bristol Fighter analogy may not altogether be fair since the turret is an infinitely more satisfactory device than the scarff ring [machine gun mounting]. There is no doubt however that the morale of fighting crews would be raised by the feeling that they were not unarmed against enemy aircraft while carrying out their attack.'

Stevenson, confronting the logical conclusion of his argument, summed up: 'The Defiant was designed for attacking unescorted bombers. If we could be certain either that bombers will be unescorted or that an adequate eight-gun fighter force would be available at the right place and time to contain the escort while the Defiants got on with shooting down the bombers, we could be satisfied with the present armament of the Defiant. In the hard reality of war experience however we know now that we cannot guarantee this anywhere in the British Isles and therefore I think we must agree the necessity to provide forward armament for the Defiant at the expense of the performance which would be lost by fitting the additional guns. This last point maybe offset to a large extent by fitting the Merlin XX [Rolls-Royce's more powerful engine]. I recommend that a four-gun set is considered.'[9]

Stevenson and the Air Staff's assessment of the Defiant may have embraced the reality of modern aerial warfare but it still clung to the outdated lessons of the past.

Three days later Douglas wrote to Boulton Paul asking for their views on fitting additional forward guns. Specifically, he wanted to know what impact this would have on the Defiant's performance, particularly its rate of climb.[10] In the meantime the Air Ministry went ahead with more orders, adding another 280 to the original Defiant commission, bringing the total order to 930.[11]

Stevenson and Douglas reassured themselves that the new models would greatly benefit from the Merlin XX engine, which had a two-stage super-charger giving it up to 1390 hp with a 12 lb boost.[12]

A prototype of the Mark II Defiant, without forward guns, was trialled on 20 July. But the Defiant II would be too late to re-equip RAF squadrons before the end of the Battle of Britain.

* * *

From the start of July, the Luftwaffe had been probing Fighter Command's defences as a prelude to launching an all-out assault. The attacks had been concentrated on the ships bringing vital supplies to Britain. But on 1 August, Hitler issued Directive Number 17, switching the thrust of the Luftwaffe's bombing operations and paving the way for Operation Sealion. Now he ordered the obliteration of all RAF aircraft, ground units and supply organisations, as well as the destruction of the British aircraft industry.

The Battle of Britain was about to enter its most critical phase.

Yet as Britain prepared to face its gravest hour, the Air Ministry was distracted, dithering over whether it should retain the services of Hugh Dowding as the head of Fighter Command. It wasn't until 5 July that the commander-in-chief was formally told that he was not to be retired on 14 July, as he had previously been informed, but would keep his job until at least the end of October.[13]

Francis Wilkinson, Dowding's closest aide, had this to say about Dowding's treatment at the hands of the Air Staff: 'It was fantastic that a commander-in-chief with all the burdens of the world on his shoulders and fighting one of the major battles of the world should not know if he was going to be kept on and have to haggle about whether he was to relinquish his command or to retire altogether from the service. It was absolutely incredible.'

On 13 August 1940, the Germans launched Adlertag (Eagle Day), a full-frontal attack against RAF airfields. This was repeated five days later on 18 August, when the Luftwaffe made an all-out effort to destroy Fighter Command. The air battles that took place on this day were amongst the largest aerial engagements in history. Both sides suffered heavy losses. In the air, the British shot down twice as many Luftwaffe aircraft as they lost. However, many RAF aircraft were destroyed on the ground, so that overall British and German aircraft losses were even. Further large and costly aerial battles did take place after 18 August, but both sides lost more aircraft combined on this day than at any other point during the campaign, including 15 September, the Battle of Britain Day, generally considered the climax of the fighting. For this reason, the air battles of 18 August 1940 became known in Britain as 'The Hardest Day'.

In the thick of the fighting was III/JG 51, led by Hannes Trautloft, the vanquisher of No. 141 Squadron, who had been escorting Ju 88s on bombing attacks against the RAF fighter stations. One of his veteran flight commanders, Arnold Lignitz, was also proving to be a deadly fighter pilot and on 15 August claimed his tenth kill, shooting down a Hurricane near Folkestone.

On 13 August, III/JG 51 was given the job of escorting Ju 88s on a raid against RAF Kenley whose fighters protected the southern approaches to London. The Surrey airfield hangars had already been badly damaged in an earlier low-level raid by nine Dorniers, one half being shot down by ground fire and Hurricanes from the indomitable 111 Squadron.

When the Ju 88s and Trautloft's 109s arrived there was a pall of thick smoke hanging over the airfield, preventing clear visibility of the target. As the German bombers milled above Kenley searching for the best bombing line they came under intense ground fire, forcing the bombers to head off in the direction of a new target, West Malling aerodrome in Kent. After passing Biggin Hill on their way to West Malling more AA fire targeted the formation. One Ju 88 was hit, forcing

Trautloft to fly closer to offer better protection to the displaced bombers. But as he dropped down into position, the formation was jumped by Spitfires and Hurricanes and several Ju 88s were sent down. By the time the Luftwaffe commander had responded to the new threat the British fighters had gone. Trautloft and his Messerschmitts returned in the late afternoon to escort another bombing raid against RAF stations. This time one of his own 109s was shot down by British fighters.

Altogether, the Luftwaffe lost between sixty-nine and seventy-one aircraft destroyed or damaged beyond repair as a result of its operations over Britain on 18 August 1940. Fighter Command flew 403 sorties to meet the major German attacks, nearly all of which successfully intercepted the enemy. The RAF suffered losses of between twenty-seven and thirty-four RAF fighters, eleven British fighter pilots killed and another nineteen pilots wounded, eleven so seriously that they did not take part in the rest of the battle.

And so the air battle raged on through August. Each day the Luftwaffe would send four or five bombing raids of three to four hundred aircraft to southern England and the RAF would do their best to meet them before they reached their targets. More often than not the Luftwaffe bombers got through and released their bombs, but it always came at a price. On 20 August Churchill made his most famous speech of the battle in which he told the House of Commons 'never in the field of human conflict was so much owed by so many to so few'[14]. But Churchill's words were uttered in desperation rather than celebration, intended to inspire his fellow countrymen to even greater endeavour as the fighting reached its most critical stage.

Despite the intensity of these full-scale engagements and the increasing strain placed on the pilots of Fighter Command, Dowding continued to hold back Hunter's Defiants from the front line. Instead 264 Squadron carried on flying a combination of day and night patrols over the North Sea. Between 1 and 11 August, 264 took part in forty-two sorties giving cover to east coast convoys without sighting a single enemy aircraft.

Jim Bailey's recollections of those days working up and down the East Anglian coast were of the expectation of an invasion at any moment: 'We waited for the invasion, not greatly perturbed. No one that I knew expected defeat, although propaganda is seductive to a young mind. I did not myself have enough history to be able to put this historic battle into perspective; instead I was aware that the German Army and the German Air Force were much more numerous than our own. I knew that they commanded the resources of all Europe and were backed by a Treaty of friendship with Soviet Russia . . . The grey-clad Wehrmacht had rolled across Europe as it pleased. It will be hard then to explain to someone only concerned in the war after the Germans have been measured up to, how truly frightening it is to be a youngster pitted against a measureless enemy with his rumoured exhibitions of vast military might, an unknown leviathan and armoured behemoth.'[15]

Dowding, who knew the actual, rather than phantom, strengths of the Luftwaffe's forces now confronting the RAF, was in no less awe of the enemy.

On 15 August PO 'Bull' Whitley and Sgt Robert Turner carried out a night sortie over the east coast two miles south of North Coates, Lincolnshire, when they began receiving incoming fire. Whitley steered his aircraft towards the source of the tracer and found a He 111. Turner fired his guns before the enemy was lost in clouds. The Heinkel was later confirmed destroyed.[16] It was the first night kill by a Defiant in more than three months of operational flying, a lamentable record that would come to haunt Dowding.

Throughout August, Fighter Command had fended off concerted attacks on its airfields and defence system. But the dwindling number of experienced fighter pilots upon whom Dowding could call on to send up against the bomber formations now threatened to wear down the RAF. Between 8 and 18 August, 154 RAF pilots were killed, severely wounded, or missing, while only sixty-three new pilots entered training.[17] If Fighter Command continued to sustain pilot casualties at this rate the Luftwaffe would clear the skies of Spitfires and Hurricanes well before the end of the summer.

On 21 August, Philip Hunter finally got what he had been hoping for – the call from group HQ. The squadron was to be recalled to front-line combat service operations, stationed at RAF Hornchurch, a key sector airfield with 11 Group, covering south-east London. They were to replace the Spitfires of 266 Squadron which had suffered badly in the battle, losing seven of their twenty pilots in the last ten days. At Hornchurch, Hunter's reputation preceded him. No. 264 Squadron still held the record for the most kills in one day and among the other RAF squadrons the Defiants were known as 'Hunter's circus', a flattering nod in the direction of Baron von Richthofen himself.

On 23 August Göring further turned the screw on the RAF by issuing another directive ordering ceaseless attacks on Fighter Command's ground bases. The Luftwaffe Reichsmarschall hoped this would force Dowding to send up his fighters into the waiting arms of his wolf packs which lay in wait in high altitude above the bombers.

Hornchurch, deep inside Essex, was outside the range of the

Me 109 flying from their bases in France. But on 23 August Hunter was told to prepare to fly at first light to the forward base at Manston, the same airfield he had operated from so successfully during the Dunkirk campaign. Manston, part of the first line of defence on the Kent coast called 'hellfire corner', lay in the direct path of the channel-hopping German bombers and their deadly fighter escort. As the first squadron in, the Defiants would be expected to be up first to face whatever attack the enemy was going to throw at one of Fighter Command's key home defence stations.

Not all the 264 pilots were happy about this tactical use of the RAF's bomber destroyer. Some of the crews wondered whether it would be better to have held the Defiants back to intercept the German formations after they had been broken up by the Spitfires and Hurricanes. Given the experience of 141 Squadron and Keith Park's concerns about the Defiant's vulnerabilities,[18] there was a strong case to provide 264 with a protective squadron of Spitfires or Hurricanes.

There was one more obvious handicap afflicting a Defiant squadron assigned to a front-line fighter base. Because the aircraft had a pilot and a gunner it could take up to twice as long to scramble a Defiant than a Spitfire or Hurricane squadron.

That evening one of the pilots decided to share his personal reservations with his commanding officer. Philip Hunter was due to hand over command of 264 after the next day's sorties, which was to be his farewell flight with his old squadron.[19] Perhaps this was why Jim Bailey plucked up the courage to raise questions about the Defiant tactics. Bailey found his commanding officer after dinner, drinking coffee outside the mess hut. The young pilot later recalled in his autobiography:

'We began to chat informally and I suggested to him that it was quite wrong that a Defiant squadron should be the first off against the enemy, as we would be expected to be the next morning. The Defiant was slow, had a low rate of climb, was helpless against enemy fighters but was a magnificent destroyer of bombers. We should be the last, not the first squadron, I argued. Philip Hunter did not deny the facts but he said that we were in the place of honour and must accept it. I think that by this he means we threw away the advantage of our peculiar aircraft, and from this our misfortunes stemmed.'[20]

It was the break of dawn when 264 Squadron left Hornchurch for Manston as planned. At 08.00 hours three sections were ordered to patrol over the airfield. B flight's new leader was twenty-three-year-old Flt Lt Ernest William Campbell-Colquhoun. He had only been posted to the squadron on 21 August from 66 Squadron which had been operating Spitfires from Duxford. Campbell-Colquhoun was an experienced pilot who had seen action in Dunkirk when his Spitfire had shot down an Me 109.[21] But he had not yet acclimatised to Defiants and that morning had difficulty starting his engine. It took him a few minutes to take off and he was the last to leave the airfield. As he climbed out to meet the rest of the squadron he thought he saw his number 2 and number 3 waiting for him. So he flew in front of them and waggled his wings. But to the British pilot's frightened surprise the two aircraft were not friendly Defiants at all, but rather very hostile 109s on an early morning strafing raid of the station. German cannon shells ripped into Campbell-Colquhoun's fuselage just behind his gunner PO Gerald Robinson, igniting a packet of Verey cartridges.

Fearing they had been badly hit, Robinson started to bail out, only to change his mind when he realised his pilot still had control of the aircraft. Campbell-Colquhoun put the Defiant into a steep dive and managed to use the early morning mist to slip away from the German fighters.

The Messerschmitts were not alone, and as Campbell-Colquhoun came down to land he could see bomb craters starting to appear along the runway. As soon as the Defiant reached a shuddering halt, pilot and gunner jumped free and ran for the air raid shelters, each expressing surprise that the other was still alive. The remaining airborne Defiants now came face-to-face with the German fighters. It was Freddie Sutton's first sighting of the enemy. He later recalled in his diary: 'We intercepted by chance a dozen of the Me 109s. It so happened that we were flying on almost reciprocal courses and met very nearly head on. The Huns flew clean through our formation and no one of either side fired a shot in the brief space of time we were close enough. I expect they were as startled as we were. Our converging and passing speed must have been relative from 400 to 500 miles an hour and how there were no collisions I don't know.'[22]

At 11.30 hours the Defiants were ordered back to Hornchurch, but later redeployed to Manston to bolster the airfield's defence against further attacks. Around lunchtime, and with no enemy sighted, nine of the Defiants landed for refuelling, leaving Eric Barwell's section to continue patrolling above.

The Germans had mostly carried out feint attacks during the morning, hoping to draw the British fighters into combat. But by 1 p.m. Fighter Command's radar stations had started to pick up five formations massing along the French coast between Dunkirk and Dover. The armada of more than three hundred bombers and fighters crossed the Kent coast at Deal, close to

Manston. Among them were twenty Ju 88s of KG76. No. 11 Group was at full stretch with squadrons either up protecting airfields or already engaging the raiders.

Nine of the 264 Defiants were still on the ground when the German bombers appeared high above the north Kent airfield and began diving from a height of around 13,000 feet. The Defiants were immediately scrambled just as the bombs started falling on the aerodrome. Two of the nine Defiant pilots had trouble starting their engines, yet somehow all twelve aircraft were soon in the air able to meet the German bombers. Hunter had no time to adopt a standard attack formation and so engaged the enemy in twos and threes, each Defiant following a section leader.

As the bombers levelled out of their attacks their underbellies presented good targets for the machine guns of the climbing British fighters fearlessly led by Hunter. The chase was on as the faster Defiants made ground on their now exposed prey. Four of the fleeing Ju 88s were caught and brought down, two by the experienced pairings of Thorn and Barker and Whitley and Turner and two more by John Banham and Barrie Baker and the new acting Squadron Leader George Garvin, a Belfast man, and his gunner Flt Lt Robert Ash, from Fife in Scotland.

But high above the 88s was a fighter force of III/JG 51, the same group that had inflicted such devastating losses on the RAF's other Defiant squadron on 19 July. They were led by Arnold Lignitz, the experienced fighter pilot who knew all about the RAF's turret fighter after taking part in the 'slaughter of the innocents' just a few miles along the Kent coast the previous month.

Eric Barwell turned his Defiant to confront the new threat and beckoned the rest of his section to follow him: 'We chased after the bombers as they headed for France. It was a long stern chase before we were near enough to engage them and I then spotted five enemy fighters that must have been lying in wait. I at once called up Jones "bandits in line, astern evasive action!" and turned as hard as possible as they attacked.' Unfortunately, the rookie crew of PO Joseph Jones and PO William Ponting, who were following on behind Barwell, reacted too slowly to their flight commander's warning and, unable to turn hard enough, were shot down. Lignitz's 109's quickly dispatched a Defiant flown by Flying Officer Ian Shaw and Sgt Alan Berry.

Remembered Barwell: 'All five enemy aircraft then concentrated on me and as each came in I turned hard giving my gunner, Sgt Martin, a straight on deflection shot. I saw strikes on three of them.' Barwell was turning and stalling his aircraft at such acute angles that Martin blacked out for a short time before recovering just in time to take back control of his machine guns. 'We were some miles out at sea,' recalled Barwell, 'and it meant that I had to keep turning hard as each plane attacked and I began to think we would never get back to base on the Kent coast.' But as suddenly as the attack had started the German fighters broke off the combat. 'I like to think we had damaged the other four aircraft but more probably they ran out of fuel and ammunition,' said Barwell.[23]

The Defiant pilot steered his aircraft safely back to base. By engaging the 109s and drawing them away from the bombers, 264 had opened the way for the arriving Hurricanes of 501 Squadron who now had a free hand with the remaining Ju 88s. Nevertheless, the Nazi bomber force had done its work and Manston had taken a beating, leaving burning hangars and cratered runways.

The surviving Defiant crews were now all down and taking

stock of their own losses and damaged aircraft. It soon became apparent that 264 Squadron had suffered more gravely than initially realised. Squadron Leader Hunter, on his last day in charge before officially handing over to Garvin, had led the chase after the Ju 88s out across the Channel where he ran into the waiting German fighters. His loyal officers and NCOs now waited anxiously for news of his Defiant. But after an hour or so had passed it began to dawn on the rest of the squadron that their brave leader's plane was not coming back.

Freddie Sutton recalled in his diary: 'Twelve Defiants went up but only eight came back. And as we learnt what had happened our hearts were very heavy indeed. The CO had gone. Someone has seen him going into the Channel and even as he plunged to death Freddy his gunner was blazing away at the Hun who had shot them down. The CO gone! One somehow never thought that there was a Hun born who could get our Philip. And who else? Artie and Peter. Taffy and Bill . . . Poor old Bill that was his first scrap. This was hellish. For the rest of the day we were very subdued. These were our friends and they took off and didn't come back. Those bloody Hun bastards.'[24]

Hunter and his gunner, Alfred King, were reported missing in action[25]. Neither their bodies nor their aircraft were ever recovered. It is likely that Hunter and King pressed home their attack against the fleeing bombers as far as they could and then, trapped between the sea and the battle-hardened fighter escort, led by Arnold Lignitz, were shot down. Arnold Lignitz knew all about the Defiant and he would not have mistaken Hunter's Defiant for a Hurricane.

The German log shows that Lignitz claimed at least one Defiant that day, and if this aircraft was Hunter's, it was then perhaps a fitting way to end the life of one of the RAF's greatest Battle of Britain pilots – in gladiatorial combat with an equally determined adversary.

Hunter was a remarkably brave pilot who had almost single-handedly shown that the Boulton Paul Defiant deserved its place alongside the Spitfire and the Hurricane in the Battle of Britain. His death was more than just a personal loss to his family. Hunter had developed the fighter tactics for the new Defiants and brought 264 Squadron to combat readiness. Over Dunkirk he had achieved the greatest success for a single RAF squadron in one day's action. But even more than this, Hunter was loved, admired and respected by his fellow pilots and gunners who had willingly followed him into battle, often against overwhelming odds. Group Captain Peter Townsend, who had first met Philip Hunter at Martlesham and survived the war to become a boyfriend of Princess Margaret, described him as a 'gentle parfit knight, a man of quiet and selfless courage'. It was left to Trafford Leigh-Mallory, the head of 12 Group, to write to Hunter's window at the family home, Woodborough Hall, Nottingham: 'I can't quite tell you how much I admired Sq Ld Philip Hunter's efficiency and gallantry as a squadron commander. I regarded him as exceptional in every way and consider him to be a very great loss to the service. I understand that his father is still alive and I hope you will show the letter to him as I would like him to know in what high regard he was held. His exceptional gallantry and efficiency will be remembered by his squadron long after his death and will act as an inspiration to them. I would be very much obliged if you would let me know where he had a photograph taken lately as I would like to present one to his squadron in memory of him.'[26]

Hunter's death left 264, whose number included only a handful of survivors from the Dunkirk days, bereft of experienced leadership and was a stinging reproach to Fighter Command's tactic of deploying Defiants without suitable fast fighter cover. In fact Keith Park and the over-stretched Fighter Command had redirected a squadron of Hurricanes to Manston to come to 264's aid – but once again they arrived too late. In the day's battle the RAF lost three Defiants in return for one Me 109 and five Ju 88s shot down, including one accounted for by Hunter and King.

The next day Göring called Lignitz and a number of other senior Luftwaffe fighter commanders to a meeting in which he accused them of deliberately leaving the bombers unprotected just so they could rack up their personal scores. From now on they would fly much slower and closer to the bombers. Had Göring's order come a day earlier it might have saved Hunter and the two other Defiants.

The surviving crews of 264 Squadron were given precious little time to mourn the loss of their leader. At 15.00 another Luftwaffe raiding party of fifty Dorniers and Heinkels escorted by Me 110s approached the Kent coast. Four of No. 11 Group's squadrons were already up patrolling on the southern and eastern approaches to London. Two of these made contact with one section of the enemy bombers which were heading for another bombing run against Manston. But the attacking force broke through the RAF defence and this time Manston was put out of action for the rest of the day. A second group of bombers, which had also managed to evade the RAF fighters, was approaching Hornchurch where the surviving Defiants were regrouping after their combat less than two hours earlier.

Jim Bailey, the junior pilot of the squadron, watched the bombers appear over the aerodrome: 'I had been able to follow the fighting from the tannoy system [which relayed the progress of the fighters and defenders as the dogfights developed]. Then I watched the formation of Dorniers, tiny specks, glinting lethally in the sunlight, approaching on its bombing run, where we were the target. As the formation drew overhead we crowded into the bomb-bays . . . the long stick of bombs began to burst running up towards us. A voice cried "Lie down", panic scythed the crowd and all lay as one man. The explosions stopped short of us. The stick killed six civilians and three cows.'[27]

The station commander, in complete panic, shouted down the tannoy for 264 to scramble, as if they needed telling. Barwell blames the commander's panicked orders for two of the taxi-ing Defiants colliding with one another: 'As the rest of us took off,' remembered Barwell, 'bombs were falling just about where we had been a moment before. A formation of Heinkel bombers were overhead at 10,000 to 15,000 feet. We didn't have a chance of catching them.'[28]

But seven Defiants, determined to avenge the loss of Hunter, were off the ground, climbing towards an attacking force made up of Ju 88s which they caught at a lower altitude. Once again the Defiants made quick kills. The squadron's new leader, George Garvin, aged twenty-three, and his thirty-one-year-old gunner Flt Lt Clifford Ash, attacked the main formation and shot down two Ju 88s. PO Terence Welsh and LAC Lawrence Hayden brought down a straggler in a classic crossover attack. Veteran 264 ace PO Michael Young had become separated from the rest of the Defiants but still managed to find a solitary He 111 which he and his gunner, New Zealander Sgt Leslie Russell, shot down in an overtaking attack.

But once again the Messerschmitt escort, in defiance of Göring's new orders about sticking close to the bombers, had hung back hoping to swoop on the distracted British fighters. Twenty-one-year-old PO Richard Gaskell valiantly fought off a dozen of the Me 109s before succumbing to overwhelming firepower. His gunner, Sgt William Makin, died from bullet wounds sustained in the action but Gaskell survived and even managed to crash-land his badly damaged Defiant.

However, the German fighters didn't have it all their own way. Return fire from Welsh and Hayden claimed one of the escorts. Of the seven Defiants, six returned to Hornchurch safely. They had acquitted themselves well with a tally of three Ju 88s, one Heinkel and one Me 109 for a loss of only one of their own machines and one airman killed.

By the close of 24 August Fighter Command had flown 936 sorties. No. 264 Squadron had played a significant part in the combat, shooting down eight Ju 88s, one He 111 and two Me 109s. But the Defiants had also sustained significant casualties. They had lost their charismatic talisman squadron leader and six other crewmen.

At Hornchurch the hushed mood among the crews spoke volumes. It was during these solemn moments that Jim Bailey reflected on what type of man made a good fighter pilot. He considered what qualities allowed some to survive and others to die. 'I found, for example,' he said, 'that only-children, pilots without brothers or sisters, were particularly helpless. When a new pilot came to us, I would try to guess after a day or two whether he came from a large family or not and then go and ask him. If he did, he had a better chance to survive. Good pilots are common, good fighter pilots were rare . . . In the course of time it appeared that men who had a private axe to grind beyond the public axe of the King's enemies were especially successful. In a secular sense it is indeed true to say that "the Lord gets his best soldiers out of the highlands of affliction".'[29]

That evening Göring sent a force of seventy He 111s to bomb the oil refineries at Thames Haven on the Essex coast. But some of the Nazi bombers took a different course, flying up the Thames and into central London where they dropped their ordnance, killing a number of civilians. Hitler, who reportedly still held out hope that Britain could be persuaded to settle for peace, had issued strict orders that only he could authorise an attack on the British capital. Whether the Heinkel crews recklessly, deliberately or accidentally ended up bombing London we will probably never know. The fact that there were casualties as far west as Twickenham suggests their actions were not solely caused by navigational error as many believe. Whatever the reasons for the attack, it so angered Winston Churchill that he ordered a retaliatory raid on Berlin, the imperial heart of the Third Reich. The next night a force of over seventy Armstrong Whitworth Whitleys, Handley Page Hampdens and Vickers Wellingtons set out for the German capital, targeting armament factories in the north of the city and Tempelhof Airport.

Due to the overpowering anti-aircraft fire and cloud cover the British bombers were forced high above the city and were unable to hit their targets accurately. As a result damage was slight and the only German casualty was an elephant in the city's zoo. But the psychological impact on the German population, who had been told by Göring that they could call 'me Meier' (German idiom for something being impossible) if one single bomb fell on Berlin, was wholly disproportionate. It also incensed Hitler, who now ordered the Luftwaffe to deviate from its strategy. Instead of targeting the RAF airfields, aircraft factories and the home defence of Fighter Command, Göring's bombers must throw all its weight into the destruction of London and the civilian population.

Neither side knew it then but it was to be the turning point of the Battle of Britain. After weeks of slugging it out with wave after wave of Nazi attackers, Dowding's fighter squadrons had been at breaking point. Many front-line airfields like Manston had been badly damaged, aircraft production was struggling to keep pace with the number of destroyed fighters and, most critical of all, there was now a shortage of RAF pilots to fly the Hurricanes, Spitfires and Defiants. By diverting the Luftwaffe bombers from the RAF airfields to the cities, Hitler had lifted his foot from Dowding's throat and given the RAF the vital breathing space it needed to regroup and meet the new threat. The change in tactics didn't happen all at once and Göring continued to harass the RAF in its bases, but he now had to split his forces between these twin objectives.

The Battle of Britain was far from over, and 264 Squadron and the RAF's third fighter still had one final part to play.

# Chapter 14

# DEFIANTS' LAST STAND

TWO DAYS AFTER the tragic loss of their leader, 264 Squadron was ordered back into the fight. Once again they were to fly from Hornchurch to Manston and just before midday vectored to intercept a large formation of Dorniers approaching Folkestone, 25 miles further down the coast.

The squadron's acting commanding officer for the day was Flt Lt John Banham who had only joined the squadron in June, a few days after the Dunkirk evacuation. He was already an experienced Spitfire pilot who had made his first kill in a Defiant during the German raid on Hornchurch on the afternoon of 24 August.

Banham was in the air with his flight of Defiants protecting Manston when the order came through to intercept a formation of enemy bombers. The approaching Dorniers, (nicknamed the 'flying pencils' because of their slim fuselages) had closed on the aerodrome more quickly than expected, and were almost upon Manston as the Defiants rose to meet them. But Banham, now joined by the other nine aircraft, had scrambled with enough time to lead the Defiants in vics, line astern, towards the bomber formation. According to the 264 combat intelligence report they even had time to perform a series of very well-executed crossover attacks (pioneered by Philip Hunter during the Dunkirk combats).[1]

As the Defiants came in range of the German formation they started setting about the bombers. PO Desmond Hughes with gunner Sgt Fred Gash, in their first-ever combat, made an immediate impact. 'The CO ordered line astern formation,' remembered Fred Gash. 'I looked to my left and there were Dornier 17s in neat formation and all the [Defiant] gunners in line with them opened fire . . . we were 60 yards away. I hit one in the right engine, saw smoke and he went nose down and dived. We moved up to the next flight then saw the next line of Do 17s. I saw one firing and so deliberately aimed at the cockpit and saw the canopy and bits and pieces flying off into the air. He went into a steep dive.'[2]

Banham and his gunner, Barrie Baker, quickly shot down one of the Dorniers. PO Howard Goodall and gunner Sgt Robert Young claimed another. Flt Lt Ernest Campbell-Colquhoun saw two airmen jumping from his German target just before it burst into a ball of flame and plunged into the sea.

This was Gash's second kill, recorded in PO Desmond Hughes' unpublished memoirs: 'Fred Gash took as his target the second Dornier and made no mistake – his De Wilde incendiaries twinkled all over it but particularly on its engine. It began to fall out of the formation, the hatch was jettisoned, two parachutes streamed as little dark figures bailed out and the stricken aircraft went down increasingly steeply with its starboard engine well alight.'[3]

The first Dornier attacked by Hughes and Gash was badly damaged, but the pilot tried to save his four-man crew by steering the aircraft towards the Goodwin Sands which were exposed at low tide. Luftwaffe pilot Willi Effmert, a married twenty-four-year-old from a spa town near Hanover, attempted to make a controlled landing but as the heavy bomber touched down on the soft sands, covered by shallow water, it somersaulted and fell into the sea on its back. Only two of the crew survived. Effmert and the Dornier's observer, twenty-one-year-old Hermann Ritzel, from Frankfurt, were rescued by a passing British ship. The bodies of their two colleagues washed up on opposite sides of the North Sea.

But that was not the end of the Dornier's story. Seventy-three years later (2013) the aircraft was recovered from the sands and strapped to a salvage vessel so it could complete the last eight miles of its journey to the English coast. Its final resting place is alongside a Boulton Paul Defiant in the RAF Museum at Cosford – the only surviving aircraft of their types left in the world.

While the Defiants battled with the remaining bombers eight miles out to sea they were once again set upon by up to fifty high-flying 109s. Banham vividly recalls: 'I attacked and shot down one of the bombers and then got badly hit and were set on fire ourselves. Eventually I managed to turn my machine upside down and fall out. Unhappily my gunner, who I thought had already jumped, was never seen again.' Banham spent over an hour in the Straits of Dover before being pulled out of the water by a friendly fisherman.

Flying Officer Ian Stephenson, a vicar's son who had trained with the London University Squadron before the war, was also hit and safely bailed out over the sea. His gunner Sgt Walter Maxwell, from Moels, in Cheshire, was reported missing. He had only joined the squadron on 4 August.

The veteran pairing of Ted Thorn and Fred Barker had taken full advantage of the initial free kills, bagging two Dorniers of their own. But they had also attracted the attention of one of the German fighters who blasted them with his cannon, causing oil and glycol to pour out of the Defiant's engine. Thorn tried desperately hard to shake off the 109 in the hope of making a crash landing near Herne Bay. But the German pilot was determined to finish off the British fighter. The two aircraft raced towards the Kent coast with the Defiant continuing to take hits. Barker, desperately seizing his guns, took one careful aim at the chasing German and, just as they passed over the cliffs, fired off his final rounds, striking the 109 with a direct shot. This gave Thorn a slim chance of steering their damaged aircraft to a belly-landing in an open field. As the British pilot and gunner clambered out of their crumpled aircraft they had the satisfaction of watching the 109 crash into the sea. The two men caught the train back to Hornchurch.

During the afternoon's combat the squadron had lost three Defiants and two gunners were killed. But they had once again scored highly against the German bombers, accounting for seven Dorniers as well as Barker's Me 109. In terms of the many engagements of the Battle of Britain it was a good return and the Defiants had once again proved they were an excellent destroyer of bombers. But by sending them up without a squadron of Spitfires or Hurricanes, they had been left exposed to the waiting *rotte* packs of 109s. This was an observation subtly, but pointedly, made by the Hornchurch intelligence officer's report which noted that the 'fifty Me 109s which kept on diving on them [the Defiants] appeared to be otherwise unengaged'[4].

It was now apparent that when the unprotected Defiants were engaging the bombers they were at their most vulnerable – and the German pilots and gunners knew it. Recalled Banham many years later: 'When it was first in action over Dunkirk the Defiant gave the Nazis a nasty surprise to see that something was firing out of its side. But German pilots twigged what was going on. If a Defiant was firing at the side towards an enemy aircraft the other side was exposed to a beam attack from the Messerschmitts. Your attention was totally distracted to attacking the bomber.'[5]

The action was to be the last for Banham in a Defiant. He was switched to Hurricanes and given command of 229 Squadron at Wittering. He survived many summer dogfights only to be shot down just before the close of the Battle of Britain on 15 October. Although his Hurricane was in flames he managed to bail out, landing in an apple tree in Kent. But he had suffered terrible burns and was sent to East Grinstead for treatment by Doctor Archibald McIndoe who carried out pioneering experimental plastic surgery. There Banham was welcomed into the Guinea Pig Club – a club comprised mostly of RAF aircrew who had been treated by Dr McIndoe.

He remains the only Battle of Britain pilot to have flown all three of the RAF's front-line fighters: the Spitfire, Defiant and Hurricane. Banham returned to active duty in early 1941 and served until July 1945 when he was released from the RAF. He died in 1987.

On 27 August the Luftwaffe flew fewer raids and 264 Squadron, which had been sent to RAF Rochford in Essex, was only called upon to perform a single patrol, out to the Thames Estuary in the early evening.

No. 264 took full advantage of the lull in hostilities. Most of the crew spent the evening dancing and drinking at a local hotel. Freddie Sutton, who along with his pilot had been held in reserve since their first flashing encounter with the 109s on 24 August, described the party in his diary: 'We ate drank and made merry and a band, which ignored the close proximity of the Hun, played on for dancing. So, finding that the local ladies shared the Women's Auxiliary Air Force (WAAF)'s penchant for aircrew, a great evening was had.' The new squadron leader's gunner, Flt Lt Clifford Ash, led the partying. 'I always remember how Clifford enjoyed himself. We had never seen him unbend in such a manner before, and he proved to be the life and soul of the place. Good old Clifford!'[6] It was to be his last dance.

While the pilots partied, work continued on patching up the airfield. In between the raids the Defiant ground crews helped out with the back-breaking business of filling in the bomb craters. Throughout the Battle of Britain these men showed extraordinary dedication to their aircraft, often working sixteen-hour days without a rest. Hunter had made sure that they were always kept informed of the combats and the fate of the crews shot down. By treating them no differently to the aircrew he was able to maintain strong morale among the ground and flying crews.

The pilots and gunners, on scramble alert outside the dispersal hut, played cards, draughts or darts, anxiously waiting for the telephone to ring. Remembered Fred Gash: 'We argued and talked. A lot of horseplay, knocking someone's hat off for the hell of it. We were like schoolboys if you like. We would have a few beers. I wasn't a drinking person. But no drunkenness. We had our favourite haunts, three or four of us would go to the pictures, dance halls or the pubs looking for female company.'[7]

Death was, it seemed, something that happened to other pilots or gunners – never them.

'We did not make a will, you did not look to die,' Gash explained years later. 'I remember at Duxford when one of the gunners said "I don't think I will be coming back from this one." He was nineteen or twenty years old and maybe he did have foresight because he was shot down and didn't come back. But there was no grieving or morale hitting the floor or depression. There was sorrow in the backs of our minds. But you just had to carry on and go out on the next flight and hope it wasn't me. I had confidence in my pilot and my aircraft.'[8]

The next day Göring resumed the attacks on the RAF airfields. At 08.00 hours Fighter Command plotters had detected a large formation of bombers with a fighter escort gathering over the French coast. No. 264 was ordered to intercept a group of twenty He 111s above Folkestone on their way to inland targets. This time the Defiants were not alone and were accompanied by three other RAF fighter squadrons.

It was to be a big day for Jim Bailey, the junior pilot who had so often answered the scramble only to be big-footed by a more senior airman. Recalled Bailey: 'I had over two hundred hours flying and a great deal more confidence in my ability than my ability warranted . . . I remember that we crossed the Thames and the Medway, leaving the towns with their moorings of toy balloons far beneath. But we were not climbing fast enough.'[9]

It was a big day too for Freddie Sutton and his pilot, Flt Lt Peter 'Ponky' Bowen. Bowen had been with the squadron since late May but had missed out on the Dunkirk operations. He had been very close to Philip Hunter, an older school friend from their days at King's School, Canterbury.[10]

At the sound of the scramble Bowen and Sutton were eating breakfast. Recalled Sutton: 'Ponky and I had to run right across the aerodrome and arrived too breathless to get our harness on. However our ground crew was there and like the esquires of old dressed us and more or less lifted us into our aircraft.' Even so, the squadron was in the air in four minutes, receiving radio instructions to reset a southerly course, climbing steadily.

The Defiants, led by Squadron Leader Garvin, spotted the Heinkels high above Folkestone at 17,000 feet. Bailey remembers looking ahead at the commanding officer's Defiant and noticing his dangling wheels which he had been unable to lock into the undercarriage.

Then Bailey saw them: 'There they are, there they are,' he shouted excitedly. A flock of Heinkels were coming in over Folkestone closely followed by trailing white puffs of smoke. 'We were at 17,000 feet, three-and-a-half miles up; but far above us, still small black motes in the empyrean, the top cover of Messerschmitts drove in.'

Sutton had also seen them: '. . . I swallowed several times, for this was to be my first fight. There was something over forty He 111s and milling all around them was an escort of about one hundred Messerschmitt 109. There were just eleven of us, as Mike had been compelled to turn back with engine trouble. I felt that somehow things were going to be a trifle warm and I was not very far wrong. They had the advantage of height and from the angle of our interception it was necessary to make a climb while turning in order to engage them. Poor old Gavvy! It was bad luck for him that the first time he should lead us it was into a big show with everything on the side of the enemy.'[11]

Meanwhile Bailey was just managing to keep his place in the formation. As he glanced up again he saw the welcome sight of the Hurricanes attacking the top cover. He thought to himself: 'The plan was excellent but we ourselves were too low, too low. And then it happened. I was on the right side of our formation, my left, gauntleted hand upon the throttle, the cockpit hood back a space to allow an uninterrupted view. A fighter – ours or theirs I did not see – a casualty from the fight above, dropped past me, quite close in perpendicular dive for the ground. I watched him, fascinated, peering over the side to keep my eye on him. He never paused, never halted but accelerated and accelerated for the deck . . . A crimson light flashed through a green Kentish wood almost before he hit.'

The Defiants continued to fly a half circle under the Heinkels, flying in sections of three, line astern. As Bailey came underneath one of them his gunner Sgt Oswald Hardie let rip with his four machine guns. 'I concentrated on keeping formation,' recalled Bailey, 'confident that the whole of B flight was behind, protecting my tail. The four Brownings stuttered above my head. I became excited. "Bull" Whitley moved over and sat just in front of me. Both Bill Carnaby and ourselves pulled Heinkels out of the formation. Our one – I never saw – fell out with flames pouring from one engine, or so Hardie told me later. Then Hardie started to fire at a second. The Heinkels looked as big as elephants.'

Carnaby's success was particularly gratifying as the young pilot's only previous claim to fame had been writing off his aircraft when he crashed into another Defiant during a practice take-off just after he joined the squadron in June.

Sutton and Bowen, flying as 'arse end Charlie', prepared to take their first shot of the war. Recalled Sutton: 'I fired a burst at one of the Heinkels. To my amazement, nothing happened at all. I had read so many reports of combat in the papers and had so many wonderful lines being shot from the BBC, that I expected to see at least three hundred Huns plunge to their doom almost before I pressed the trigger. This was disconcerting to say the least, particularly as I had just realised that all those sparks flying around us were not sparks at all but tracer bullets from the Heinkels.'

This time Sutton took a deep breath and steadied his aim: 'Ah, that was much better. Our opposite number in the Hun formation dropped his undercarriage and discarded quite a lot of Perspex as he straggled away from his friends. That's a damaged, any old how.'

But what Sutton, Bailey and the rest of the Defiant crews couldn't have known was that the threat posed by the Me 109s was now deadlier than ever.

Above them were the three fighter squadrons of III/JG 26 led by Major Adolf 'Dolfo' Galland, one of the greatest German aces of the Second World War. A veteran of the Spanish Civil War and every campaign since, Galland had chalked up twenty-four kills and would go on to become the highest-scoring fighter pilot on the Western Front. He was accompanied by Werner Molders, who had shot down the first Hurricane on 22 December and had only officially returned to combat that day after being wounded during a dogfight with a Spitfire on 29 July.[12]

Galland now led his fighters into the attack, diving onto the preoccupied British fighters. His 109 leapfrogged the straggling line of Defiants, seeking out the lead aircraft, flown by Squadron Leader Garvin, and raked it with machine gun fire. But Garvin and his gunner, Clifford Ash, weren't going down without a fight and Ash landed hits on Galland before the Defiant's petrol tank burst into flames. Pilot and gunner bailed out in the nick of time.

But the veteran 264 Squadron pairing of 'Bull' Whitley and his gunner Robert Turner were not so fortunate and were shot down and killed near Molash, Kent.[13] The same fate befell PO Peter Kenner, twenty-one, and his gunner thirty-five-year-old PO Charles Johnson when their aircraft crashed near Hinxhill in Kent. It was their first combat. Johnson is buried at Hawkinge Cemetary alongside 'Arch' Hamilton, a pilot with 264's sister squadron 241.

When four 109s turned their attention on Bailey and Hardie it seemed certain that the squadron's other rookie crew would be next.

Bailey felt the first 'jolts and rattles' on the aircraft and then a voice seemed to say down the intercom: 'I'm wounded.' Bailey flicked over, pulled back on the stick, and then spiralled to the ground in a controlled blackout. At ground level he straightened out and shouted: 'Are you alright?' Hardie replied: 'Quite all right.' Bailey had misheard Hardie's original call. Seeing the four German aircraft, he had shouted 'Turn to starboard,' not 'I'm wounded.'[14] Nevertheless, his call had achieved the intended result and probably saved both their lives.

Bailey's Defiant was just 200 feet over the Kent countryside when its engine finally died: 'I moved the throttle but there was no response . . . so I looked for a convenient field, finding them all however studded with poles to forestall German gliders. It had been a warm August, the Kentish day was dry and caked. I had earlier resolved if I had to make an emergency landing, I would, for comfort, cushion it into the brush top of a hedge. Just such a hedge was handy, so we dodged between the poles, crashed through the brush and landed comfortably on the verge at the other side. [Defiant] gunners had earned a reputation in our squadron of being out of the turret of a crashed aircraft before it had actually crashed. Hardie was no exception. He was peering into my cockpit before I had raised my cut nose from the instrument panel into which it had banged.'

While the two friends exchange gasps of relief the dogfights continued in the sky above them. 'We heard a blue note and the rattle of machine guns . . . a Hurricane was hard on its tail pumping lead into him. The pilot parachuted in the nick of time, his aircraft plunging into the earth three fields away.'

Bailey and Hardie eventually found the downed German pilot detained in a horsebox guarded by a detachment of regular soldiers. Bailey was keen to engage his mythical adversary in conversation. The Nazi pilot proudly told him that he had shot down a Defiant: 'He said in general he judged Spitfires to be better than Messerschmitts, Hurricanes not so good and Defiants no good at all. This summary grieved me. But he alarmed me by his appearance, for in the place of the muscle-knotted Siegfried I've come to expect of the Nazis, he seemed to be the typical jeweller from the Old Kent Road. Had I seen him first I should never have allowed a middle-aged character like that to shoot me down.'[15]

No. 264 was not yet done. Bowen and Sutton were still in the fight and holding their own, although now on the receiving end of an awful lot of cannon and machine gun fire: 'The German fighters,' Freddie Sutton later recorded, 'were hammering away all this time, and it occurred to me that I would probably serve the chaps better from my position if I concentrated on them. Accordingly I spun around in my turret taking quick shots at yellow noses, but never able to observe the effects of my fire, so quickly did they come and go.'

Against such mounting odds the brave Defiant crew were

now in mortal danger. Bowen opened his in-flight intercom and calmly suggested to his gunner: 'You know, I think we'll get out. All the others have gone.'

Just before they made good their escape Sutton was presented with one last shooting opportunity: 'At that moment,' he recalled, 'I was given the target all air gunners' pray for. A 109 dived down on our tail holding his fire. At the last moment he obviously realised he was attacking a Defiant, which could shoot backwards and not a Hurricane. In a second of panic he made the elementary mistake of pulling back on his stick, with the result that he presented a large belly just about 50 yards to the rear and above me. I couldn't miss and poured a nice burst into him. I just had time to see smoke coming from him as he fell over on his back.'

Before Sutton could enjoy his victory the British fighter found itself on the wrong end of a fusillade from a Messerschmitt: 'In one second I was being thrust by invisible hands through my seat – the next my neck was trying not to break as my weight was being thrust in the same way through the roof of my turret. I just caught a few disjointed words from Ponkey – "hit – fire – jump" – there was an awful roar and whistling in my ears and I shrieked at Ponky to find out what was going on. I could hear no reply so thought he must have jumped for it and tried to get out . . . in a second or so I was exhausted. I was far too puny to beat the laws of centrifugal force, and so just settled down to wait for the bump.'

The Defiant had taken a direct hit from a cannon shell, setting fire to the engine and causing the aircraft to go into an inverted spin. Damage to the electric circuit had left Sutton partially trapped in the turret as the Defiant spun down to earth.

Fortunately Bowen had realised that his gunner was unable to respond and so instead of bailing out tried to regain control of the badly damaged Defiant. At around 5000 feet the pilot finally succeeded in arresting the spin of the British fighter and got it to level out. But Bowen and Sutton were not out of danger. Seven 109s had followed the Defiant down, exchanging fire with the RAF gunner, before finally breaking off and heading back to France.

Then it was the RAF's turn to try to bring down the doughty Defiant. Recalled Sutton: 'We limped back to base somewhat shaken but very thankful to be alive, until this Hurricane crossed our path and gave us a burst as he went. I expect he was sorry when he recognised us but I feel it was lucky for him that my turret was now useless, the electrical system having gone completely.'

Bowen somehow managed to guide the Defiant back to Rochford. Their machine had taken an extraordinary amount of punishment, including a line of bullets running all the way along the fuselage before coming to a merciful stop just as it reached Sutton's turret. Two further bullet holes had penetrated the Perspex turret just above Sutton's head and one had lodged in his parachute.

Both sides had suffered losses in the day's desperate fighting but the RAF were unable to stop the Heinkels reaching their intended target, the airfield of Eastchurch, where the bombers caused considerable damage. Peter Townsend, who four times that day had led 85 Squadron against the Luftwaffe attacks, later lamented: 'If only the British fighters could have fought off the Me 109s the Defiants might have routed the Heinkels before they bombed Eastchurch.'[16]

As it was, 264 Squadron claimed four Heinkels. But they

had lost four of their own aircraft and five crewmen. The fifth confirmed fatality was Flt Lt Ash who had bailed out with Garvin. The squadron leader suffered only minor injuries but when they found Ash's body it had three bullets in it.[17] The only logical conclusion was that Ash had been machine-gunned by one of Galland's pilots as he helplessly floated down to earth. Suspicion immediately fell on Galland and Molders.

In his memoirs Galland went out of his way to vent his disgust for the shooting of pilots after they had bailed out of their aircraft. He claimed that Göring had once asked him his opinion of killing RAF pilots in this way. Galland said he replied, 'I should regard it as murder, Herr Reichsmarschall. I should do everything in my power to disobey such an order.'

Three days later, on 31 August 1940, the question of machine-gunning parachutists came up when Dowding dined with Winston Churchill at Chequers. Indeed the conversation may well have been prompted by the death of Flt Lt Ash. To Churchill's surprise Dowding suggested that German pilots were perfectly entitled to shoot RAF pilots parachuting over Britain as they were still potential combatants, while RAF pilots should refrain from firing at German pilots as they were out of the battle and presented no threat. Churchill was appalled by this suggestion, arguing that shooting a parachuting pilot 'was like drowning a sailor'. Had Galland or Molders machine-gunned the defenceless Ash, Dowding's interpretation of the rules of war provided a complete defence to a charge of murder.

Of the eight Defiants that landed at Rochford after the morning's fighting only three were serviceable.[18] At noon, Fighter Command radar stations picked up another enemy formation heading towards the south coast. As the German aircraft closed in, the plotters could see the Luftwaffe was heading straight for Rochford. Despite interceptions by several RAF squadrons the German force of twenty-seven bombers maintained its course for the Essex airfield. Only the badly battered 264 stood in their way.

The operations room had no trouble persuading the depleted Defiant squadron to scramble and mount a last-ditch defence. News of the machine-gunning of Flt Lt Ash had filtered through and their blood was up, eager to avenge their brave colleague in any way they could. Three Defiants were airborne just before the bombs started to fall. But despite their best efforts they were too late to catch the raiders and the bombers escaped out to sea. Throughout the afternoon sections of Defiants were sent up to patrol skies above the airfield until the threat subsided. One of them was a Defiant piloted by nineteen-year-old Richard Stokes. And sitting in his turret was the irrepressible fifty-year-old Sid 'Timbertoes' Carlin, hoping for a chance to shoot down a German and claim victories in both World Wars.

By the end of the day only Hughes and Gash had a serviceable Defiant. Yet the Luftwaffe still kept coming and so up they went again. Remembers Fred Gash: 'We were told there were a hundred Germans flying towards the east coast. The only Defiant left was our own so we set off to meet them. But after half an hour we were told to go back because they had turned back. We were quite relieved. God knows what would have happened if we had met them.'

During the air battles of 28 August the RAF lost sixteen fighters, including the four Defiants, while the Luftwaffe had thirty aircraft destroyed.[19] Fighter Command may have been knocking out enough of the enemy's bombers, but in fighter-to-fighter engagements it was losing as many of its own aircraft as the enemy. By 28 August the heavy attrition in Defiants had reached unsustainable levels. Over a period of ten days, in fourteen sorties and in four daylight combats, 264 Squadron had lost eleven aircraft and thirteen crew were killed.

Because the Defiant carried a pilot and a gunner these casualty figures were worse than other front-line fighter squadrons. They had also claimed nineteen kills of their own which was higher than most squadrons involved in similar combat. But the number of available replacement Defiants had now become a critical factor.

Beaverbrook and the Air Ministry had never been able to significantly improve the rate of production for Defiant aircraft. On 26 July, seven days after the destruction of 141 Squadron in the Channel, Fighter Command had twenty-six serviceable Defiants. On 31 August there were now just seventeen shared between the two squadrons.[20] After the war, evidence emerged that this deplorable shortage in Defiant fighters may well have been the result of design rather than accident. Since his appointment in May, Beaverbrook had fallen out with the overly bureaucratic Air Ministry, working much more closely with Fighter Command. In an interview in 1961 Keith Park told the BBC that from day one he had a direct line to Beaverbrook's office: 'He used to ring my house every evening at midnight and ask what replacements were required the next day. It was very heartening to have the head of aircraft production on the phone. I was never grounded through lack of aircraft.' Given what we now know about Park's antipathy towards the Defiant it is easy to understand why Beaverbrook, influenced more by Fighter Command than the Air Ministry, didn't prioritise them.[21]

With the Defiants almost out of production Keith Park and Hugh Dowding were able to assess the aircraft in much more objective terms, knowing that they need not fear the Air Ministry's empty promise of equipping Fighter Command with eight full squadrons of turret fighters.

Dowding later claimed in his official report to the government on the Battle of Britain that he had always maintained an 'open mind' about the Defiant, saying that although the aircraft had proved successful against unescorted bombers over Dunkirk he had waited to see how the aeroplane fared in 'short range' fighting. After the August combats he concluded that they were simply 'too expensive' and withdrew them from the front line of the campaign.

In August 1941 he wrote to the Secretary of State for Air justifying this and other decisions relating to his conduct of the Battle of Britain: 'It [the Defiant] had two serious disabilities; firstly, the brain flying the aeroplane was not the brain firing the guns: the guns could not fire within 16 degrees of the line of flight of the aeroplane and the gunner was distracted from his task by having to direct the pilot through the Communication Set. Secondly, the guns could not be fired below the horizontal, and it was therefore necessary to keep below the enemy. When beset by superior numbers of fighters the best course to pursue was to form a descending spiral, so that one or more Defiants should always be in a position to bring effective fire to bear. Such tactics were, however, essentially defensive, and the formation sometimes got broken up before they could be adopted.'[22]

Dowding's claim to having an open mind in respect of the Defiant is hardly credible. In 1938 when Stevenson and Douglas had committed Fighter Command to fifteen squadrons of turret fighters, he told the Air Staff in very blunt language that he thought the aircraft type was already obsolete. It was a view he maintained when corresponding with Professor Melvill Jones, saying he could see no other use for the Defiant other than as a trainer or target aircraft.

But when Britain faced the imminent and potentially overpowering threat of unescorted bomber fleets, his attitude softened and he was prepared to give the Defiant at least a fighting chance. He supported the AFDU and Philip Hunter in the development of the fighter, although he rebuffed the Air Ministry's demands to rush the Defiant into combat duties. Dowding was pragmatic and he realised that should the Luftwaffe start protecting the rear of the bombers with armour and heavy metal plating, beam attacks or belly attacks would have to be considered.

Park was far less compromising. The head of No. 11 Group, which had met the full force of the Luftwaffe attacks, had shown his opposition to the fighter even after the outstanding leadership of Hunter and his squadron's performance in battles with both German bombers and fighters over Dunkirk. Park's closed mind and his deployment of the Defiant at the frontline fighter stations of Manston and Rochford, where he sent them up without Hurricanes or Spitfires, betrays a reckless handling of the brave crewmen of 264.

Overall figures for 264 Squadron's combat record were as impressive as any of the more glamorous Spitfire squadrons. Since Hunter's first kill on 12 May over Dunkirk, the squadron had shot down 102 Germans for the loss of thirty Defiants. But by the end of August 1940 Dowding and Park were of the same mind and agreed that both Defiant squadrons should be withdrawn and consigned to night fighting and 'the attack of unescorted bombers'.[23] At the end of the month 264 were ordered back to Kirton-in-Lindsey, Lincolnshire, where they were relegated to convoy protection patrols in the North Sea.

This decision was greeted with dismay by the proud Defiant aircrews who regarded the squadron's transfer to the backwaters of the battle an admission of failure. For Freddie Sutton and the rest of the surviving 264 crews it came as a devastating blow: 'The thought that we had been withdrawn because we were unable to cope upset us. We would have gone on until there was none left to fly rather than be brought out in disgrace. Blast it all, we had held our own! Fourteen dead – oh god! we knew that, but we were certain of sixteen Huns, not counting the probables and damaged. And the fourteen who could not report to the intelligence officer presumably had hacked something down in payment for their lives. We had turned back raids. We knew we had pulled our weight. The Hurricane and Spitfire boys – were they not getting killed also? We went to bed feeling rather bitter about things.'[24]

Jim Bailey felt betrayed by Dowding and Park. He recalled that despite the losses 'morale remained excellent', adding: 'We were all convinced that given proper leadership, we would do as well over London as the squadron had previously done during the week over Belgium and Holland. I think that our squadron scored in that week [in August] of fighting around London, nineteen German aircraft destroyed, with six other German aircraft damaged or probably destroyed.'[25]

Fred Gash loyally defended the Defiant: 'I thought it was a wonderful aircraft . . . The Defiant was a little bit slow but I don't think it was used as it should have been used. We should have been used to attack the German bombers solely . . . we should have been allowed to go into the bombers and let the Spits and Hurricanes take care of the fighters.'[26]

When at the close of the Battle of Britain the Air Ministry sent a team of inspectors to interview some of the Defiant crews they reported back that 'without exception they speak very highly of both aircraft and turret'.[27]

The next morning the Air Officer Commanding (AOC), No. 12 Group, flew down to Rochford to personally address 264 Squadron. Trafford Leigh-Mallory may also have harboured serious doubts about the Defiant as a fighter but he could not deny the valour of the aircrew or the part they had played in the critical phase of the Battle of Britain.

All the crews were ordered to assemble at dispersal. Remembered Freddie Sutton: 'There we found the AOC. No ceremony parade this. We were all just lying on the grass in the sun, and the AOC took off his tunic and cap and sprawled with us as he talked. And as he talked so our spirits soared. He first of all congratulated us. It seemed that the powers were pleased with us. The squadron which held the daytime record score has not soiled its record. Gradually we realised that he was not just putting sugar on the pill. We were not in disgrace. We had put up a bloody good show! That was different.'[28]

A Battle of Britain fighter squadron relied on its veterans: four or five experienced hands who could be trusted to go up, return safely and occasionally shoot down a German. Most important of all these seasoned fighters, through leadership and practice, passed on the tricks of the trade which kept the rookie pilots alive.

At the end of August 1940, 264 Squadron was running low on veterans. Of the original pilots and gunners who saw action at both Dunkirk and in the Battle of Britain only four remained with the squadron. One of those survivors was Eric Barwell. Having destroyed six enemy aircraft during the spring and summer of 1940, Barwell was awarded a DFC. After the Battle of Britain he married a WAAF cypher officer, Ruth Birchall. And on 10 April 1941 he achieved his first night-time success when he and his gunner destroyed one Heinkel bomber and claimed a second probable. He later transferred to Beaufighters and in his first combat in the aircraft on 1 July 1942 claimed a Dornier as a probable.

But that victory was eclipsed by the news that on the same day his elder brother Philip, group captain commanding the fighter base at RAF Biggin Hill, had been shot down over the Channel by friendly fighters. Barwell was given six months' rest before he returned in March 1943 to No. 125, a Mosquito squadron. Eric and Ruth Barwell later named their only son after Eric's brother.

At the end of the war he rejoined Barwell Engineering, the family firm near Cambridge, which specialised in tyre retreading. Ruth Barwell was an accomplished artist, glass engraver and enamel worker. When in later life she was confined to a wheelchair her husband spent the summers driving his wife, with a caravan in tow, all over the continent to allow her to paint her various subjects. He died in 2007 aged ninety-four.

Michael Young, the longest-serving member of the squadron who claimed 264's first kill on 12 May 1940, went on to fly a number of successful night-fighter missions before being posted to the Middle East in September 1940 where he joined 73 Squadron as a flight commander before taking command of 213 Squadron. Adding to his tally he claimed a damaged Ju 88 and a damaged Me 109. Like Barwell he also survived the war, and for his gallantry was awarded the DFC. He was released from the RAF in 1946 as a squadron leader. He later studied brewing at Birmingham University and worked in the beer brewing industry before retiring. He died in January 1998.

Freddie Sutton became 264's most senior gunnery officer flying with Squadron Leader Phillip Sanders. The night-fighting pair shot down two He 111s in 1941. Sutton was posted away from 264 on 16 May 1942 and went to Canada as a gunnery instructor, returning as an instructor at RAF Penrhos. He left the RAF in 1945 and later became manager with the National Westminster Bank and a founder of the RAF Air Gunners Association. He died in June 1981 in Kingston upon Thames.

His old friend Peter Bowen joined a Mosquito squadron. At 01.05 hours on 13 February 1944 Bowen and his navigator, PO John Latimer Atkinson, took off from RAF Little Snoring on a training flight. While making a tight turn during a target run the Mosquito crashed into the sea two miles off Burnham in Norfolk, killing both men.

Jim Bailey, a friend of Peter Townsend who the night before the fateful mission of 24 August tried to warn his commanding officer about the dangers of sending up 264 Squadron without any Spitfire or Hurricane cover, survived the war. He later wrote about his experiences as a Battle of Britain pilot in the critically acclaimed *The Sky Suspended*. After the Battle of Britain he transferred to 85 Squadron, a night-fighter unit led by Squadron Leader Townsend which had switched from Hurricanes to Defiants.

Bailey was later moved to the Mediterranean Theatre where he flew Beaufighters during the Anzio landings. In the Italian campaign he shot down two Ju 88s, two Ju 87s and a Me 110 and he was awarded the DFC in 1944. He also acquired an interest in beekeeping and kept a swarm of bees which he moved from airfield to airfield, although he said he didn't manage to collect a single drop of honey. Bailey's mother was determined that her son had done his bit for the war effort and during a private meeting with Winston Churchill persuaded the Prime Minister to intervene to have Bailey returned to Britain.[29] Back in Blighty Bailey found himself assigned to the Air Ministry where he was given the job of streamlining bureaucracy in the RAF.

After the war Bailey moved back to South Africa where he used his father's fortune to campaign against the country's apartheid laws. He established a magazine for black Africans called *Drum* and became a close friend of Nelson Mandela. Townsend later wrote of Bailey: 'The best airmen are mostly simple, who having been overwhelmed by their love for flying that it has driven some of them to drink, others to silence . . . But occasionally there arises one, a poet, a philosopher, who succeeds in lending coherent reason to their love. This you have certainly done for me and I believe for every airman of our age you have given wings to their thoughts.'[30]

The veteran pilot/gunner duo of Ted Thorn and Fred Barker had survived a number of close shaves and at the end of August 1940 were one of only two intact pilot/gunner pairings from 264 Squadron to have seen combat in both the Dunkirk and the Battle of Britain campaigns.

They ended their partnership with a score of thirteen enemy aircraft, making Barker the highest-scoring gunner of the Second World War. In recognition of their success and outstanding bravery during the Battle of Britain both Thorn and Barker were awarded a Bar to their DFCs. In the middle of a field in Surrey, just two miles from my house in Godalming, stands a lonely statue of a Second World War airman, marking the location of their last victory, a Heinkel shot down on the night of 9 April 1941. The statue is of a German navigator, the only member of the crew to survive the crash landing.

Shortly after this success the partnership was broken up. Thorn, who had come through the ranks, was commissioned as a pilot officer on 11 October 1941 and assigned to No. 32 Squadron RAF flying Hurricanes. Barker remained with 264 squadron for two more years before becoming an instructor in the Middle East.

On 6 July 1942 Thorn was appointed acting squadron leader commanding No. 32 Squadron, seeing heavy action during the Dieppe Raid commando landings on 19 August. On 22 September he was decorated with the DFC for his achievements in command and particularly for his bravery over Dieppe. Posted to No. 169 Squadron as a flight commander he led night-fighting and night-intruder missions in Mosquitoes against the Luftwaffe over occupied Europe. For his achievements in this role Thorn was awarded a Bar to his DFC on 8 December 1944. At the end of the war in Europe he was transferred to command a training unit. On 1 January 1946 he was again mentioned in dispatches for his skill and dedication as a flying instructor and commander.

But less than one year after the close of hostilities tragedy struck. On 12 February 1946 Thorn was flying a Gloster Meteor F.3 of the Empire Central Flying School when his aircraft dived out of a cloud and crashed at Rectory Farm near Landbeach, Cambridgeshire. He was killed outright.

Thorn's old friend and gunner, Alfred Barker, who had been commissioned as a flying officer in April 1944, was so deeply affected by Thorn's death he decided to leave the RAF. The close bonds formed during their combat operations in the Battle of Britain meant Thorn was never far from Barker's thoughts. Barker died peacefully on 18 September 2008 in his home in Romford.

And what of Sydney 'Timbertoes' Carlin – the fifty-year-old veteran gunner who had been shot down and lost a leg in the First World War only to join up again in 1940? After the Battle of Britain he continued serving as a gunner with 264 Squadron, claiming at least one kill before transferring to 151 Squadron, another Defiant unit, in January 1941. Based at RAF Wittering, he resumed night-interception missions against enemy bombers attacking the Midlands. He kept up his friendship with Squadron Leader Percy Pickard from their time in Kenya, and even persuaded him to let him volunteer as an unofficial rear gunner with 311 Squadron in one of Pickard's Wellingtons during bombing raids over Germany.

On the evening of 8 May 1941 RAF Wittering was attacked by a single Ju 88 that swept in low over the airfield. It strafed 'A' flight dispersal hut and dropped a stick of eight anti-personnel bombs. Instead of taking cover, Carlin managed to clamber onto a bicycle and pedal furiously out to his parked Defiant. He climbed into the turret and cocked the Browning machine guns ready to repel the German bomber. After the raid had passed, his pilot, Harry Bodien, who was on foot running to the plane, found Carlin mortally wounded, his right arm clean blown off by one of the bombs.[31]

# Chapter 15

# DIVINE INTERVENTION

THE FIRST DAYS of September 1940 saw no let-up in the Luftwaffe offensive. Göring continued to send large formations of bombers and fighters in daylight raids. But Hitler's order to unleash the bombers on London and other British cities meant attacks on Fighter Command airfields were not as concentrated and lacked the penetration of the previous weeks.

The Nazi leadership hoped the new strategy might result in London's eight million population 'going mad'. This new night offensive, which became known as the Blitz, did kill Londoners in their tens of thousands and quite a few people were sent mad. But overall it only served to stiffen the British fighting spirit.

By mid-September Hitler could see his air victory slipping away. On the afternoon of 14 September, the Führer met his commanders at the Reich Chancellery to discuss the future strategy of the war against Britain. The Luftwaffe had not achieved any of the objectives with which they had started when the Nazi leader had authorised Operation Sealion. But rather than recognise the strength of his opponent's air force he blamed the failure to achieve more decisive results on inclement weather. A decent spell of clear bright days was promised, especially over southern England. Hitler ordered a concerted effort to win the battle.

On 15 September the Luftwaffe began one of the biggest attacks on Britain since the start of the war. In a two-pronged offensive the bombers targeted London's railway communications in the morning and in the afternoon the dock areas of the East End of London. The German bomber crews had been told the RAF was down to its last reserves and that one more assault would clinch victory. They were in for a nasty shock.

The battle would be fought between Luftflotte 2, commanded by Generalfeldmarschall Albert Kesselring, who was responsible for the bombing of south-east England, and No. 11 Group headed by Keith Park. Kesselring could call upon thirteen hundred machines including 500 Me 109s, 100 Me 110s, 51 reconnaissance and 484 medium bomber aircraft. But crucially he didn't have sufficient crews to fly them. The squadrons of Dorniers, Heinkels and Junkers were now only 60 per cent operational.

Anticipating the attrition in personnel, Dowding had introduced a 'stabilisation scheme' for regrouping squadrons by pilot experience. This provided some relief to his own hard-pressed aircrews while also maintaining combat effectiveness. On 15 September No. 11 Group had 310 fighters, including 92 Spitfires and 218 Hurricanes. Almost all had pilots. Park could also call upon other squadrons from other groups if needed (including the Defiants, but only as a very last resort).

During the morning attack on the railway system the Luftwaffe lost six bombers and twelve Me 109s but shot down thirteen RAF fighters. In the afternoon assault on the docks the RAF destroyed twenty-one bombers and twelve fighters for the cost of fifteen Hurricanes and Spitfires. During these two main engagements, involving nearly fifteen hundred aircraft from both sides, the fighter losses had been about equal. At one point in the afternoon all of Park's squadrons were engaged. The big difference was the number of bombers being shot down and destroyed by the RAF. The more bombers Kesselring sent over southern England, the more were lost.

Kesselring was in no better position than he had been at the start of the offensive. Park's handling of the operation had been a masterclass of aggressive defence. In August the relentless assaults against his airfields had made organised defence almost impossible. September's big set-piece offensive played into his hands.

On 19 September Hitler quietly ordered the scaling down of Sealion while publicly maintaining its broad objectives. But the country remained on invasion alert and Fighter Command was more or less oblivious to Hitler's tacit admission of defeat.

The Luftwaffe continued to mount attacks against industry and airfields by day and the civilian population by night. Dowding knew the key to winning the Battle of Britain was to ensure that the RAF remained capable of being an aggressive fighting force. At the beginning of October the large number of Spitfires and Hurricanes able to confront the bombers and their Messerschmitt escorts showed Fighter Command had more than achieved that objective. As the winter months closed in, it was clear the Germans would be unable to mount an invasion.

Dowding noted in his dispatch to the Air Ministry the next year: 'Night attacks by Heavy Bombers were continuous throughout the operations, and, although they persisted and increased in intensity as day bombing became more and more expensive, they had an essentially different purpose, and the "Battle of Britain" may be said to have ended when the fighter and fighter bomber raids died down.'[1]

Dowding could do little to deter, never mind stop, the night-time bombing, and he knew it. Without in-flight radar, his night fighters failed to make any impact on the German raiders.

In the middle of a period of intense night bombing towards the end of August, Dowding was working late at Bentley Priory. One bomb had landed close enough for the explosion to disturb him. 'Did you hear that?' he asked his senior staff officer, Air Vice Marshal Douglas Strath Evill. 'I did sir,' replied Evill. 'Tell them to stop it,' said Dowding. 'Of course sir, I'll write to Fighter Command about it.' Dowding smiled back.[2] But this languid approach to a nightly terror which killed thousands of civilians made Dowding appear remote and out of touch with the British public.

The press began asking awkward and often charged questions about the conspicuous absence of the RAF night-time fighter force. The government, which faced equally difficult questions in the House of Commons, came under political pressure to encourage Dowding to take some action which might assuage the wrath of the bombed-out Londoners.

One advantageous consequence of Dowding's decision to withdraw the Defiants from the front-line of the battle was that he had released two squadrons of ready-made night fighters. No.s 264 and 141 had been undertaking night sorties since the first few weeks of the war. But they had just one victory to their name, PO 'Bull' Whitley and Sgt Turner, who shot down an enemy bomber on 15 August. Before the Defiants entered the fray half a dozen Blenheim squadrons, carrying a primitive radar, had performed the night-fighter role. But because the Blenheim was often slower than the enemy bomber it was chasing, these units had never been very effective.

Jim Bailey recalled the Defiants' new role during September 1940 when the squadron was assigned to protect Hull and the Humber and the industry of the Midlands: 'We improved and our equipment improved and as we improved we began to fly in thicker weather. That winter I seemed to watch from the air most cities in England flame, but there was as yet little any of us could do about it.'[3]

In fact the Defiant would go on to prove to be a very good night fighter, shooting down more enemy aircraft than other RAF aircraft kitted out for the role. It even became a firm favourite of Group Captain Peter Townsend who flew them with Jim Bailey when they were both assigned to 85 Squadron.[4] But the Defiant alone could not stop the Luftwaffe onslaught.

The nation owed a great debt to Dowding. Without his meticulous, strategic planning and willingness to battle the Air Staff as much as the Luftwaffe, the outcome of the Battle of Britain could have been very different. But his prickly relationships with those who opposed his forward-thinking ideas on modern fighter aircraft and tactics had left him isolated.

On the evening of 17 October Dowding and Park were both summoned to the Air Ministry to answer questions about their handling of the Battle of Britain. Present were the Air Minister, Sir Archibald Sinclair, the newly appointed Chief of the Air Staff, Sir Charles Portal and, chairing the meeting, Dowding's old adversary, Deputy Chief of the Air Staff, Sholto Douglas. Dowding and Park had fully expected to be asked to explain to the air chiefs how the battle was won. But this was far from the purpose of the meeting, which instead had the atmosphere of a court of inquiry. Douglas appeared determined to hold both men to account for their failure to deploy 'big wing' formations of large numbers of fighters against the enemy.[5] A big wing strategy, championed by fighter ace Douglas Bader and the commander of No. 12 Group, Trafford Leigh-Mallory, was regarded as a better tactic for defeating the Luftwaffe than the piecemeal squadron defence employed by Park and Dowding. But since the Luftwaffe had already been defeated this was a problematic argument to run. When this became all too apparent the Air Staff looked for another means of deposing of Dowding.

So they switched their attack to Fighter Command's failure to combat the Luftwaffe night raids. Here Sholto Douglas felt he was on much firmer ground. German bombs were falling on British cities almost every night and the Battle of Britain did not feel much like a victory to the suffering urban populations of England. When Douglas had suggested in September that Dowding use the Defiants in conjunction with Hurricanes, which would act as 'night eyes' for the turret night fighters, the head of Fighter Command dismissed the idea as too dangerous.

Now Douglas returned to the subject with fixed intent. Churchill had remained loyal to Dowding. But Douglas and Portal had managed to persuade Lord Beaverbrook to join their cause. Although the charismatic and influential minister had worked closely with Dowding to boost the supply of Hurricanes and Spitfires, at the cost of the Defiants, Beaverbrook had long supported the case for a more dynamic leader of Fighter Command to take the fight to the enemy.[6]

Beaverbrook came up with the idea of establishing a committee to investigate the night-fighting problem to be chaired by one of Dowding's fiercest critics, Sir John Salmond. In the interwar years Salmond and his brother, a former Chief of the Air Staff, had clashed with Dowding over the development of Fighter Command and the deployment of the new turret fighter. Douglas and Stevenson now made sure John Salmond would determine Dowding's fate.

Salmond duly delivered a damning critique which personally held Dowding accountable for not making adequate provision for night-fighting squadrons which could be independently coordinated by a new command. Dowding was directly accused of not releasing sufficient fighter aircraft, like the Defiant, for night duties. While this may have been true it was hardly Dowding's fault alone. Throughout the Battle of Britain the Air Ministry had insisted the Defiant should be used as a daytime fighter to shoot down bombers in the Battle of Britain. Instead of turning out a first-class night fighter, Douglas and Stevenson had pressed ahead with developing a new version of the Defiant fitted with forward guns.[7]

None of this would save Dowding. Salmond scrawled[8] all over his final report 'Dowding should go' and then wrote personally to Churchill setting out his reasons: 'I am most anxious to put to you the case for a change in the holder of the important position of C-in-C Fighter Command. Recently on Lord Beaverbrook's instructions, I have carried out an enquiry into night air defence, the result of which, together with what has since occurred, makes a change, in my opinion, imperative. This opinion is also very strongly held by most, if not all, service members of the Air Council.'[9]

Churchill asked Dowding to respond to Salmond's official

findings. The head of Fighter Command conceded that despite everyone's efforts no one had come up with a means of defeating the German night bombers. He repeated his conclusion that until airborne radar was more effective sending up fighters at night would only be successful if they made a 'lucky encounter'.[10] In fact night-fighting provision had been so badly neglected that well into 1941 the crews were still being issued with 'bucket loads of oranges and carrots' to improve their night vision before they went out on sorties.[11]

The deployment of the Defiant had been the first of many contentious air defence issues over which Dowding and the Air Ministry had disagreed. And it was to be the last.

On 17 November Hugh Dowding was removed from his post to be replaced by Sholto Douglas, the ambitious air marshal who had coveted the job for so long. At the same time Donald Stevenson was promoted to head of No. 2 Group (Bomber Command) where his willingness to risk the lives of RAF crews on futile low-level bombing missions earned him the nickname 'butcher'. The historian Max Hastings described Stevenson as 'an arrogant, ruthless man . . . who regarded No. 2 Group's operations solely in light of the value to his own advancement'.[12] Stevenson later suffered the loss of his son Peter, who was shot down in his Spitfire on a sweep over Boulogne in 1943.[13]

The following year the Air Ministry published its official account of the Battle of Britain. There was no mention of Dowding, nor indeed of Keith Park. But the Boulton Paul Defiant was given equal billing alongside the Spitfire and the Hurricane as one of three RAF fighters that had saved Britain in its hour of need.

The glaring omission of Dowding in the official account

provoked Churchill to write directly to the head of the Air Ministry, Archibald Sinclair: 'This is not a good story . . . The jealousies and cliquism which have led to the committing of this offence are a discredit to the Air Ministry, and I do not think any other Service Department would have been guilty of such a piece of work. What would have been said if the Admiralty had told the tale of Trafalgar and left Lord Nelson out of it?'[14]

But Dowding was determined to have the last word. In October 1941 he wrote his own unvarnished, warts-and-all account of the Battle of Britain. It included his personal views of the Air Staff, the choice of fighters and the real reason the RAF had beaten Göring's Luftwaffe. However, this version was deemed so sensitive that the government censors intervened and blocked publication until a year after the end of the war.

Dowding called his book, a mixture of memoir and military review, *Twelve Legions of Angels*. When it was finally cleared for publication in 1946 it was already out of date and of no interest to a nation that wanted to move on from the privations and horrors of war. As a result it quickly went out of print. But there is a single copy held at the British Library. And it contains the most valuable insight into how the Commander-in-Chief of Fighter Command fought the Battle of Britain.

In it, Dowding forcefully made out his final case for his fixed-gun fighters, the Hurricane and the Spitfire, in preference to the turret fighter. With a clear advantage of hindsight, he wrote[15]: 'In the first place every turret involves the addition of one member to the crew and detracts from the performance of the fighter by its head-resistance and weight. I cannot afford to increase the size and weight or to reduce the performance of my standard fighter, which will be required in maximum numbers.' And he now stressed the 'necessity for having all the functions of a day fighter controlled by a single brain,' adding that the 'manoeuvring of the fighter and the firing of the guns are so intimately connected that no system of communication between two individuals can serve the purpose'.

Putting the debate to bed, he concluded: 'In saying that I cannot accept turret guns as the main armament of the standard day, I am not just giving you my personal opinion – my views are based on practical experience.'

Still smoldering with resentment over the trumped-up justification for his removal from Fighter Command, Dowding claimed it had not been possible to use the Defiant as a night fighter until it had been equipped with in-flight radar sets. He argued: 'My interception system, although very effective, will not suffice to put me so close that I can see the bomber on a dark night, so I must have some form of detector in the fighter in order that the fighter may be able to carry out the final stages of the approach.' He also firmly dismissed Sholto Douglas's idea of deploying Hurricanes in this role because there was insufficient room for a 'detector'.

And in a chapter provocatively titled 'Why are senior officers so stupid?' Dowding mounted a broader and thinly veiled attack on the Air Staff. He accused them of being blinkered, lacking imagination and engaging in groupthink which he blamed on 'public schools, where the individualist is suppressed and the good citizen is mass produced'.

He then finally turned to the question that military experts and historians have been quarrelling over ever since the end of the war: how did we win the Battle of Britain? Dowding's answer is truly astonishing. Instead of citing the Spitfire, radar or his brilliant home defence system, Dowding, a punctilious military leader famed for his reliance on scientific experiment, claimed that God had personally intervened on the side of the RAF. But this was not simply a pious military leader honouring his Christian faith, the Commander-in-Chief of the RAF candidly claimed he had personal experience of this divine intervention.

He revealed: 'I had this personal experience in the Battle of Britain. I wish I could tell you about it, but the story, or series of events, is intensely personal and others besides myself are concerned. It will never be published – at any rate not by me. I pay my homage to those dear boys, those gallant boys, who gave their all that our nation might live; I pay my tribute to their leaders and commanders; but I say with absolute conviction, and but for God's intervention, the Battle of Britain would have been lost. Now therefore as I lay down my sword I take up my pen and testify.'[16]

# EPILOGUE

Britain went to war with Germany fielding three front-line fighters. If the Air Staff had got its way, twenty of Fighter Command's squadrons would have been equipped with the Boulton Paul Defiant. But due to the hostility of Hugh Dowding and Keith Park, combined with chronic production hold-ups at the Boulton Paul factory, only two squadrons of turret fighters ever fought in the battle.

The contrasting fortunes of those two units tell us as much about the tactical failures of Fighter Command in the deployment of the Defiant as it does about the performance of the aircraft.

At Dunkirk, Defiant crews serving with 264 Squadron had done all that was asked of them, shooting down sufficient numbers of German bombers to justify the aircraft's principal purpose as a bomber destroyer. During Operation Dynamo it had arguably performed this role better than the Hurricane or the Spitfire.

Destroying thirty-eight German aircraft in one day, with no loss, was an extraordinary combat record which gave the British public something to cheer about when very little else was going Britain's way. Initially the Defiant may have been mistaken for a Hurricane so that Messerschmitt fighter pilots accidentally flew into a hail of rear-gun fire. But there are three reasons why this is not an adequate explanation for the Defiant's 'surprising' success. By mid-May 1940 the Luftwaffe already knew all about the Defiant's formidable fire power. No. 264's record haul of kills on 29 May included more bombers than fighters. And Hunter's tactics meant that the enemy fighters were deliberately drawn into the turrets' arcs of fire.

The sudden appearance of the Defiant over the skies of continental Europe in spring 1940 also had an indirect impact on the fighting capability of the enemy. We will never know how many Hurricane pilots owe their lives to the reluctance of German fighters to launch a stern attack out of a fear of making themselves a target for the turret gunner. Even a split-second hesitation would have given a Hurricane enough time to get away.

More significantly German high command knew that if Operation Sealion, the invasion of Britain, was going to be successful the Luftwaffe would need to first secure air superiority. Fighter Command's new turret fighter presented the Luftwaffe with a very different challenge, helping to convince Hitler that the RAF posed a potent threat to his invasion plans.

But the combat effectiveness of a modern fighter in 1940 was much more than just a streamlined, armoured hulk of metal.

When Dowding delivered his report to the Air Ministry in 1941 on Fighter Command's conduct of the Battle of Britain he emphasised the importance of individual leadership. He stressed that 'Some of our worst losses occurred through defective leadership on the part of a unit commander, who might lead his pilots into a trap or be caught while climbing by an enemy formation approaching "out of the sun".'

In Philip Hunter, 264 Squadron had one of the best commanding officers of the Battle of Britain. Under his brave and resourceful leadership, the Defiant crews had shown the new fighter was only as good as the pilots and gunners who flew them. Yet all Hunter's success seemed to achieve was to antagonise Fighter Command. Keith Park's explosive memo to Dowding setting out his negative critique of the aircraft during Dunkirk does not cast the air vice-marshal in a very favourable light.

When it came to the turn of the second squadron of Defiants, 141, Fighter Command's decision to send the unblooded crews into combat unprotected was shameful. If Park really believed what he had written in his memo to Dowding in June why did he order 141 to Fighter Command's most exposed airfield, Hawkinge, and then on 19 July allow the Defiants to be scrambled to face the enemy without any fighter cover? Was this because the Air Ministry and Fighter Command had still not addressed the radio communications problems which had plagued the development of the Defiant? Had it been secretly decided that there was little point in providing the Defiants with a protective cover of Hurricanes or Spitfires if the two squadron leaders were unable to talk to each other once airborne? And what excuse was there for not fitting the Defiants with bulletproof glass cockpits and constant speed propellers which would have aided their performance? Dowding and Park, who both resented having to use other fighter units to protect Defiants, must shoulder some of the blame for the massacre that followed.

When 264 Squadron was recalled to the fray in August, Park and Dowding had no hesitation in repeating this tactical blunder, deploying the Defiants to Kent's 'hellfire corner' where they were ordered to protect RAF Manston. Once again they were repeatedly scrambled without any fighter cover.

Yet throughout ten days in August, 264 Squadron performed no worse against the German fighters than any other RAF squadron. But when read against Hurricane and Spitfire pilot losses, the Defiant's two-man crew inflated the fatality rate. After the Defiants were finally withdrawn on 28 August it became apparent the squadron had scored highly but suffered terribly. This was partly because in the four major battles in which they took part they ran up against some of the Luftwaffe's most experienced aces and, in Arnold Lignitz, a fighter pilot leader who knew all about shooting down Defiants.

Fighter combat orthodoxy has long held that the Boulton Paul Defiant was a flawed and anachronistic aircraft borne out of a stubborn and misguided preservation of the division of roles between the pilot and the gunner. Eighty years later it is easy to accuse the armchair air marshals of being out of step with modern fighter technology because their own experience was grounded in the air combat tactics of the First World War. But during the interwar period the British military and the public lived in fear of a terrifying and devastating attack from the air. These fears were stoked by reports of a super-bomber force being developed in Germany, capable of long-range attacks on the British mainland. In that context it seems quite rational to want to develop a specialist bomber destroyer capable of neutralising this threat.

After the First World War, the Air Ministry invested all of this thinking in the Boulton Paul Defiant. But the Defiant became a political pawn in a power struggle between Hugh Dowding and the Air Staff. Dowding and his number two, Keith Park, had resolutely concluded the turret fighter was obsolete before it had a chance of firing its four Browning machine guns in anger. Dowding, ex post facto, tried to claim he had always kept an open mind about the Defiant. And there is some evidence to show that during the Phoney War, when the RAF didn't know whether their fixed-gun fighters could cope with the German bomber force, the commander-in-chief was prepared to let the aircraft prove its worth. But by then Dowding enjoyed the luxury of knowing that the Boulton Paul factories could never trouble his squadrons with anything like the number of Defiants the Air Ministry had threatened him with.

At the height of the Battle of Britain the Defiant, like the Hurricane and the Spitfire, was vulnerable to the latest variants of the Me 109, the best fighter of its day. In the end Fighter Command's final decision to retire the Defiant as a front-line day fighter at the end of August 1940 was not just a reaction to mounting losses but a reflection of the unavailability of replacement aircraft.

So where does all this leave the Boulton Paul Defiant's role in the Battle of Britain?

Fewer than one hundred pilots and gunners served with the two Defiant squadrons during the main battle. They accounted for no more than twenty-three German aircraft in around twenty days of active service on the front line in July and August. The combined losses for 141 and 264 Squadrons is seventeen aircraft. Of course the figures for 264 Squadron alone are much more impressive, especially as they were fighting during the most critical phase of the Battle of Britain. Even so, it is clear that after Dunkirk and the tragedy of 141 Squadron, the Defiant played a very limited role in the main battle. So then the question becomes more abstract. What would have happened if the Defiant flew in the numbers the Air Ministry intended?

Some have argued that had Dowding and Park not resisted the Air Ministry's ambition of equipping a third of Fighter Command with Defiant squadrons the RAF would have lost the

Battle of Britain. Given what we know of 264's combat statistics I'm not sure that is a fair assessment. I believe that with proper fighter protection and the advantage of fighting on home territory, rather than at the limit of its range over Holland and in the Dunkirk theatre, the Defiant would have acquitted itself well.

The Luftwaffe might have even lost more bombers more quickly, giving the enemy a short sharp shock. But the Defiant was never allowed to exploit its tactical advantage in the Battle of Britain. It was deployed to the front-line fighter stations where it was miscast as an independent fighter, instead of a bomber destroyer which operated best in tandem with squadrons of Hurricanes and Spitfires. This was a fact that Philip Hunter conceded when he discussed squadron tactics with Jim Bailey on the night before his death.

Britain won the Battle of Britain and five years later secured ultimate victory over the Nazis. The Defiant, along with many different RAF types, played its part. Yet very little has been written about the Defiant and the brave airmen who crewed them.

Instead, history has treated the aircraft as a military design failure and its participation in the battle as an unmitigated disaster, costing the lives of dozens of young pilots and gunners. This version of the Battle of Britain underplays the heroism of the airmen who flew the Boulton Paul Defiant against all the odds. It also fails to show how the Defiant was as much a victim of political infighting and mismanagement as it was of the much faster German Messerschmitts.

Indeed the concept of the two-seater fighter survived the Battle of Britain. The UK's Tornado fighter bomber and the US F 14 Tomcat interceptor became two of the most successful fighters of the twentieth century. The Defiant and its crews deserve to be counted among them.

# ACKNOWLEDGEMENTS

THE SEEDS OF this project were sowed in a diary extract written by George Heseltine, my great uncle who, after recovering from wounds sustained in the Gallipoli campaign, volunteered for the Royal Flying Corps. He was typical of the young men of the First World War who calmly accepted the horrors of war as part of the performance of their duty in the service of the nation. When I read about his courageous aerial exploits as the pilot of a novel but under-powered fighter aircraft I was hooked and wanted to know the whole story. It was a quest which led me from Uncle George's single-engined two-seater fighter, the Fe2d, to its natural conclusion, the Boulton Paul Defiant, and the brave airmen who flew this aircraft when Britain faced its gravest hour twenty-five years later.

I wish also to acknowledge my father's contribution to this book. Born in Kent in 1929, he was part of a generation whose youth meant they could only watch in awe as the RAF slugged it out with the Luftwaffe in dogfights above the fields of southern England during the summer of 1940. After the war my father flew gliders from the same Kent airfields (West Malling and Hawkinge) which only a few years earlier had been used as front-line fighter stations. He passed on the flying bug to me, although I only ever mastered the piloting of balsa-wood model aircraft.

It would have been impossible to write this book without the resources and assistance of the National Archives, Imperial War Museum, Kent Battle of Britain Musuem, Hawkinge, RAF AIR Historical Branch, Battle of Britain London Monument and the RAF Museum in Hendon and Cosford. Special thanks to Gordon Leith for his help at Hendon.

I wish to pay particular thanks to Meg Sparks and John Richardson (children of Sq Ld William 'Dickie' Richardson), Group Captain Patrick Tootal OBE, secretary of the Battle of Britain Memorial, Les Whitehouse, archivist of The Boulton Paul Association, Neil MacDougall, John Dimmock, John Moles and Ben and Sarah Nicholls (granddaughter of Philip Hunter) for providing information about Boulton Paul and the crews who flew with 141 and 264 Squadrons.

And last, and my no means least, I owe a special debt of gratitude to Duncan Proudfoot, whose boundless encouragement and wise editorial direction has kept the project on the road. In the same vein I wish to say thank you to my agent Piers Blofeld, armchair air marshals, Jonathan Ames, Dan Hayes, Michael Hamblin and Paul Ferris; pilot of my life, Linda King and rear gunners, Stanley and Walter Verkaik.

# NOTES

## 1 First of the few

1 Ian Castle *London 1917–18: The Bomber Blitz* p. 8.
2 Robert Wright *Dowding and the Battle of Britain* p. 36.
3 Cyril Newall replaced him.
4 Vincent Orange *Dowding of Fighter Command: Victor of the Battle of Britain* pp. 31–2.
5 Graham Wallace *RAF Biggin Hill* p. 28.
6 https://www.kentonline.co.uk/folkestone/news/a-quiet-spring-day-then-126206/
7 https://www.military-history.org/articles/strategic-bombing-gothas-over-london.htm
8 https://www.rafmuseum.org.uk/blog/the-forgotten-father-of-the-royal-air-forc/
9 Wallace p. 36.
10 Wallace p. 36.
11 Author's interview with John Dimmock, son of Norman Dimmock. Wallace p. 38.
12 Peter Townsend *Duel of Eagles* p. 13.
13 Townsend p. 14.
14 Townsend p. 16.
15 Wallace p. 39.
16 Wallace p. 41.

## 2 Rearmament

1 Townsend p. 31.
2 Townsend p. 39.
3 AIR 10/199 RAF notes for airmen on demobilisation, 1919.
4 Townsend p. 35.
5 Townsend p. 42.
6 John T. LaSaine *Air Officer Commanding: Hugh Dowding, Architect of the Battle of Britain* p. 30.
7 Townsend p. 46.
8 Townsend p. 48.
9 Hannes Trautloft and Bob Hans-Ekkehard *The War Diaries of Hannes Trautloft: Kommodore of JG54 Grunherz.* Townsend p. 84.
10 http://www.airpages.ru/eng/ru/lipetsk.shtml
11 Interview with the family of Sq Ld William Richardson.
12 Robert Jackson *Men of Power: The Lives of Rolls-Royce Chief Test Pilots Harvey and Jim Heyworth.*
13 Townsend p. 95.

## 3 Bombers in command

1 Harold Macmillan *Winds of Change* p. 522.
2 Neville Jones *The Beginnings of Strategic Air Power* pp. 160–3.
3 Alan J. Levine *The Strategic Bombing of Germany, 1940–1945* p. 16.
4 Colin S. Sinnott *The RAF and Aircraft Design: Air Staff Operational Requirements 1923–1939* p. 119.
5 John Salmond was a former Chief of the Defence Staff who had worked closely with Keith Park after the First World War to bolster Britain's air defence. His daughter married the son of the British Nazi sympathiser Sir Oswald Mosley.
6 Alec Brew *The Turret Fighters* p. 13.
7 Alec Brew *Boulton Paul Aircraft: An Illustrated History* p. 5.
8 http://britishaviation-ptp.com/jd_north.html
9 AVIA 46/111 Ministry of Supply 1946 report on the origins of the Defiant. Brew p. 21.
10 AVIA 46/111 Extract from notes prepared by Mr J. D. North. Boulton Paul Aircraft Ltd, Wolverhampton.
11 Brew *The Turret Fighters* p. 20.

12 AIR 2/1599 Air Ministry papers. Defiant single engine, two-seater day and night fighter. Specification: F.9/35. 8.4.35.
13 AIR 2/1599.
14 AVIA 46/111 Extract from notes prepared by Mr J. D. North. Boulton Paul Aircraft Ltd. Wolverhampton. 'Used my contacts at the ministry . . .' probably Edward Derek Davis.
15 Sinnott p. 126.
16 AIR 2/1599.
17 AVIA 46/111.
18 AIR 2/1599.
19 AVIA 46/111.
20 AIR 2/1599.
21 AIR 2/1599.

**4 March of the Messerschmitt**

1 Townsend p. 106.
2 Hansard HC Deb 30 July 1934 Vol. 292 cc. 2325–447.
3 Townsend p. 124.
4 Hannes Trautloft *Als Jagdflieger in Spanien* [*As a Fighter Pilot in Spain*].
5 Trautloft.
6 Trautloft.
7 Stephen Bungay *The Most Dangerous Enemy* p. 50.
8 http://www.luftwaffe.cz/trautloft.html
9 Jim Bailey *The Sky Suspended: A Fighter Pilot's Story* p. 17.
10 Jim Bailey *The Sky Suspended: A Fighter Pilot's Story* p. 12.
11 Jim Bailey *The Sky Suspended: A Fighter Pilot's Story* p. 13.
12 *Guardian* Obituaries 3 March 2000. https://www.theguardian.com/news/2000/mar/03/guardianobituaries
13 www.oldcranwellians.info/ca/ca-home-menu.html
14 John E. Mack. *A Prince of Our Disorder: The Life of T. E. Lawrence* p. 421.
15 https://www.iwm.org.uk/collections/item/object/80006615
16 Interview with the family of Sq Ld William Richardson.
17 John Terraine *The Right of the Line: The Role of the RAF in World War Two* p. 44.
18 Bungay p. 85.
19 Jim Bailey *The Sky Suspended: A Fighter Pilot's Story* p. 18.

20 Bungay p. 171.
21 https://www.independent.co.uk/news/obituaries/group-captain-john-gardner-new-zealand-fighter-pilot-who-fought-in-the-battle-of-britain-2288114.html
22 Townsend p. 145.
23 Orange p. 99.
24 Orange p. 89.
25 Townsend p. 145.
26 http://www.inventricity.com/rdf-and-radar
27 Orange p. 93.
28 AIR 2/2165.
29 https://www.baesystems.com/en/heritage/vickers-supermarine-spitfire
30 It was later decided to double the number of guns carried by the Spitfires and Hurricanes so they had four .303 Browning machine guns in each wing.
31 Orange p. 102.
32 AIR 2/2964.
33 AIR 2/2964.
34 AIR 2/2964.
35 Sholto Douglas with Robert Wright *Years of Command* p. 18.
36 Douglas p. 14.
37 Douglas p. 57.
38 Orange p. 103.
39 Sholto Douglas with Robert. Wright Years of Command p. 172.
40 AIR 2/2964.
41 AIR 2/2964.
42 Orange p. 103.

## 5 Three fighters

1 https://www.iwm.org.uk/collections/item/object/80006615
2 Townsend pp. 149 and 156.
3 Townsend p. 160.
4 John Banham interview with Imperial War Museum (27.4.1983) reel 1 https://www.iwm.org.uk/collections/item/object/80006615
5 Orange p. 115.
6 Orange p. 94.
7 Memo to Neville Chamberlain from Winston Churchill 12 March

1938. Robert Rhodes James *Churchill: a study in failure, 1900–1939* p. 263. William Manchester *The Last Lion: Winston Spencer Churchill: Alone, 1932–1940.*

8 AIR 6/33. June 1938 Douglas' letter to Dowding. Orange p. 103.

9 Michael J. F. Bowyer 'The Boulton Paul Defiant' *Aircraft in Profile, Vol. 5* London: Profile Publications Ltd, 1966. p. 4.

10 Bowyer p. 4.

11 AVIA 46/111 Ministry of Supply report into Defiant progression. Phil Listemann *Squadrons! Vol 19. The Boulton Paul Defiant: Day and Night Fighter* p. 5.

12 E. R. Hooton *Luftwaffe at War: Gathering Storm 1933–39 Vol. 1.*

13 Hansard 9 March 1939.

14 *Yorkshire Post* Wednesday 1 February 1939.

15 *Liverpool Daily Post* Wednesday 1 February 1939.

16 Listemann p. 3.

17 *Aberdeen People's Journal* Saturday 8 April 1939.

18 Robert Wright *Dowding and the Battle of Britain* p. 73.

19 *The Journal of the Cambridge University Engineering Society* 1952 pp. 14–17. http://cues.soc.srcf.net/downloads/magazine/1952small.pdf

20 Report by Bennett Melvill Jones Gunnery Research Office. A&A.E.E., Royal Air Force, Boscombe Down, Amesbury, Wiltshire 7.11.39.

21 AIR 16/130.

22 Orlebar's flying pedigree was peerless and he had been at the forefront of the early development of the Supermarine Spitfire. Between 1927 and 1931 he was Officer Commanding and pilot with the High Speed Flight, the RAF's team for the Schneider Trophy seaplane races. In 1929 he set an air speed record of 357.7 mph in Supermarine S.6.

23 AIR 16/154 Correspondence between Dowding/Air Ministry and AFDE July/September 1939.

24 Orange pp. 113–14.

25 In April 1940 Ludlow-Hewitt was removed from Bomber Command.

26 Orange p. 117.

27 *The Times* 8 August 1939 p. 7.

28 PRO AIR/16/129 Preliminary Report on Home Defence Exercise 25 August 1939.

29 Wright pp. 77–8.
30 Orange pp. 122–3.
31 Listemann p. 3.
32 AIR 16 / 130.

## 6 State of war

1 'Date of attack September 1' Townsend p. 177.
2 www.historyplace.com/speeches/chamberlain.htm
3 Townsend p. 177.
4 Townsend p. 178.
5 https://www.iwm.org.uk/collections/item/object/80006615 https://www.rafbf.org/news-and-blogs/lucky-arthur-john-banham http://264squadron.co.uk/newsletters/
6 Banham interview with Imperial War Museum 27.4.1983 reel 1 https://www.iwm.org.uk/collections/item/object/80006615
7 https://www.iwm.org.uk/collections/item/object/80006615 https://www.rafbf.org/news-and-blogs/lucky-arthur-john-banham http://264squadron.co.uk/newsletters/
8 AIR 16/130.
9 Douglas p. 48.
10 Townsend p. 171.
11 Bailey p. 18.
12 Martin Middlebrook and Chris Everitt (2014). *The Bomber Command War Diaries: An Operational Reference Book 1939–1945*. Pen & Sword Aviation.
13 https://www.rafmuseum.org.uk/research/history-of-aviation-timeline/interactive-aviation-timeline/british-military-aviation/1939.aspx
14 John Freeborn *Tiger Club* p. 48.
15 http://blitzwalkers.blogspot.com/2013/09/the-battle-of-barking-creek.html
16 James Kightly *Aeroplane Magazine* October 2015 p. 80.
17 Turner was reported missing 11 January 1940.
18 Appleby, aged twenty-six, was killed on 23 July 1940 when his Hudson collided with a Hurricane in Wick, Scotland. William APPLEBY (42975) Wireless Op./Air Gunner Hudson p. 51–2 AIR 81/2435.
19 Kightly pp. 73–80.

20 Dowding's logic was that by letting the enemy pilots fight another day he was putting his own pilots in more danger.

21 In June 1940 Albert Leslie Womersley co-led an attack against the legendary Nazi battleship the *Scharnhorst* off Norway. Despite facing intense AA fire and the attentions of a squadron of Me 109s he managed to drop his bombs on the ship's bows but damage was only minor. At least two of the six Hudsons used in the mission were lost along with their crew.

## 7 Combat readiness

1 *The Journal of the Cambridge University Engineering Society 1952* pp. 14–17. http://cues.soc.srcf.net/downloads/magazine/1952small.pdf

2 Report by Bennett Melvill Jones, Gunnery Research Office. A.&A.E.E., Royal Air Force, Boscombe Down, Amesbury, Wiltshire 7.11.39.

3 AIR 20/6299.

4 AIR 20/6299 Dowding wrote to Melvill Jones on 8 November 1939 in reply to his letter the day before.

5 AVIA 15/398 Air Ministry Memorandum on Programmes 5.4.40.

6 http://www.historyofwar.org/articles/timeline_spitfire.html

7 AVIA 46/11 Ministry of Supply 1946 report on the origins of the Defiant.

8 AVIA 15/398 Internal Memo Directorate of Aeroplane Production 15.5.40.

9 AVIA 15/398.

10 AVIA 15/398.

11 http://www.rafweb.org/Biographies/Hardy.htm
http://www.rafweb.org/Squadrons/COs/OCs_261-299.htm
http://264squadron.co.uk/wp-content/uploads/2012/04/history-of-264.pdf

12 AIR 16/154 Stevenson's letter to Dowding 17.12.39.

13 Listemann p. 20. In 1940 Hardy was station commander at RAF Coltishall; he died in April 1945. http://www.rafweb.org/Biographies/Hardy.htm

14 AIR 16/154.

15 https://www.iwm.org.uk/collections/item/object/80019802

16 http://264squadron.co.uk/wp-content/uploads/2018/02/Squadron-News-69.pdf

17 AIR 16/154.

18 AIR 16/154.

19 AIR 16/154 Letter from Donald Stevenson to Hugh Dowding 17.12.39.

20 AIR 16/154 Memo from Hardy to Wing Commander D. V. Carnegie at Fighter Command.

21 AIR 20/6299 Dowding's memo to Melvill Jones on 8 November 1939 in reply to his letter the day before.

22 AIR 16/154 Keith Park wrote to Dowding 16.1.40.

23 *Aberdeen Press and Journal* 2.2.40.

24 AIR 16/154.

25 Dowding's micromanagement of the Defiant tests extended to him setting out the precise level of harmonisation for the gun sights.

26 AIR 16/130 Memo to Air Ministry 19.1.40.

27 AIR 16/130 19.1.40.

28 Memos written by Park to Dowding 19.2.40 and 7.2.40.

29 I. McInnes and J. V. Webb *A Contemptible Little Flying Corps* pp. 118–19.

30 AIR 16/130 Wing Commander G. H. Vasse AFDU. *Report number 21 on free gun fighter tactics – Defiant* Air Fighting Development Unit RAF Station Northolt 5.5.40.

31 Greg Baughen *The RAF in the Battle of France and the Battle of Britain* p. 85.

32 In his tactical memorandum 27.4 40 AIR 16/154 Hunter pointed out that due to the Defiant's poor rate of climb (20,000 feet took seventeen minutes) it was practically impossible to attack any aircraft flying faster than 180 mph because in endeavouring to get in position one would probably lose sight of the enemy and also lose distance. 'In view of the experience of this Squadron gained at Air Fighting Development Unit, Northolt, the following attacks have been produced. The minimum number of aircraft for day flying is two aircraft. The reason for this is that a Defiant can be placed on either side of the enemy target. If there was only one aircraft then the enemy aircraft could escape.'

33 AIR 16/154.

## 8 Baptism of fire

1 This appears to be a mistaken assumption on Mayfield's part that the Defiant had a forward-firing machine gun operated by the pilot.

2 Guy Mayfield *Life and Death in the Battle of Britain* pp. 61–2.
3 AIR 16/154.
4 Minutes of conference on free-gun fighter attacks. Fighter Command HQ 9.5.40.
5 Diagrams of Defiant fighter attacks sent to Dowding in July 1939. Dowding describes 'overtaking attack' as an 'excellent' idea. In a further letter to Group Captain Orlebar dated 17.9.39 Dowding describes how Defiants can provide 'broadsides' that pour 'enfilade and raking fire' into the enemy aircraft.
6 AIR 16/154.
7 AIR 50/104/154 combat report. AIR 27/1553 264 Operations Record Book.
8 Cooke's combat report. AIR 50/104/24
9 IWM https://www.iwm.org.uk/collections/item/object/80019802
10 Listemann p. 22.
11 Hugh Harkins *Defiant Mk 1 Combat Log* p. 16.
12 http://264squadron.co.uk/wp-content/uploads/2012/04/squadron-history-3.pdf
13 AIR 50/104/115.
14 AIR 50/104/62.
15 Jan Jolie *Luchtgevechten boven West-Brabant en de Biesbosch.*
16 WO 416/150/111.
17 http://www.aircrewremembrancesociety.co.uk/styled-5/styled-7/styled-441/index.html
18 AIR 50/104/160.
19 AIR 50/104/66.
20 CAB 66/7/38 Weekly Résumée (No. 37) of the Naval, Military and Air Situation from 12 noon 9 May to 12 noon 16 May 1940.
21 http://www.aircrewremembrancesociety.co.uk/styled-5/styled-7/styled-438/index.html
22 John A. Chambers *Defiant: The True Story* p. 23.
23 http://www.aircrewremembrancesociety.co.uk/styled-5/styled-7/styled-250/index.html
24 AIR 27/1553 264 Operations Record Book.
25 AIR 27/1553 264 Operations Record Book.

## 9 Dunkirk mission

1 In the air, the Allies were outnumbered. The Armée de l'Air had 1562 aircraft, and RAF Fighter Command committed 680 machines, while RAF Bomber Command could contribute some 392 aircraft to operations.
2 AIR 14/449.
3 D. Harvey (October 1990). 'The French Armée de l'Air in May–June 1940: A Failure of Conception' *Journal of Contemporary History* p. 448.
4 Tony Holmes *Hurricanes to the Fore* pp. 48–9.
5 Denis Richards, in his 1953 contribution to the official British account History of the Second World War.
6 Bungay p. 136.
7 Townsend p. 221.
8 Townsend p. 219.
9 Derek Dempster and Derek Wood, *The Narrow Margin* p. 97. Pen & Sword Aviation, 2010.
10 Townsend p. 222.
11 Simon Parry and Mark Postlethwaite *Dunkirk Air Combat Archive* p. 8.
12 Townsend p. 225.
13 Townsend p. 225.
14 Orange p. 159.
15 Townsend p. 226.
16 Parry and Postlethwaite p. 23.
17 AIR 50/104/199.
18 Parry and Postlethwaite p. 52.
19 The trial took place on 6 April 1940.
20 Tony Bartley's letter to his father June 1940. Norman Franks p. 25.
21 AIR 27/1553 No. 11 Group Intelligence Fighter Command combat report. 24.5.40 Operations Record Book.
22 AIR 27/1553 264 Operations Record Book.
23 Parry p. 58.
24 Orange p. 166.
25 AIR 27/155 264 Operations Record Book.
26 Parry and Postlethwaite p. 63.
27 Townsend p. 229.
28 Welsh and Hayden survived Dunkirk and the Battle of Britain, as

did Thorn and Barker. http://www.bbm.org.uk/airmen/Hayden.htm They claimed a scalp on 27th. Off Dunkirk on 27 May they shared in the destruction of an He 111 and on the 29th destroyed a Me 109, a Me 110 and two Ju 87s. On 24 August they destroyed a Ju 88 and damaged a Me 109 in the Hornchurch area.

29 AIR 27/1555 264 Operations Record Book. AIR 50/104/154 Young combat report.

30 AIR 50/104/154 Young combat report: 27.5.40. Took off Manston at 11.20 landed Manston at 13.15 12 Heinkels. Height: 7000 ft. Enemy sighted: 12.30 West of Dunkirk. Enemy casualties: One shared with Red leader.

31 AIR 50/104/24 N. Cooke combat report. Blue Section leader. 27.5.40.

32 AIR 50/104/143 Parry and Postlethwaite p. 103. Harkin pp. 32–3.

33 http://www.bbm.org.uk/airmen/Stevenson.htm

34 AIR 16/870. Orange p. 170.

35 Franks p. 33.

36 Philip Hunter's son Nigel became a qualified doctor and had a family of his own. His daughter (Philip Hunter's granddaughter) Sarah lives in Hampshire.

37 Scott sailed with the British team at the 1936 Olympics in Germany.

38 https://www.cwgc.org/find-war-dead/casualty/1078765/lippett,-albert/

## 10 Day of the Defiant

1 Parry and Postlethwaite p. 117.

2 Citation DFM Air Ministry 14 June.

3 Parry and Postlethwaite pp. 126–7.

4 AIR 27/1555 264 Squadron report.

5 AIR 50/104/154 Young/Johnson combat report.

6 AIR 50/104/25 Cooke/Lippett combat report.

7 Interestingly, I can't find any German record of Me 110s damaged that day, which suggests that the Gruppe did not file a report or it has been lost. It seems incredulous to think that not a single Me 110 suffered any damage. There are reports for the Heinkels and the 109s of the day.

8 Eric Barwell. Sound recording. Catalogue number: 20981 Imperial War Museum 20.1.01.

9 Citation from Hunter's DSO medal.
10 Parry and Postlethwaite p. 134.
11 Guy Mayfield *Life & Death in the Battle of Britain* p. 75.
12 Parry and Postlethwaite p. 138. Harkins p. 35.
13 AIR 16/1170-3. Orange p. 171.
14 Press Association Air Correspondent Saturday 1 June 1940.
15 Belfast Newsletter.
16 AIR 27/1555.
17 Brew p. 63.
18 Gordon Kinsey *Boulton & Paul Aircraft* p. 116.

## 11 Deliverance

1 Chambers p. 32.
2 That left a third brother alive fighting in the deserts of north Africa.
3 Parry and Postlethwaite p. 153.
4 Young combat report. AIR 50/104/154
5 Parry and Postlethwaite p. 154.
6 AIR 50/104/199.
7 AIR 81/928.
8 https://www.iwm.org.uk/collections/item/object/80019802
9 https://www.iwm.org.uk/collections/item/object/80019802
10 AIR 81/728.
11 Mayfield p. 76.
12 *The Times*, 31 May, 1940, p. 6.
13 AIR 16/216.
14 Orange says 2 June but others say 4 June.
15 Vincent Orange *Dowding of Fighter Command* p. 170.
16 AIR 24/524 p. 7.
17 Orange p. 168.
18 Parry and Postlethwaite p. 191.
19 AIR 27/1553 264 Operations Record Book.
20 AIR 16/216.
21 Bungay pp. 84 and 156; also Seely debate.
22 Phil Listemann and Andrew Thomas *Allied Wings Series. Boulton Paul Defiant* p. 6.
23 Martyn Nutland *Brick by Brick: The biography of the man who really made the Mini – Leonard Lord* p. 108.

24 AVIA 15/398 23.5.40.
25 AVIA 15/398 1.6.40 A. E. Heyward, Assistant Director of Aeroplane Production.
26 Orange p. 172.
27 Orange p. 175. German figures show Luftwaffe in early June had 4663 aircraft. Flint p. 89.
28 Banham Reel: 2 IWM.
29 Trumble left the squadron later in July after the start of the Battle of Britain and was in command of the RAF airfield in Crete which was captured by German paratroops in 1941. https://www.telegraph.co.uk/news/obituaries/1461860/Group-Captain-Tony-Trumble.html
30 Listemann p. 19.
31 Bailey p. 31.
32 http://www.bbm.org.uk/airmen/ScottWJ.htm
33 Adam Claasen *Dogfight: The Battle of Britain* p. 113.
34 Bailey pp. 31–2.
35 AIR 24/526.
36 Bailey p. 33.
37 Bailey pp. 33–5.
38 Brew p. 64.
39 AVIA 15/140 Fighter Command to the undersecretary of state at the Air Ministry. Written by Wing Commander R. M. Clarke on behalf of Dowding. 31.5.40.
40 AIR 24/526 Letter from Air Chief Marshal Air Officer Commander -in-Chief, Fighter Command, signed by David Carnegie, to Secretary of State for Air Ministry. 1.7.40.
41 AIR 24/526 Secret memo from number 264 Squadron, Duxford. Squadron Leader Philip Hunter. Operations Record Book. Fighter Command. 3.7.40.
42 J. M. Spaight *The Sky's the Limit: A Study of British Air Power* p. 122.
43 AIR 16/216.
44 AIR 81/1145.
45 AIR 24/526 Operations Record Book. Fighter Command. July 1940.
46 Bungay p. 137.
47 Peter Flint *Dowding and Headquarters Fighter Command* p. 97.
48 Bungay p. 156. Colville p. 228, pp. 142–3.

49 Brian Lavery *Churchill Warrior: How a Military Life Guided Winston's Finest Hours* p. 361.
50 Spaight p. 68.

## 12 Slaughter of the innocents

1 https://www.dailyrecord.co.uk/news/uk-world-news/incredible-story-of-first-world-war-1039510. It was from Leuchars in Fife, east Scotland, that my Great Uncle Leslie led his flight of Hudsons which were credited with shooting down the first Nazi plane by British-based aircraft.
2 AIR 27/969/3 RAF Form 540 Operations Record Book. No. 141 Squadron. July 1940. National Archives catalogue.
3 Don F. Aris *History of 141 Squadron*. Imperial War Museum, 2006. Catalogue no LBY06/1373.
4 http://www.bbm.org.uk/airmen/HamiltonAC.htm
5 Kenneth G. Wynn *Men of The Battle of Britain: A Biographical Dictionary of The Few* p. 165.
6 Robert McGugan interview with the Imperial War Museum. 6.9.1988.
7 Aris.
8 141 suffered its first losses on 15 May 1940 when Sgt Stephen Keene and his gunner A. C. David Whightman crashed during a training flight near RAF Turnhouse, Scotland.
9 John Chalmers *Defiant, The True Story*.
10 Orchard died in 1943. https://www.forces-war-records.co.uk/records/2332884/flight-lieutenant-james-ronald-ritchie-royal-air-force-volunteer-reserve-royal-air-force-volunteer-reserve/
11 Brew *The Turret Fighters*.
12 Report written by 264 Squadron Leader Philip Hunter to Fighter Command HQ 6.4.1940.
13 AIR 27/969/3 RAF Form 540 Operations Record Book. No. 141 Squadron. July 1940.
14 Dennis Knight *Harvest of Messerschmitts. Chronicle of a Village at War – 1940. Diary of Mary Smith* p. 72.
15 Two years later he was mysteriously killed when his RAF Short Sunderland flying boat crashed into a hillside near Dunbeath, Caithness, Scotland, while flying from Invergordon, Ross and Cromarty, to Iceland.

16 Author's interview with Rudal Kidson's uncle.
17 http://www.historyofwar.org/air/units/RAF/111_wwII.html
18 AIR 27/866/11 RAF Form 540 Operations Record Book. No 111 Squadron. July 1940.
19 Knight p. 73.
20 Brian Cull *Battle for the Channel: The First Month of the Battle of Britain* p. 225.
21 Robert Forczyk *We March Against England: Operation Sea Lion, 1940–41.*
22 Hannes Trautloft *The War Diaries of Hannes Trautloft: Kommodore of JG54 Grunherz.*
23 Author's interview with Neil MacDougall, son of I. M. MacDougall.
24 I. M. MacDougall combat report 19.7.40.
25 John Moles, nephew of Peter Atkins. http://www.bbm.org.uk/airmen/Atkins.htm
26 http://tauranga.kete.net.nz/remembering_war/audio/show/12-shot-down-during-the-battle-of-britain
27 https://www.independent.co.uk/news/obituaries/group-captain-john-gardner-new-zealand-fighter-pilot-who-fought-in-the-battle-of-britain-2288114.html
28 AIR 81/1145.
29 I. M. MacDougall combat report 19.7.40. AIR 50/61/2.
30 Knight p. 74. http://www.bbm.org.uk/airmen/Stevenson.htm
31 AIR 81/1150 Air Ministry report into Donald and Hamilton deaths.
32 Copeman was killed on 11 August in a dogfight near Margate, his Hurricane seen crashing into the sea. His body was washed ashore in Belgium and he is buried in Middelkerke Communal Cemetery.
33 Trautloft's diary continued: 'After landing I got out of my aircraft as soon as possible I could still smell burning and didn't want to be inside if the airplane exploded. Only after I've got out could I see my radiator been shot to pieces. A young lieutenant from a nearby flak battery came towards me and asked if I was ok. He had also seen a German air sea rescue aircraft take off from Boulogne to pick up the pilot who had ditched and follow the track of another aeroplane that had disappeared behind the hill near the coast. It had been trailing smoke and could only have been Kath. I got into a

truck and drove in the direction is indicated. From a vantage point on a small hill I surveyed the countryside and spotted Kath's aircraft which had landed intact in. Soon he stood in front of me and told me how he shot down a Defiant and that his aircraft has been damaged in almost identical fashion to my own.'

34 AIR 27/921.
35 AIR 81/1150.
36 AIR 27/866.
37 AIR 24/526.
38 AIR 24/526 Fighter Command Operations Record Book July 1940.
39 AIR 24/526 Fighter Command Intelligence Report.
40 AIR 27/969 141 Operations Record Book. 19.7.40.
41 Imperial War Museum. Catalogue no: LBY K. 06/1234.
42 Knight p. 74.
43 AIR 24/526.
44 https://www.upi.com/Archives/1940/07/19/Hitler-offers-Britain-peace-or-destruction/6824181303557/
45 Interview with the Richardson family.

## 13 Death of a hero

1 Wright p. 146.
2 Jim Bailey says the squadron had been sent to reinforce London against a German attack but were pulled back after news broke of the losses suffered by 141 Squadron. Bailey p. 38.
3 AIR 27/1553 264 Operations Records Book.
4 Bailey p. 48.
5 Private paper of Sq Ld Harry Bidien. IWM catalogue no. 17660.
6 Freddie Sutton *We Defy* p. 59.
7 AIR 24/526 Secret memo from Dowding to Under Secretary of State Air Ministry 19.7.40.
8 AVIA 15/600 Stevenson, Director of Home Ops, minute to Douglas 1.8.40.
9 AVIA 15/600.
10 AVIA 15/600 Air Ministry letter to Boulton Paul 4.8.40.
11 Brew p. 67.
12 Brew p. 67.
13 Wright p. 139.

14 HC Deb 20 August 1940 vol 364 cc1132-274.
15 Bailey p. 36.
16 Alec Brew *The Turret Fighters* p. 67. Harkins p. 59.
17 Denis Richards, in his 1953 contribution to the official British account *History of the Second World War*.
18 Park had written to Dowding in June setting out his very serious concerns about Defiants operating unescorted.
19 Townsend p. 346.
20 Bailey p. 38.
21 http://www.bbm.org.uk/airmen/Campbell-Colquhoun.htm http://battleofbritaincombats.blogspot.com/2012/12/ernest-william-campbell-colquhoun.html
22 Sutton p. 29.
23 Chambers p. 39.
24 Sutton p. 31.
25 AIR 81/2766 Sq Ld Hunter and F King missing believed killed; presumed shot down, enemy action, Defiant N1535, 264 Squadron, 24 August 1940.
26 AIR 81/2766. The death of an airman could leave a family impecunious. Alfred King's widow was forced to write to the Air Ministry asking for the £5 he was due for his DFM and a £40 grant for his uniform which she said she still hadn't been paid even as late as September 1940. She wrote again in 1961, from California where she had emigrated after the war, asking the Air Ministry to confirm her 'missing' husband as officially dead so she could make a claim on his RAF pension.
27 Bailey p. 40.
28 Chambers p. 39.
29 Bailey p. 7.

## 14 Defiants' last stand

1 Harkins p. 67.
2 Reel 1. https://www.iwm.org.uk/collections/item/object/80011890
3 https://www.telegraph.co.uk/history/world-war-two/10122414/The-doomed-flight-of-the-last-Dornier.html
4 Banham interview with Imperial War Museum 27.4.1983 reel 1 https://www.iwm.org.uk/collections/item/object/80006615
5 RAF Hornchurch archives.

6 Sutton p. 31.
7 Imperial War Museum audio record of interview with Fred Gash. https://www.iwm.org.uk/collections/item/object/80011890
8 https://www.iwm.org.uk/collections/item/object/80011890
9 Bailey p. 40.
10 King's School Canterbury biography http://www.hambo.org/kings-canterbury/view_man.php?id=19
11 Bailey p. 40. Private papers of Frederick 'Freddie' Sutton IWM Catalogue No:12645.
12 Christer Bergström *Battle of Britain: An Epic Conflict Revisited* p. 161.
13 AIR 812/955.
14 Bailey p. 40.
15 Bailey p. 43.
16 Townsend p. 356.
17 After the war, Flt Lt Ash's father wrote to the Air Ministry to ascertain the circumstances of his son's death but could be told no more than death was due to 'gunshot'.
18 Reel 1. https://www.iwm.org.uk/collections/item/object/80011890
19 http://worldwartwodaily.filminspector.com/2016/08/august-28-1940-call-me-meier.html
20 Bungay p. 425.
21 http://www.bbc.co.uk/archive/battleofbritain/11422.shtml
22 Supplement to the *London Gazette* of Tuesday 10 September 1946. http://www.wwiiaircraftperformance.org/Battle_of_Britain-Dowding.pdf
23 Supplement to the *London Gazette* of Tuesday 10 September 1946.
24 Private papers of F. C. Sutton pp. 41–2. https://www.iwm.org.uk/collections/item/object/1030012458
25 Bailey pp. 43–4.
26 Reel 2. https://www.iwm.org.uk/collections/item/object/80011890
27 AVIA 1540 31.10.40.
28 Private papers of Frederick 'Freddie' Sutton IWM Catalogue No:12645.
29 Bailey p. 170.
30 Bailey p. 6 (Foreword by Peter Townsend).
31 Harry E. Bodien letters to his sister. Imperial War Museum.

## 15 Divine intervention

1 Supplement to the London Gazette of Tuesday 10 September 1946. www.wwiiaircraftperformance.org/Battle_of_Britain-Dowding.pdf
2 Townsend p. 355.
3 Bailey p. 47.
4 Listemann p. 40.
5 Townsend p. 340.
6 A. D. Harvey *Collision of Empires: Britain in Three World Wars, 1793–1945* p. 654.
7 The Air Ministry finally cancelled the plan in a letter to Boulton Paul Defiant on 29.10.40. AVIA 15/600. Douglas later ended orders for Defiant night fighters because they were too slow to catch the bigger-engined Ju 88 and Do 217 which had a speed of well over 320 mph.
8 https://warfarehistorynetwork.com/daily/wwii/the-big-wing-controversy-and-hugh-dowdings-fall-from-grace/
9 Orange p. 210.
10 Orange p. 212.
11 https://www.iwm.org.uk/collections/item/object/80011890
12 Max Hastings *Bomber Command* p. 39.
13 On 11 August PO Peter Stevenson was shot down in the Channel one mile off Dover following a solo attack on twelve Me 109s, one of which he probably destroyed. He bailed out of his Spitfire and was rescued from the sea by a Motor Torpedo Boat (MTB) after firing his revolver to gain the crews' attention. He was killed on 13 February 1943, as a Flight Lieutenant with 64 Squadron, shot down in a Spitfire during a sweep over the Boulogne area.
14 Richard Hough and Denis Richards *The Battle of Britain* p. 324.
15 Air Chief Marshal Lord Dowding *Twelve Legions of Angels* pp. 24–5.
16 Air Chief Marshal Lord Dowding *Twelve Legions of Angels* p. 76.

# BIBLIOGRAPHY

*Air Member for Training* Air Ministry Pamphlet 156. The Battle of Britain, 1943

Air Ministry. *Pilot Notes. The Defiant II Aeroplane. Merlin XX Engine* Air Publication, 1941

Bailey, Jim. *The Sky Suspended: A Fighter Pilot's Story* Bloomsbury, 1990 (first published under the title *Eskimo Nell* in 1964)

Baughen, Greg. *The RAF in the Battle of France and the Battle of Britain* 2019

Bergström, Christer. *The Battle of Britain. An Epic Conflict Revisited* 2015

Bishop, Edward. *Book of Airmen's Obituaries* Bounty Books, 2002

Bishop, Patrick. *Fighter Boys: The Battle of Britain, 1940* Viking, 2003

Bosman, Martin. *Voices in Flight. RAF Fighter Pilots in* WWII Pen & Sword, 2015

Bowyer, Michael. 'The Boulton Paul Defiant' *Aircraft in Profile, Vol. 5* Profile Publications Ltd, 1966

Brew, Alec. *Boulton Paul Defiant: An Illustrated History* Amberley Publishing, 2019

Brew, Alec. *The Turret Fighters* Crowood Press, 2002

Brickhill, Paul. *Reach for the Sky: The Story of Douglas Bader* Odhams Press, 1955

Bungay, Stephen. *The Most Dangerous Enemy* Aurum, 2000

Caygill, Peter. *Flying to the Limit: Testing World War II Single-engined Fighter Aircraft.* Pen and Sword Aviation, 2005

Chambers, John. *Defiant – The True Story* BJ and M Promotions, 1997
Churchill, Winston. *The Second World War Vol. II Their Finest Hour* Cassell & Co., 1949
Claasen, Adam. *Dogfight: The Battle of Britain* ReadHowYouWant, 2012
Cull, Brian. *Battle for the Channel: The First Month of the Battle of Britain* Fonthill Media, 2017
Deighton, Len. *Fighter, the True Story of the Battle of Britain* Jonathan Cape, 1977
Dempster, Derek and Wood, Derek *The Narrow Margin Pen & Sword* Aviation, 2010.
Douglas, Sholto. *Years of Combat Vol. 1* Collins, 1963
Douglas, Sholto. *Years of Combat Vol. 2* Collins, 1966
Dowding, Hugh. *Twelve Legions of Angels* Jarrold Publishers, October 1941
Flint, Peter. *Dowding and Headquarters Fighter Command* Airlife, 1996
Forczyk, Robert. *We March Against England: Operation Sea Lion, 1940–41* Osprey Publishing, 2016
Franks, Norman. *Air Battle for Dunkirk. 26 May–3 June* Grub Street, 2000
Freeborn, John and Christopher Yeoman. *Tiger Club* Pen & Sword, 2009
Harkins, Hugh. *Defiant Mk 1 Combat Log* Centurion Publishing, 2014
Harvey, A.D. *Collision of Empires: Britain in Three World Wars, 1793–1945* Orion, 1994
Hastings, Max. *Bomber Command* Michael Joseph, 1987
Hendrie, Andrew. *Seek and Strike: The Lockheed History in World War II* William Kimber, 1983
Hillary, Richard. *The Last Enemy* Macmillan, 1942
Holland, James. *Battle of Britain: Five Months that Changed History* St Martin's Press, 2011
Holmes, Tom. *Hurricanes to the Fore* Delprado Publishers, 1999
Hooton, E. *Luftwaffe at War: Gathering Storm 1933–39 Vol.* 1 Classic Publications, 2007
Hough, R. and Richards, D. *The Battle of Britain* Norton, 1989
Humphresy, Roy. *Hawkinge 1912–1961*. Meresborough Books.

James, T.C.G. *Growth of Fighter Command, 1936–1940* (Air Defence of Great Britain Vol. 1) Frank Cass Publishers, 2000

Jolie, Jan. *Luchtgevechten boven West-Brabant en de Biesbosch* Lorelax Productions, 2000

Jones, Neville. *The Beginnings of Strategic Air Power: A History of the British Bomber Force 1923–1939* Routledge, 1987

Jullian, Marcel. *The Battle of Britain* Jonathan Cape, 1967

Kinsey, Gordon. *Boulton & Paul Aircraft* Terence Dalton, 1992

Knight, Dennis. *Harvest of Messerschmitts. Chronicle of a Village at War – 1940. Diary of Mary Smith* Wingham Press, 1990

Lavery, Brian. *Churchill Warrior: How a Military Life Guided Winston's Finest Hours* Casemate, 2017

Listemann, Phil and Thomas, Andrew. *Boulton Paul Defiant* Allied Wings Series, 2009

Listemann, Phil. *Squadrons! Vol. 19. The Boulton Paul Defiant: Day and Night Fighter* 2017

McInnes, Ian and Webb, J. V. *A Contemptible Little Flying Corps* London Stamp Exchange, 1991

Miller, Russell. *Trenchard: Father of the Royal Air Force* Weidenfeld and Nicolson, 2016

Ministry of Information. *The Battle of Britain* Crown Publishers, 1941

Newton Dunn, Bill. *Big Wing: The Biography of Air Marshal Sir Trafford Leigh-Mallory* Airlife, 1992

Nutland, Martyn. *Brick by Brick: The Biography of the man who really made the mini – Leonard Lord* Authorhouse, 2012

Orange, Vincent. *Dowding of Fighter Command: Victor of the Battle of Britain* Grub Street, 2008

Orange, Vincent. *Park: The Biography of Air Chief Marshal Sir Keith Park* Methuen, 1984

Overy, Richard. *The Battle of Britain* Penguin, 2010

Parry, Simon. *Battle of Britain Combat Archive. 10 July–22 July 1940* Red Kite, 2015

Parry, Simon. *Battle of Britain Combat Archive. 19 August–25 August 1940* Red Kite, 2015

Parry, Simon and Postlethwaite, Mark. *Battle of Britain Combat Archive. 21 May–2 June 1940* Red Kite, 2015

Ray, John. *The Battle of Britain: Dowding and the First Victory* Cassell, 2002

Ritchie, Sebastian. *Air Historical Branch. The RAF, Small Wars and Insurgencies in the Middle East, 1919–1939* Centre for Air Power Studies, 2011

Sarkar, Dilip. *The Few: The Story of the Battle of Britain in the Words of the Pilots* Amberley Publishing, 2009

Sinnott, Colin. *The RAF and Aircraft Design: Air Staff Operational Requirements 1923–1939* Routledge, 2000

Spaight, J.M. *The Sky's the Limit* Hodder and Stoughton, 1940

Terraine, John. *The Right of the Line* Hodder and Stoughton, 1985

Townsend, Peter. *Duel in the Dark* Harrap Publishers, 1986

Townsend, Peter. *Duel of Eagles* Weidenfeld and Nicolson, 1990

Townsend, Peter. *Time and Chance* Collins, 1978

Trautloft, Hannes. *Als Jagdflieger in Spanien* 1939

Trautloft, Hannes. *The War Diaries of Hannes Trautloft: Kommodore of JG54 Grunherz* Cerberus Publishing Ltd, 2005

Wallace, Graham. *RAF Biggin Hill* Putnam & Co., 1957

Warner, Carl (Mayfield, Guy). *Life and Death in the Battle of Britain* IWM, 2018

Wellum, Geoffrey. *First Light* Viking, 2002

Wright, Robert. *Dowding and the Battle of Britain* Macdonald and Co., 1969

# INDEX